J A
and                    phy

bal Age

Rupert Hart-Davis
Educational Publications

© J Alexander and F G Murphy 1970

Published by Rupert Hart-Davis
Educational Publications
3 Upper James Street Golden Square
London W1    01 734 8080
Photoset by BAS Printers Limited, Wallop, Hants
and printed by Compton Printers Limited, Aylesbury,
Bucks

SBN 247 98623 2

COVER PHOTOGRAPH

The National Aeronautics and Space Administration
of the USA, which has given permission for the
reproduction of the photograph on the cover of this
book, has supplied the following caption:

The rising earth is about five degrees above the lunar
horizon in this telephoto view taken from the Apollo 8
spacecraft near 110 degrees east longitude. The horizon,
about 570 kilometres from the spacecraft, is near the
eastern limb of the moon as viewed from earth. Width
of view at the horizon is about 150 kilometres.
On the earth, 384,000 kilometres away, the sunset
terminator crosses Africa. The south pole is in the white
area near the left end of the terminator. North and
South America are under cloud. The lunar surface
probably has less pronounced colour than indicated
by this print.

# The Global Age

# The Glo

The Twentieth Century to 1967

# Authors' note

The authors are deeply indebted to Geoffrey Warner, Reader in Politics at Reading University, for detailed suggestions, criticism and guidance.

Mr Murphy wishes to thank Jasmine Gale, in charge of picture research, and Karen Bishop, picture librarian, both of BPC Publishing, for their generous help in finding photographs; also Mr Olgun Halil for help with proof reading; and students at Peckham Manor School for advice on difficult words.

# Acknowledgements

For permission to reproduce the photographs on the pages indicated acknowledgement is made to the following: Associated Press Ltd pages 159, 183, 197, 200, 211, 227, 235; Mr Alexander ben Bernfes pages 150–151; Black Star Publishing Co Ltd pages 75, 171, 213; BPC Publishing page 63; Bundesarchiv Koblenz page 120; Camera Press Ltd page 167; Henri Cartier-Bresson and the John Hillelson Agency pages 164–165, 218; Central Press Photos Ltd pages 127, 145, 221, 263; Bernard B. Fall Collection pages 224–225; Hulton Picture Library pages 22–23; Imperial War Museum pages 25, 26–27; Keystone Press Agency Ltd pages 138–139, 146–147, 153, 161, 189, 201, 202–203, 207, 209, 257; Popperfoto (Paul Popper Ltd) page 32; SCR Photo Library pages 30–31; Syndication International pages 28–29; Thames & Hudson page 239; US Air Force page 148.

Maps and diagrams were drawn by T. R. Allen.

# Contents

# Chapter 1
# Introduction

What sort of person are you? The answer to this question obviously has a lot to do with the sort of people your mother and father are – but that has a lot to do with their parents and the world they grew up in; and so on, as far back as you like to go. It is hard to tell just where the history of anything really starts. Suppose you wanted to study the history of the atomic bomb. Would you start from scientific discoveries of fifty years ago or from the invention of gunpowder a thousand years ago?

In this chapter we are going to look at some of the developments which, once they are understood and remembered, make the whole story that follows easier to fit together. But we have to remember that they have their beginnings a long time before our century, and will probably go on being important for a long time after it.

## 1  The Industrial Revolution

Machines for making clothes and steam engines to drive them; great coal mines to feed the engines and great iron-works to make them; a transport revolution based on steam engines that moved themselves along; the spread of machine methods from clothes to nails, to motor-cars, to farming, to nearly every human activity; the use of electricity to store power, to drive machines even faster and cheaper, to send messages and pictures at the speed of light; these make up the greatest historical event of our times.

It is still an event which we are at the beginning of, something still happening. The machines have made possible the aeroplane and the refrigerator, and they must have many more things to make yet, perhaps so fast that we will have great trouble living with our own inventions.

Before it all started, for eight out of every ten men and women there was only one way of life, and that was

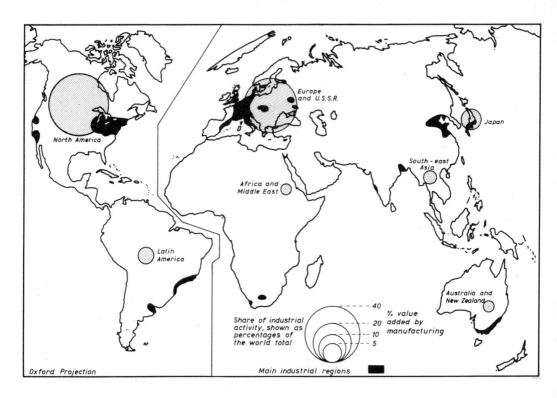

North America

Europe and U.S.S.R.

Japan

South-east Asia

Africa and Middle East

Latin America

Australia and New Zealand

Share of industrial activity, shown as percentages of the world total

40
20
10
5

% value added by manufacturing

Oxford Projection

Main industrial regions

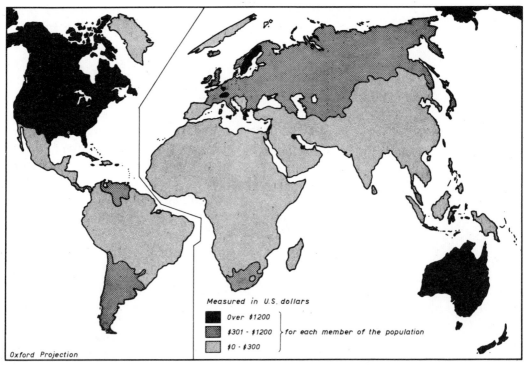

Measured in U.S. dollars

■ Over $1200
▨ $301 - $1200 } for each member of the population
▦ $0 - $300

Oxford Projection

toiling over a few hectares of land to grow the food that kept them alive. This was true from the open field villages of Britain to the rice-paddies of China. Life was hard, disease-ridden, narrow, and, to our eyes, monotonous.

Then came the machines, and where they came, great changes. In the fields, fewer men were needed. But there was work serving the machines in the mines and factories, and there the people went, no longer to grow their own food, but to buy it with their wages.

The move to the town often enough also meant living in crowded slums and working under cruel conditions. Struggles for better housing, hours, wages, health and education took place, and still go on. But what we must remember is that this tremendous change in man's way of life, with its mixture of hard realities and dreams of machine-made plenty, which started in our part of the world, is spreading all over it. Everywhere in the world mankind is becoming less a farmer, more a town-dweller. This move from growing food to making goods in factories is called Industrialisation.

Industrialisation spread at first because inventive men could make great fortunes out of it, and because governments wanted the ships and guns that factories could give them. But it is also very popular. Where industrialisation has not yet arrived, and men are still tied to their rice-paddies and maize-fields, they know about the new way of life, of towns and machines, and, right or wrong, they have often decided that they want this for themselves.

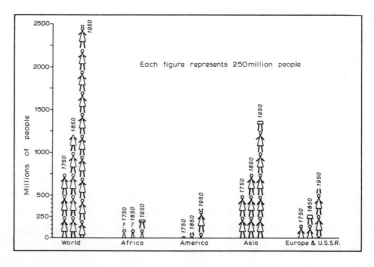

Each figure represents 250 million people

*The Population Explosion*

The graph on p. 11 shows the tremendous changes in modern times in the numbers of people alive in the world. This did not happen because more people were being born, but because fewer and fewer of them were dying while they were young children. As far as can be discovered, before this increase started something like six or seven out of every ten children born must have died before they reached the age of ten.

This population explosion has two effects on our period of history. At first, it happened in Europe. Notice how European nations dominate everything that happens in the world during the twentieth century, until about 1940. This was because Europe had the industrial power of the machine age and plenty of spare manpower. Great numbers of Europeans spilled over into parts of the world where they found room or could make it, into places like North and South America, Eastern Russia, Southern Africa and Australia. After 1940, the picture begins to change. In Europe, the number of people goes on increasing, but more steadily. Instead of Europe, Asia becomes the scene of a dramatic increase in the population.

## 2  The dominance of Europe

In 1492 Columbus landed in the Americas. In 1498 Vasco da Gama reached India by the sea route, around Africa. These two events began a process of discovery and conquest in which the peoples of Europe used their navies and armies to seize and govern most of the rest of the world.

The European nations were able to do this because of that same gift of technical inventiveness which made the Industrial Revolution. The gun and the great ocean-going sailing ship were European inventions. A much more complicated question is, why did they want to make these conquests?

One reason was the great fortunes that could be made by individual adventurers. The Spaniards who went to South America were looking for gold, and found silver. The new lands had novel products which could be sold in Europe for great profit: products like spices, sugar, tea and rubber. British India was for a long time ruled not by the British government, but by a commercial firm, the British East India Company. A similar Dutch firm ruled the wealthy

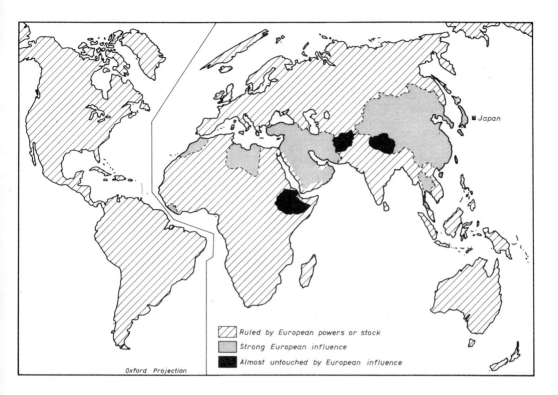

Legend on map:
- Ruled by European powers or stock
- Strong European influence
- Almost untouched by European influence

Oxford Projection

Japan

*The world dominance of Europe, about 1900*

islands which are now Indonesia.

Of course it was not long before the governments began to interest themselves in this wealth, and to take notice of the doings of the adventurers. For not only did valuable things come out of the colonies, they were also a market—a place to sell the machine-made goods. It was important not only to trade with the new lands, but also keep other European nations out of your market. The most effective way of doing this was to occupy the territory by force and take over its government. (A territory thus taken over is called a colony, and the colonies of any country together form its empire.)

Sometimes areas were seized not for their own wealth, but because they controlled the routes to wealthy areas, or because they provided harbours and fuelling stations. The Suez Canal and the Cape of Good Hope were examples of this.

There were often other reasons besides the acquiring of wealth. The Pilgrim Fathers, for example, founded colonies in North America so that they could practise their religion in peace. Along with the gold-hungry Spanish and Portuguese adventurers went priests intent on carrying European religions to the new lands. Some of Britain's empire-making in Africa was aimed at stamping out the slave trade, and was inspired not only by adventurers chasing riches, but also by men like David Livingstone, the Scottish missionary, and William Wilberforce, the leader of the anti-slavery movement in England.

In 1898 the United States of America joined in the overseas empire-building business by taking Cuba and the Philippine Islands from Spain. Was it done to free the Cubans and the Filipinos, or to make money out of them, or simply to give the American fleet a coaling station in Asia? Or did the American government simply want some excitement to attract the voters' attention away from home troubles? No one to this day can really say with certainty which of these reasons was the most important.

The USA's empire has in the twentieth century included colonies in South America in which there is no apparent armed conquest, nor any take-over of the government. The empire-building is done by American companies which build, manage and maintain so much of the economy of a country, that they may be said to own it. Although this method of empire-building (imperialism) is not only an American activity, it is often known as dollar-imperialism.

The European nations, the USA (and for a time Japan, see Chapter 5) multiplied their wealth and power by building empires; but the empires also created dangerous competitions and jealousies which became one of the main causes of the two world wars which occurred in the twentieth century. The very existence of the great empires meant that any fighting between European countries would bring in the whole world.

Just as important as their effect on Europe is the effect of the empires on the subject peoples of the colonies. From the European rulers, traders and missionaries they learned European ideas. They learned about firearms and railways. They heard of new European ideas about democracy and equality (see p. 19). They saw what industrialisation could do. They discovered, among many things, how and why the Europeans conquered them. And of course, the quickest learners were those who hated their European masters.

Resistance against European rule was always present. Sometimes hardly noticeable, sometimes widespread and violent, it was increasingly successful. This is true both of colonies where the people were mostly themselves European by origin, and where they were the native people of the territory.

As early as the 1780's the Europeans in North America threw off the British in a revolutionary war and became the independent United States of America. The Spanish and Portuguese governments lost control of the South American mainland in the early nineteenth century. In 1857 the British were badly shaken by an unsuccessful revolt in India. Africa was seldom a peaceful continent even while the Europeans ruled. At the beginning of the twentieth century, nationalism, the idea we must look at next, was already present among the subject peoples as well as their masters. Part of the story of the century is the rising power of nations outside Europe and North America, until Europe is no longer the centre of world history.

## 3   Nationalism

Everyone belongs to many different groups and organisations, and has a sense of loyalty, or belonging, to them. You are a member of your family, and perhaps a football team. You also belong to a country, and you are a member of the human race.

If you wanted, you could probably make up a very long list of groups to which you belong, and to which you feel loyalty. Could you list them in order, to discover to which of them you owe the most loyalty? Which would come first if you had to choose between them? In some cases, of course, you would not be able to make a free choice unless you were ready to break the law!

To understand the history of any group of people anywhere in the world, you must try to answer that same question for them.

Think of a typical English village in medieval times. To whom would the people there have given their loyalty if they had had to make a choice? To their king? Or their feudal lord? Or their priest? It is not easy to say, but it is hard to imagine that the answer 'England' would have been on their list at all.

In modern times it has become more and more the case that for most men the greatest loyalty they have is to their

**God save the King**
Great Britain
1745

*God save our gracious King,*
*Long live our noble King,*
*God save the King.*
*Send him victorious,*
*Happy and glorious,*
*Long to reign over us,*
*God save the King.*

*O Lord our God arise,*
*Scatter his enemies,*
*And make them fall.*
*Confound their politicks,*
*Frustrate their knavish tricks,*
*On Thee our hopes we fix,*
*God save us all.*

*Thy choicest gifts in store*
*On him be pleased to pour.*
*Long may he reign.*
*May he defend our laws,*
*And ever give us cause*
*With heart and voice to sing*
*God save the King.*

**Hail Columbia**
United States of America
1798

*Hail! Columbia, happy land!*
*Hail! ye heroes, heav'n-born band!*
*Who fought and bled in freedom's cause,*
*And when the storm of war was gone,*
*Enjoy'd the peace your valour won;*
*Let Independence be our boast,*
*Ever mindful what it cost,*
*Ever grateful for the prize,*
*Let its altar reach the skies.*

*Firm, united, let us be,*
*Rallying round our liberty,*
*As a band of brothers join'd,*
*Peace and safety we shall find.*

*Immortal Patriots rise once more,*
*Defend your rights, defend your shore,*
*Let no rude foe with impious hand*
*Invade the shrine where sacred lies*
*Of toil and blood the well-earn'd prize.*

*While offering peace sincere and just,*
*In heav'n we place a manly trust*
*That truth and justice will prevail,*
*And every scheme of bondage fail.*

**La Marseillaise**
France
1792

*Ye sons of France, awake to glory,*
*Hark, hark, what myriads bid you rise:*
*Your children, wives and grandsires hoary,*
*Behold their tears and hear their cries!*

*Shall hateful tyrants mischief breeding*
*With hireling hosts, a ruffian band*
*Affright and desolate the land*
*While peace and liberty lie bleeding?*

*To arms, to arms, ye brave!*
*Th'avenging sword unsheathe!*
*March on! march on!*
*All hearts resolve*
*On victory or death.*

*O sacred love of France, undying,*
*Th'avenging arm uphold and guide.*
*Thy defenders, death defying,*
*Fight with freedom at their side.*

*Soon thy sons shall be victorious*
*When the banner high is raised*
*And thy dying enemies, amazed,*
*Shall behold thy triumph, great and glorious.*

*To arms, to arms, ye brave! (etc)*

nation, the country and people to which they belong. Men have come to feel more strongly for their nation than for their religion, their political party, or any other organisation which might have a claim on them. Less than two hundred years ago, a Dutchman, and after him a German, could become King of England; a Scot could become a leading member of the French government; in 1862, the Prussian ambassador to Russia, Bismarck, was leaving Russia to become Prime Minister of Prussia, when the Czar offered him a job working for Russia. Bismarck refused, but he wasn't surprised. Such things would now be considered very odd indeed.

The first steps towards making the nation the most important thing in people's lives were taken by kings who made themselves safe from their enemies by winning the loyalty of their people to themselves instead of the local baron. Much later, in the last quarter of the eighteenth century, came two matters of greater importance to modern history, the American War of Independence and the French Revolution.

In 1776, the peoples of the British colonies in North America, peoples of many different nationalities and religions, rebelled against British rule, and fought a long war against it, the War of Independence. They had a lot of help from France, and in the end they won. But they were helped too by the idea of sticking together against Britain, of having their own flag and nation to unite behind. And it worked! Against all the odds they beat the armed might of one of the most powerful nations on earth. Their success helped them shortly after to unite their separate countries into the United States of America.

A similar thing happened soon after in France, with even more astonishing results. Here the revolutionaries did away with their traditional rulers, and the government was taken over by people who saw themselves not as rulers of a land, but as leaders and representatives of the people. They announced that they were bringing the people liberty, equality and brotherhood. To what could they now ask the people to be loyal when they were attacked?

The answer was, to the idea of France, the nation. The people had to fight, not for a king, or a religion, but for themselves; to defend not what the king owned, but what they owned as members of the French nation.

And as with America, it worked! So well that under Napoleon the French conquered most of the rest of Europe. The difference between the new and the old can be seen in the words of *Hail Columbia* and *La Marseillaise*, especially when they are compared to the British national anthem, which was written in an earlier age.

The new spirit of nationalism began to catch on everywhere. Rulers liked it because they envied the new might it had given France. The people liked it because the French and Americans had linked it to the ideals of liberty and equality for all men.

The new enthusiasm came to Spaniards and Russians and Germans and helped them beat the French back to France. It came to the Italians, and created one nation, Italy, out of a hotch-potch of small countries. In the same way, in 1871, the great nation of Germany appeared on the map of Europe for the first time.

The subject peoples of the Austrian and Turkish empires entered a long struggle to create themselves anew as nations.

## 4 Liberty, equality, and government by the people

One of the things that helped to make nationalism so popular was the idea of government by the people. The difficulties come in the practical arrangements. Fifty or five hundred people can gather together to agree on laws and policies, perhaps, but fifty million cannot. The history of the twentieth century is often about the solution of this problem.

One answer, usually called democracy, is for the people to elect representatives to do the governing. This can work well, but not always. Sometimes there are deep and bitter arguments and divisions among the people, and their representatives reflect the disagreements so much that no government can be carried on; sometimes the quarrels cannot be settled without civil war, as in America in 1861 and Spain in 1936.

One way to overcome division tried in the twentieth century is dictatorship, when one man, or a group of men, claim to know what the people really want, in spite of their quarrels, and dictate the government accordingly. Here the trouble is that disagreement with the dictator has to be forbidden, and the people are not even free to tell him what it is they do want!

Communism is another approach of great importance. It is a set of ideas mostly developed from the theories of Karl Marx, a German writer of the nineteenth century. He saw the world as a place where a small number of rich people who owned the factories (capitalists) ruled over and cheated the great majority, the wage-earners (the proletariat). Equality and freedom were not matters of votes but of wealth, and he expected that one day the proletariat, the workers of the world, would rise up in anger and overthrow the rule of the capitalists. There would then be a period of ruthless dictatorship by the workers while they put paid to the capitalists and reorganised society. After that, nothing of any importance would be owned by individuals, but all property and wealth would be held in common and used equally by everyone. Once wealth was properly shared, there would be plenty for everyone. With nothing left to fight over, there would be no more crime or war. There would hardly be any need for government at all.

Followers of Marx who have tried to put his ideas into practice are called communists, and we shall see how communists have come to rule over much of the world, and how Marx's ideas have been worked out in practice. For the time being it is enough to notice that the dictatorship of the proletariat has the same practical difficulty as government by the people. You have to find a way of choosing a small number of people to do the actual governing.

A great question of our century is – what is freedom? We shall meet those who say that freedom means that people can think and say what they like, and choose what government they like by voting. Others will reply that these are foolish freedoms to men who are starving, and that freedom from hunger is the only freedom that matters. Nationalists will put freedom from foreign governments at the top of their list. We shall even meet those who say that freedom is being able to leave all the worries to the leaders, and not having to think or speak about politics at all.

These may seem to be mere arguments, theories; the fact is that these arguments are things for which men have lived, fought, and died.

# Chapter 2
# The First World War

The nations of Europe were leading the world into the twentieth century, building the new industries and the great cities; but this did not mean that the nations of Europe could give up their old habits. War was nothing unusual to them, and when another one started in the summer of 1914, it seemed serious enough, but not anything new. That summer the generals reckoned on fighting for a few months before victory: dashing cavalrymen in splendid uniforms jingled about looking for the chance to make a heroic charge; enthusiastic young men rushed into the armies to enjoy the glamour of a soldier's life; the newspapers talked of glory and justice, and explained that the enemy were cowardly and wicked. In the winter of 1918 when the war at last was mostly over, a terrible lesson had been learned. This had been no ordinary war, but something new, deserving a new name. They called it the Great War, the World War, or the War to End War. It had been a long war, full of horror. Nearly ten million people had died in it. Instead of glamour, there had been mud and machine guns and poison gas. As the years went on, every village sent its quota of men to the slaughter. As the men left the factories, women had to take their places. Bombs fell on civilians, and a new phrase came into being – the Home Front. War had become more thoroughly destructive than it had ever been.

## 1  Causes of the war

In 1871 a new nation had appeared in Europe, and it was a very strong one. A collection of small, weak countries joined themselves together under the King of Prussia to become Germany. The King of Prussia became the Emperor of Germany, or Kaiser. The Prussians achieved this by war, first by making their state the most warlike of all the German countries, then by leading the others to a tremendous victory over France.

So it was that the new Germany, made in the heat of triumph over France, spent the next years on guard against France, for there were always Frenchmen ready to preach revenge. In the Rhine valley, where the two countries met, a new war always seemed possible. To discourage the French, the Germans struck an alliance with Austria.

The rulers of Austria (sometimes called Austria Hungary), however, had their own troubles. The new German empire was made up of Germans, and nationalism (see pp. 15–19) had helped to make it. The old Austrian empire was made up of peoples of many races and languages. Nationalism was its enemy, and on the frontiers of the Austrian empire nationalism was on the march. For in the Balkans were small nations who had fought for their freedom from another empire, the Turkish. The Austrians only waited for the best moment to advance against the Balkans.

One thing made Austria hesitate, and that was Russia. Russia wanted to get into the Balkans so that she could win control of the narrow straits at Constantinople. In times of war her enemies had stopped her ships from entering the Mediterranean Sea by controlling these waters. Austria knew that when she attacked in the Balkans there was every chance that Russia would rush to the rescue. The alliance with Germany might make the Russians think twice.

But, faced with the combination of Austria and Germany, France and Russia formed their own agreement to fight together. Thus the two possible explosions were wired together. If one or other of them blew up, the other would as well.

That, however, wasn't the end of it. The new Germany offered challenges on and over the sea. She wanted an empire to support her growing industries, and this brought her into rivalry with Great Britain. The Germans had come late into the empire-building business, resented the poor share that was left, and particularly resented the size of the British empire. To help support their claim to what they called a "place in the sun", the Germans tried to build a fleet to rival the mighty British Navy. Before long the German fleet was the second biggest in the world, but the British in turn insisted on always building more

Trench warfare, 1917
Entrenched German soldiers
cut down French attackers

than the Germans. As ill-feeling grew, the British rulers drew closer in friendship to France and Russia. A quarrel anywhere might be enough to bring the most powerful nations in the world at each other's throats.

The rulers and the people were aware of the dangers, and in many ways they were spoiling for a fight. National feelings were strong, and the populations were growing. Large and enthusiastic armies could be recruited and trained. The techniques of the factories and the machine age led to competition in producing guns and ships. The new instruments of civilisation, the railways, newspapers, telegraphs, road-systems, were planned and developed as much for future wars as for other purposes. Europe was prepared for war, so that when it came after several false alarms, it was almost a relief.

It started in the Balkans. A Serbian nationalist murdered the heir to the Austrian throne in June 1914. Austria decided that the moment had come, and marched into Serbia. The Russians joined in on Serbia's side. Germany honoured her promises to Austria, declared war on Russia's ally France, and sent her armies forward through Belgium. That forced the hand of Britain, for Belgium's ports were a possible springboard for an enemy attack across the English Channel, and for this reason Britain had promised to defend the tiny country against attack.

One of the millions caught up in the agony of war – a German soldier captured by the British on the Western Front in 1917

## 2   The course of the war

The war was not decided by military conquest. In their collision, the armies, baffled by the apparently impenetrable defence of trench and machine-gun, for the most part

*First World War* – the furthest the armies could get at different times in the four years fighting.

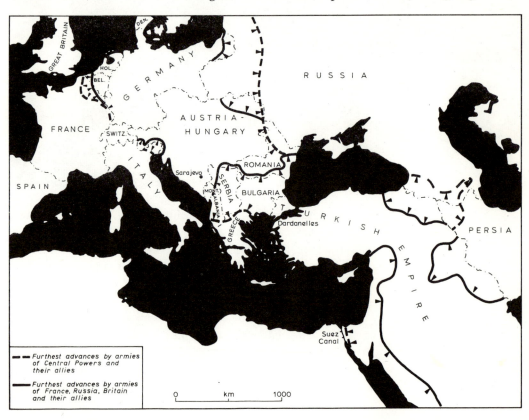

Furthest advances by armies of Central Powers and their allies

Furthest advances by armies of France, Russia, Britain and their allies

0    km    1000

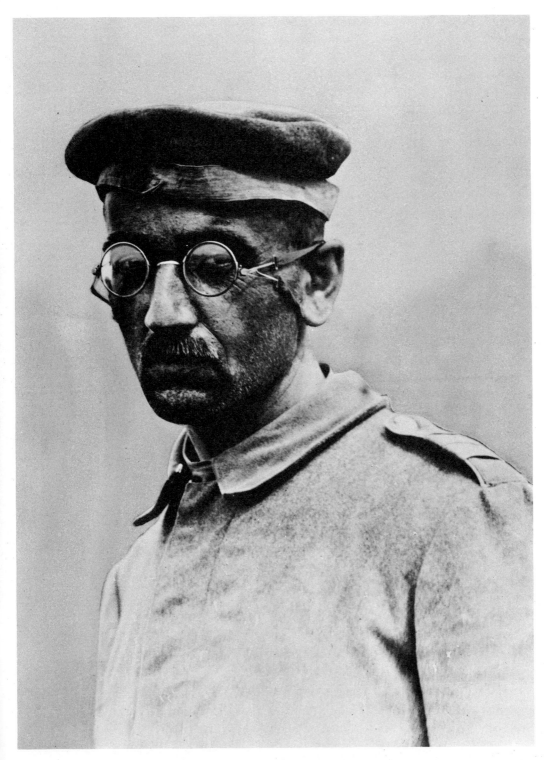

managed little but mutual slaughter. The question became not, who was going to win, but which side would be the first to cry, 'Enough'.

The map on p. 24 shows the main areas of the fighting and how little the armies achieved in four years. They made occasional advances and retreats, but they could do nothing decisive on the western, eastern and Italian fronts. The attempt of 1915 by troops of the British Empire to strike at the enemy through Turkey at the Dardanelles ended in failure. There were other more successful attacks on the Turkish Empire in the Middle East, but they had more effect on post-war history than on the war itself.

If the clash of armies could not bring the war to a decision, what could? The answer lay in the struggle for resources. Here was the essential battle. Which side could continue longest to supply the armies with men, food, clothes, weapons, transport, and the enormous quantities of ammunition they needed? Which home population would first be forced by shortages to sue for peace?

The end came when the balance finally swung against Germany and her allies. Germany's merchant fleet was early driven from the seas, and she depended for overseas supplies on neighbouring neutrals, Holland and the Scandinavian countries, until the British fleets cut off this source by blockade. The German Navy made one attempt to fight, at the Battle of Jutland in 1916. Although that fight was indecisive too, the German fleet made no more direct challenges. Instead, Germany's submarines were sent against all vessels trading with her enemies, whether neutral or not. This policy came very near to destroying Britain, but it defeated itself by so angering the United States of America, whose ships came under attack, that she was brought into the war against the German coalition; this finally tipped the scales of the battle for men and materials.

## 3   The entry of the United States

Throughout the nineteenth century, the USA had avoided any involvement in European affairs, asking only that the European powers should keep out of the New World. The bulk of the Europeans who had populated the country by emigration had little time for a Europe they had chosen

1918 – enter the American army. British soldiers look on

to leave behind, and the opening up of the American West had given people and government plenty to do. In 1914 there was little thought in the USA of getting mixed up in the war. In 1916 President Woodrow Wilson was re-elected partly because many of his supporters thought that he would continue to keep the United States out of the war.

It was clear, though, that America was a powerful nation, and likely soon to be the most powerful in the world. In this position, it was impossible for her to go on ignoring the war. A German victory, and German domination of the land-mass of the old world, could endanger the world markets of America's growing industries. Her shipping was searched by British naval patrols, which was annoying enough, but even worse was the threat of German submarine attack. American citizens of French and British descent, longer settled in the New World, held more power in government and newspapers than the German elements in the population. Clever British propaganda played on the growing anti-German sentiment, and the discovery that the Germans were guarding against American entry into the war by plotting to get Mexico interested in a war against the USA, combined with a German refusal to respect American ships trading with her enemies, finally caused the United States to declare war on April 16th 1917. Even before this date, her industrial strength had been committed to supplying Germany's enemies.

## 4 Revolution and collapse in Russia

Although the entry of the USA really settled the question of which side would stand the strain of war the longer, the first to break and withdraw from the war was one of Germany's enemies. In March 1918 Russia purchased peace at the price of giving up an enormous area of her empire in Eastern Europe.

For years the huge empire of Russia, under the rule of the Czars, had trembled on the brink of revolution. The trouble lay in Russia's backwardness. The peasants could not pay their taxes because they still used medieval farming methods and implements, but they were convinced that they could solve all their problems if they had more land of their own. They were bitterly envious of the great estates of the nobility.

Industrialisation came later to Russia than elsewhere, and when it was the turn of the Russian factory workers and miners to suffer the long hours, low pay, and brutal treatment of the Industrial Revolution, their anger was brought to life at once.

Out of the discontent and backwardness grew political parties with programmes for reforming and modernising Russia, even though such parties were illegal. Illegal news-

The Russian army breaks up, 1917.
A Russian soldier tries to stop two deserters

papers began to circulate; strikes, riots and assassinations troubled the country. A climax came in 1905, when the Czar lost control of the principal cities to striking workers, and part of the navy mutinied in sympathy with them. Only when the Czar agreed to have a Parliament to share the running of the country with him, and to allow open and legal political parties, was order restored.

The discontent was by no means ended, because the Czar gave the Duma, as the new Parliament was called, very little power. In 1914, Russia's enormous population seemed bound to do well in the war, and men talked of the Russian "steamroller"; but the truth was that Russia's millions were in no condition to give the Czar the unquestioning loyalty which four years of massacre at the front and shortages at home were to demand as the condition of success in the First World War.

Again Russia had to pay the price of backwardness and bad government. The army was short of shells, heavy guns, machine guns, medical supplies, and good generals. By 1917 it had endured terrible losses, and the troops were underfed and mutinous. In March of that year, factory workers again rioted and seized control of Petrograd, the capital, and the soldiers first refused to fire on the workers, and then joined them. The Czar had lost control completely this time, and abdicated. A committee of men from the Duma became the official government. Most power lay with the elected committee which led the soldiers and factory workers. This committee was called the Soviet.

During the next few months, the men of the Duma tried to keep the war against Germany going, but chaos grew as the peasants and workers took the law into their own hands, and the soldiers lost interest in the fight. One small group of revolutionaries who followed the sixty year old ideas of Karl Marx (see p. 19), the Bolshevik Party led by Vladimir Lenin, was carefully working its way towards seizing power for itself. First it argued and harangued and debated within the Soviet, and by September Bolsheviks were elected into control of the Soviet in the two leading cities, Petrograd and Moscow. In November they drove out the Duma committee, with an armed attack, brilliantly planned by Lenin's most talented colleague, Leon Trotsky.

The leading demands of the Bolsheviks before they came to power were for bread for the people and immediate peace; hence their popularity with the soldiers of the Soviet. In fact, in the chaos of the revolution it was impossible for Russia to continue fighting – the army had been weak enough before, but now both discipline and supplies were non-existent. On November 21st 1917, the new Russian government asked for a cease-fire, and a few months later agreed to peace on humiliating terms involving the surrender of great areas of territory. Even

New hands on the guns. Bolshevik 'Red Guards' in Petrograd

as American strength was building up on the western front, in the east Germany had outlasted one of her enemies.

## 5  The Armistice

Partly in the hope of keeping some sort of anti-German war going in Russia, partly fearing the spread of revolution to their own countries, Britain, France and the United States all maintained troops on Russian soil at some time between 1918 and 1920, to harass the new government.

They had little success, against either the Bolsheviks or the Germans. German troops released from the Russian front flowed west to reinforce the armies in France, ready for a great assault before the trickle of fresh American troops could become a flood.

The attack was made in the spring of 1918. The British and French lines reeled back, but held, and the advancing German soldiers were disheartened to discover from their prisoners how well their enemies were eating. Supplies were crossing the Atlantic in spite of the German submarines, thanks to the new system of convoys and the protection of American destroyers. Confidence mounted among the armies of Britain, France, and their allies.

A new assault in the Balkans in September led to the surrender of Bulgaria. In October, Turkey was defeated. In the same month the forces of the Austrian Empire began to give ground in Italy, and by November the counter attacks of the allies on the western front had the German army in retreat. The essential battle of supplies, manpower and morale was clearly over when revolution broke out among the hungry peoples of Germany and the Austrian Empire. The Kaiser fled to Holland, and a German delegation met the western allies to ask for peace. The firing ceased on November 11th 1918, a date still remembered as Armistice Day. The long struggle was over. As Germany had had Russia at her mercy at the beginning of the year, so now Germany was at the feet of the victorious allies, but counting on President Wilson's promise to base the peace terms on justice, not revenge.

The war had done two things which were not fully understood at the time. It had brought a new government to power in Russia which was determined to modernise the country; and a modernised Russia was bound to be the strongest of the European countries. The war had also brought into Europe another power greater than any of the Europeans. The United States of America was no longer aloof from world affairs.

What was noticed at the time was the terrible slaughter of the war, and the terrible destructive power of modern guns, tanks and aeroplanes. Could the victors so arrange affairs that such a war need not happen again?

# Chapter 3
# Peacemaking and Post-war Problems

The Great War ended as it had begun, in muddle. It was harder to stop the fighting than it had been to start, and harder still to tidy up the mess left behind. The task of working out the peace treaties took three years and no government was satisfied with the results.

Bolshevik Russia was left out of the discussions as no one else even recognised its government as legal. In Germany the peace terms were so hated that men could hardly be found to sign them. In Italy the nationalists felt their allies had cheated the Italians out of the rewards they deserved for their sacrifices. In France the generals and many others feared that Germany, too leniently handled, would soon be strong enough to fight another round. In the USA a majority of Congress felt that they could not commit their country to support the treaty at all. In Britain, educated people felt guilty about treating Germany so harshly, and hoped that Wilson's pride, the League of Nations, would heal the wounds and save the world from future wars. Twenty years ahead was a Second World War, whose roots grew from the problems which the peacemakers could not solve.

## 1   The League of Nations

President Wilson saw that no really fair terms could be made in 1919. For instance it would be fair if the German speaking people of the Austrian empire were allowed to join Germany, as they mostly wanted, but America's allies were not prepared to see their strongest enemy grow larger. So Wilson's main hope was the League, which would be the machinery for peaceful revision of the settlement when war's hatreds had cooled. Thanks to Wilson the League Covenant, a promise not to make war without having first tried to settle the quarrel through the League, was put at the top of each treaty with the beaten countries. Thus all who signed the treaties pledged their countries to try to solve international disputes peacefully and to stop trading with, or if necessary to make war on, any country judged to be an aggressor by the League. No country could resist a world in arms, so if the Covenant were faithfully kept, war would be impossible. So hoped Wilson and other supporters of the League all over the world.

Also in the treaties were outline plans for organising the League. All member countries were to send a representative to the annual Assembly. International disputes would go straight before the Council, a standing committee with a majority of Great Power members. The assembly would hear annual reports from members on how they were looking after their mandates: this was the name given to Germany's colonies and some parts of the Turkish empire, which the Allies insisted on sharing out among themselves. According to the treaty, these mandates were countries not yet ready to run their own affairs, and the allies, the advanced nations, would be responsible for guiding them to maturity. The people who lived in the mandates were not asked if they agreed with all this, and the system was little more than window-dressing to keep Wilson content while the winners shared the loot of victory.

## 2   Eastern Europe

This area was the trouble centre before both world wars. The three great empires of Russia, Austria, and Turkey which controlled it before 1914 had now all collapsed. In the peace treaties it was divided according to nationality, more or less – not exactly, as there were many areas of mixed nationality; and the prospects for these new nations were not bright – these small weak countries were sandwiched between giant neighbours, Russia and Germany, who might indeed be worn out in 1919 but would soon recover their strength.

So the Lithuanian, Latvian, and Estonian republics on the Baltic coast would be squashed as soon as Russia stirred to protect Leningrad (see Chapter 8, p. 140); and long before that they had turned into ugly dictatorships. Further north, Finland, previously part of the Russian empire but recognised as independent by the Bolsheviks, was bound

Legend:
- Territory lost by Germany
- Territory lost by Austria - Hungary
- Territory lost by Russia

0    km    500

to be overshadowed by Russia, with Leningrad so near the frontier. When war loomed again, in 1939, Russia struck. The largest new country in eastern Europe was Poland. This ancient kingdom had been shared among the three great empires, and in many areas Polish-speaking people, mostly strong Roman Catholics, were mixed among Russians, Ukrainians, and Germans. One such area was the Polish Corridor, which split Germany in two – but note that the peacemakers had to give Poland the corridor if Poland was to have the access to the sea promised in Wilson's 14 Points, which the German government accepted before the armistice. Inside the corridor was the German port of Danzig – trying to be fair to Germany, Britain's Prime Minister, Lloyd George, insisted that it should be ruled by the League of Nations, not by the Poles. Still, Poland now ruled a million Germans in the corridor, as well as 6 million non-Polish people to the east, in land seized from Bolshevik Russia. In 1919 the Bolsheviks tried to overrun Poland, hoping to bring help to the German communists. But with French help Poland's Marshal Pilsudski beat them off, and steered his country through its early years of independence. Democratic government did not develop healthily so he made himself dictator, and after his death Poland was a one-party state.

South of Poland was a country, shaped like a squirrel with a small tail, which did not seem likely to live long or peacefully. In its name, Czechoslovakia, 'Czecho' refers to the Czechs, a Slav people living in the richest industrial area of the old Austrian empire (it included Central Europe's largest armaments works, at Skoda); Slovakia refers to the Slovaks, another Slav people, mostly peasant farmers – you could compare the two peoples to the English and the Irish. If they could avoid quarrelling there would still be thousands of Hungarians, Poles, and Ruthenians within Czechoslovakia, and, the biggest headache, over 3 million Germans (generally called the Sudetens). Could this assortment hold together? There were reasons for hope in the wealthy, civilised Czechs, with their gifted leaders who had won powerful friends in the United States, Britain and France; and in fact, until Hitler interfered, their country was happy enough, and democracy's only East European showpiece.

Hungary was treated as an enemy, and lost fringe areas to its neighbours. It became a republic ruled by a proud class of great landowners. The provisional president in 1919 set an example by giving away his estates to his tenants, but this did not save him from overthrow in a communist rising. Czech and Romanian armies soon turned the communists out, and Horthy, once an admiral in the Habsburg fleet, set up a landowners' dictatorship.

South of Hungary and of the German-speaking Austrians are the lands of the South Slavs. To keep its grip on these, the Habsburg empire had gone to war – now when the empires had fallen they had joined Serbia to form the kingdom of Yugoslavia (South Slavs' land). The Serbian royal family controlled the government of this economically backward country. On its frontier with Italy the people

**DENMARK**

**LITHUANIA**
*Memel-land to Lithuania*

**EAST PRUSSIA**

Danzig

*North Slesvik to Denmark*

**GERMANY**

*Polish Corridor*

**No Air Force**
**Fleet sunk**
**No submarines**
**No big ships**
**Army of 100,000**
**All overseas colonies lost**
**Compensation**

**HOLLAND**

**BELGIUM**
*To Belgium*

*Rhineland*

**LUX.**

Saar

*Alsace-Lorraine to France*

**POLAND**

*Upper Silesia to Poland and Czechoslovakia*

*"Sudetens" under Czech. rule*

**CZECHOSLOVAKIA**

**AUSTRIA**
*To have no links with Germany*

**HUNGARY**

**SWITZERLAND**

**FRANCE**

*South Tirol to Italy*

**ITALY**

*1919 frontiers* — · —
*League of Nations control*
*Demilitarized zone*
*Lost by Germany as a result of 1914-18 war*

0        km        200

were very mixed and Italian nationalists invaded Fiume, a port where an Italian colony lived in a Slav area. This attack of 1919 was the first use of force against the peace terms.

With the bribe of a large chunk of Hungary, the Allies had persuaded the kingdom of Romania to join them in the war. The Romanians had lost their war and made peace, but two days before the cease-fire of 1918 they declared

*Versailles: Germany disgraced*
Text of Article 231 of the treaty:
The Allied and Associated Governments affirm, and Germany accepts, the responsibility of Germany and her allies for causing all the loss and damage to which the Allies and Associated Governments and their nationals have been subjected as a consequence of the war imposed upon them by the aggression of Germany and her allies

war again, hoping thus to qualify for the bribe. The new, enlarged Romania was a byword for its shabby politics. At first an ally of France, it got special attention from the Nazis because of its oil wells, and Romania's Nazis took their country into the second world war on Hitler's side.

## 3 Germany and the peace terms

'Vengeance! German Nation! Today in the Hall of Mirrors of Versailles the disgraceful treaty is being signed. Do not forget it! In the place where, in the glorious year of 1871, the German empire in all its glory had its origin, today German honour is being carried to its grave. Do not forget it! The German people will with unceasing labour press forward to reconquer the place among the nations to which it is entitled. Then will come vengeance for the shame of 1919.'

A German newspaper printed this statement on a front page edged with mourning black, on the day when two reluctant Germans – a socialist and a Catholic – signed the peace treaty.

These were the terms which seemed so disgraceful to the Germans:

(i) *Frontiers*
Germany lost Alsace-Lorraine to France.
The Polish Corridor split Germany in two.
The Saar coalfield was handed to France for 15 years.
German-speaking Austria was forbidden any links with Germany.

(ii) *Colonies*
All Germany's colonies, disguised as mandates (see p. 35) shared among her enemies.

(iii) *Disarmament*
No German troops or defence works west of a line 30 miles (50 kilometres) east of the Rhine.
This area to be occupied for 15 years by Allied armies .
The German army cut to 100,000 with no General Staff to plan wars, no national service to build up a trained reserve, no tanks, heavy guns, aircraft or airships.
The fleet to have no submarines or battleships.

(iv) *Reparations* (compensation for war damage)

Germany was to pay for war damage to Allied civilians and their property. The bill would be huge, since the German army had laid waste north east France and Belgium on its retreat in 1918.

(v) *War guilt*

The Kaiser and other guilty Germans were to be tried as war criminals. (The Dutch government blocked this by refusing to hand William over.) Germany was declared responsible for starting the war and banned from the League of Nations.

Wilson had called for and the Germans had looked for a fair, just peace without revenge, disarmament for all countries (not just the losers), and an impartial settlement of colonial problems. This peace was rather different! And the new German Republic was given a weak start by being forced to take responsibility before its people for accepting such terms.

## 4 Russia: communism in power

In December 1918 the elections for Russia's constituent assembly gave the Bolsheviks only 175 out of 707 seats. After the first day, the Bolsheviks would not let the assembly meet. They dropped the word "provisional" from their government's title, closed down all non-Bolshevik newspapers, and started a new political police, the Cheka, ordered to shoot at sight anyone suspected of counter-revolutionary actions. In the new Red Army which Trotsky was organising, a Bolshevik commissar was to check on each officer's every order. So, well before their Russian enemies took up arms against them, Lenin's men were setting up the dictatorship of a minority party.

Nor did the Bolsheviks keep the promises they had made to win popularity before they seized power (see ch. 2, p. 30). True, they stopped the war against Germany, but at a terrible cost. Instead of voting for peace with their feet, like the Russians, the German armies had marched on into Russia until the Bolsheviks had accepted their ruinous peace terms. This humiliation led many Russians to take up arms against the Bolsheviks. Within a year the Russians had stopped killing the Germans and were killing each other instead. So the promised peace turned sour. The promised bread was never eaten. The food situation got worse and worse as the peasants shared out the large estates which had grown food for sale, as the factories produced less and less, run by inexperienced workers and starved of raw materials, and as the richest farming area, the Ukraine, was taken over by the Germans. The workers soon lost their promised control over the factories. Seeing that "workers' control" failed to deliver any goods. Lenin ordered that the government would take charge of the basic industries and the owners run the rest. Party opinion forced him to go back on this early in 1918, when he nationalised all industrial firms – but this did not mean workers' control. The workers kept some right to share in decisions, but Lenin insisted that there must be one manager in charge of each concern, and the unions must see that he was obeyed.

All the same the Bolsheviks still had strong support from the town workers (in the election they won narrow majorities in Moscow and Petrograd). The peasant masses were never Bolshevik, and they turned right against Lenin when he tackled the food breakdown. He told the town soviets, the Red Army and the poorest peasants simply to seize all the grain they could find, leaving the growers with just enough to feed themselves and sow next year's crop – no payment need be made, and indeed there was nothing to pay with; no factory goods, and money which was worthless paper.

By mid-1918 civil war was breaking out in Russia. The humiliating treaty with Germany was a body blow to Bolshevik authority. Right wing supporters of the Czar, moderate supporters of the Duma, and left wingers who hated Bolshevik tyranny, all took up arms against the Bolsheviks. Britain, France, Poland, Japan and the USA also sent troops to fight the Reds, as they called the Bolsheviks, and support the Whites, the Bolsheviks' enemies.

How did the Bolsheviks survive this perilous year? By sheer luck, as Trotsky said? They had other assets. Trotsky himself turned out to be a military leader of genius. rumbling in his armoured train from front to front. He could do this because the Bolsheviks, like the French in 1914, had the advantage of interior lines of communication; and the Whites had nothing to offer the town workers, alarmed the peasants by promising to restore the land to its old owners, and accepted foreign help, which made them seem to be traitors. It was this which led many army officers to give Trotsky their services. The socialists of different kinds, who really won the election, lost the war through lack of toughness and organisation, and through standing by their democratic principles, whereas Lenin would scrap any principle in order to keep the Bolsheviks in power. The Bolshevik party itself was far from democratic. A handful of Bolshevik leaders controlled it. According to Lenin's notion of democratic centralism, the party central committee chose all the officials, ran the newspapers, and controlled the membership. In Lenin's lifetime ordinary Bolsheviks were allowed to discuss policy and at first he often had to follow party feeling rather than lead it. But once policy had been stated Bolsheviks were expected to silence their doubts. The leaders with real power were a minority within a minority, as the Bolsheviks themselves were only a fraction of Russia's people, who were mostly indifferent or against them.

Of course the Bolsheviks said that final authority lay with the Soviets which represented the working masses, but right from the start Lenin made sure that all the Commissars chosen by the soviets to form the actual government were Bolsheviks, and he boasted that the Soviets never even got the chance to consider a decision which the Bolsheviks had not already approved. Bolshevik Russia was no workers' democracy but the tyranny of a group of dedicated revolutionaries.

Confiscation – for instance, of the treasures of the Russian Church – and murder, stain the history of the Bolshevik revolution in the years of foreign menace and civil war. All the Czar's family were butchered: as Lenin's wife later wrote – 'The Czechoslovaks were advancing on Ekaterinberg where Nicholas II was being held prisoner. On July 19 (1919) we had him and his family shot.' The royal family were killed with Lenin's consent, to discourage the Whites and show the Reds that there could be no turning back – so Trotsky later explained. Nicholas, of little use to his people while alive, died nobly trying to shield his son from the murderers' bullets.

But Lenin did not mean to unleash mass looting and murder. True, the communists held that property was a a bourgeois notion, but he reminded them that bourgeois civilisation was better than no civilisation at all. As he came to realise that building socialism in Russia would take many years, he insisted that during those years the old civilisation must be protected. The old law courts were scrapped, but replaced with working-class courts, which were to see that property was protected.

The gravest charge against Lenin is that he caused millions of deaths by violence and starvation as a result of confiscating the peasants' crops. In 1919 the peasants simply did not grow any food except for themselves. By 1921 Russia was growing less than half as much food as before 1914! So in the towns there was nothing to eat; the agony would have been worse without the famine relief work of the League of Nations organised by an American engineer, Herbert Hoover.

By 1921 Lenin had little to fear from the White armies, but the food situation was desperate, and the core of communist supporters was rotting.

A danger signal came from the sailors of the Baltic fleet at Kronstadt. They demanded fresh elections for the soviets, freedom for other political parties as well as the communists, and the return of small-scale private trading to improve food supplies. They trusted the Bolsheviks too much to use force against them, but Lenin had no such fine feelings; he sent the Red Army against the sailors, and after bitter fighting in which 3,500 people were killed the sailors were wiped out. Free elections Lenin did not dare allow, but after the Kronstadt battle he dropped the food confiscation policy and launched his New Economic Policy (N.E.P.) which allowed private businessmen to buy and sell food and other goods. So some kind of market revived – there was some incentive to grow crops or make goods for sale at a profit, and in the next six years Russian life began a slow, painful recovery. The return of private trading seemed treason to old-fashioned communists – Lenin showed his greatness again by being ready to swap horses in mid-stream rather than die on a drowning one. If the theory doesn't work, change it; that was his attitude. 'Grey', he liked to say, 'is every theory, but green is the eternal tree of life.'

Lenin's position as unchallenged leader of the Bolsheviks was safe, but his active career was nearly over. In summer

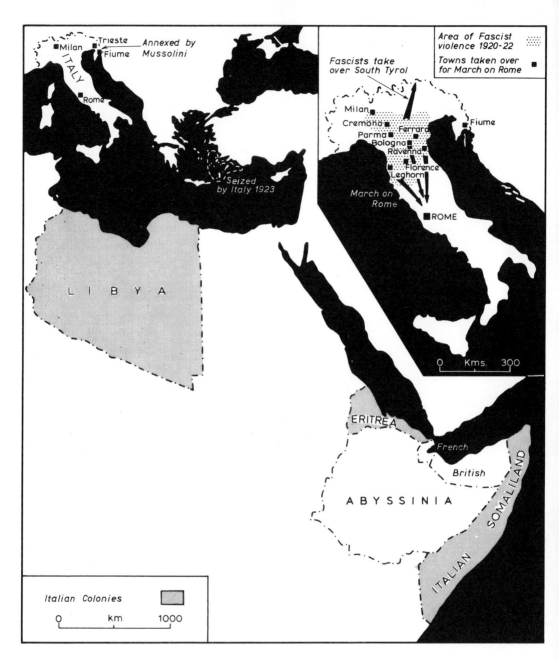

Annexed by Mussolini

Milan
Trieste
Fiume
ITALY
Rome

Seized
by Italy 1923

L I B Y A

Area of Fascist
violence 1920-22

Towns taken over
for March on Rome

Fascists take
over South Tyrol

Milan
Cremona
Parma
Ferrara
Bologna
Ravenna
Florence
Leghorn
March on
Rome
Fiume
ROME

0    Kms.   300

ERITREA
French
British
A B Y S S I N I A
ITALIAN SOMALILAND

Italian Colonies

0        km        1000

1918 all political parties except the Bolsheviks had been
banned – and a woman member of the party with most
peasant support had shot Lenin and seriously wounded
him. His health never fully recovered, and a series of
strokes crippled him months before his death in January
1924. While he was dying. Stalin, a quiet, pitiless person

*The Italian Empire and the
rise of Mussolini*
Milan's most powerful
journalist became Prime
Minister in Rome; but he
looked outside Italy towards
a new 'Roman Empire' based
on the Mediterranean and
East Africa

who had steadily brought the whole communist party organisation under his own control, was inching his way towards supreme power. Lenin saw the danger – he had quarrelled with Stalin, who had crushed the Georgian nationalists of southern Russia with too bloody a hand though he was from Georgia himself. Lenin decided he was too rough and when he died was trying to have Stalin dismissed from his powerful position as secretary of the Party.

At the time of his death Russia was still an outcast among nations. Russia had suffered more than any other country in the war of 1914–18, yet the Western allies, dreading the spread of communism to their own countries and at the same time doubting whether it would last in Russia, settled the peace terms without consulting the Russian government. They did not even recognise that the Bolsheviks were the legal government of Russia.

Not until 1921 was a conference arranged to which the Russians were invited – this was Lloyd George's conference at Rapallo in Italy. Even then, the Russians correctly felt that they were wanted only to make a solid front against Germany over reparations, while the Russians would find the Germans supporting the allies in demanding payment of Russia's debts to foreign countries – the Bolsheviks had refused to honour these. So the two debtors made a deal together, and the German republic became the communists' first foreign friend, apart from the sections of the world's socialist parties which had accepted the Bolsheviks' leadership, and called themselves communists. All through the 1920's, Russia helped Germany to dodge the 1919 disarmament terms, while German experts and machinery helped the Russian economy to get on its feet. Not until 1924 did Britain, Italy, and France recognise the communist government.

## 5   Italy

The 1919 peace settlement could get no love or loyalty from Russia or Germany. The same can be said of another country, this time not a loser in the war, but a dissatisfied winner – Italy. Attacking the peace terms was one of the chief tactics used by the Fascist party leader, Benito Mussolini, to curry favour with the Italian nationalists

45

after 1919. Mussolini, son of a blacksmith and a school mistress, was sullen and vicious as a boy, and twice expelled from school for knifing fellow pupils. Talented only in speechifying, it seemed, he qualified as a teacher, but spent years of exile in Switzerland doing odd jobs. Before 1914 Mussolini won fame in Italy as an extreme left-wing journalist, a violent enemy of the army, royal family, church, and empire. His appetite for forceful action landed him in prison more than once, and when the war broke out he soon deserted from the Italian socialist party which held that Italy should stay neutral. While serving as a soldier he was badly wounded by an accidental explosion, and posing as a war hero he joined forces with the nationalists. Like them, he felt in 1919 that the Italian government was not being tough enough to get a fair return for the country's war effort: what was needed was a take-over of power by the new generation, especially by the ex-servicemen, instead of the respectable old politicians.

He started a network of *fasci*, groups of men who felt this way. They paraded in black shirts, copied from the *arditi*, the Italian commandos. The Fascists rejoiced at the invasion of Fiume (see p. 38) – but in elections they fared badly and Mussolini saw that peaceful methods alone would not bring them to power. The socialists gave him his opportunity. They launched a new series of major strikes and tried to take over the running of the factories – and Mussolini shouted that they wanted to bring Italy to the same shocking state as Russia. The Fascists took the lead in the upper and middle class struggle against social-ism; they beat up socialist councillors, burned down socialist clubs and co-operative farms, broke up socialist meetings; they used ex-army weapons and the police and army never tried to interfere. The socialists answered violence with violence – hundreds were killed. In fact the Italian socialists had no idea of launching a Bolshevik revolution, from which Mussolini claimed to be saving Italy. The claim was enough, though, to bring him into friendly co-operation with the old-style politicians, who dreaded socialism. Once they had accepted him, he was in a position to take over the government peacefully, but the Fascists wanted to play it rough and Mussolini as their leader had to follow them. He agreed to a March on Rome by blackshirt columns from all over Italy. While they marched he sat in his Milan office waiting to be invited properly, by the King, to form a government.

The politicians now thought Fascism looked too ugly and they wanted to use the army against the advancing blackshirts – but the King would not support this so Mussolini got his invitation. Wearing a bowler hat and a black shirt he set out for Rome by train. There he paraded the marchers and sent them home.

As Prime Minister he worked with the other political parties at first, and seemed reasonably mild. He launched a strict government economy campaign and did not prevent people from criticising him. But the next elections were rigged to make sure that the Fascists got a big majority, and there was much threatening of voters by the Fascists. A socialist named Matteotti collected evidence to prove this; he was kidnapped and murdered by the Fascists. This made headlines all over Europe; Mussolini's popularity slumped and he thought of resigning. In the end he accepted full responsibility for the murder and for the rest of Fascist violence. He used the continuing attacks on his methods as an excuse for banning all opposition parties and starting a strict press censorship.

So was born Europe's first Fascist dictatorship – an answer from the Right to Lenin on the Left. When Lenin died Mussolini had achieved little, beyond destroying political freedom in Italy.

## 6 The United States of America

What of the USA, whose President had tried to force the 14 Points on the allies as a basis for the peace terms, and championed the League of Nations as an authority to revise them without war? Wilson returned to Washington in 1919 to present the Versailles treaty to the Senate. He admitted that old entanglements had stood in the way of a triumph of freedom and right, and that it had been difficult to graft the new ideas on to the old, so the fruits might be bitter for a time; yet he felt that his new ideas would prevail. Though the politicians might be unfriendly, the hearts of the people yearned for a new start, he reckoned. Yet Wilson's own people did not back him up. In 1918 they had voted his party, the Democrats, out of control of Congress, and his opponents, the Republicans, in.

Wilson did nothing to make the Republicans feel it was their treaty as well as his. Before leaving for Paris he refused to take any leading Republicans with him. When he came back he would not allow any changes in the treaty to meet Republican complaints.

Seeing that Congress was unlikely to pass the treaty as it stood, Wilson made a last appeal to the people, a heroic speech-making tour of America. With his health cracking, he could hardly climb on to the platform at Pueblo, Colorado, for his 37th speech in 22 days. The 14 Points, he claimed, were not his ideas but his effort to read the thought of the people of the USA. In tears he reminded his audiences of their pledges to 'those dear ghosts that still deploy upon the fields of France', where he had seen French women each day leaving flowers on the graves of American soldiers; he called on America to 'see the thing through' and 'make good their redemption of the world.'

That same evening Wilson collapsed in his train, and soon he was crippled by a severe stroke. His wife kept this a secret. Soon he was just well enough to sign official documents (but one was brought out of his bedroom signed at the top instead of the bottom). Desperately the sick man clung to every letter of his treaty. Congress threw it out. The Republicans considered that Wilson had not lived up to his own programme. In particular he had not protected China from Japanese greed (see Chapter 5, pp. 82–83). By pledging the US to the Covenant he risked dragging his country into quarrels that were of no concern to it.

American interest was now focussed on home affairs. As in Europe the post-war years were troubled. In the North there were race riots where negroes had moved from their homes in the South to take jobs in war industries. Wage cuts were answered with strikes and factory bosses hired gunmen to use against strikers. In New York the actors struck, in Boston the police. America was bitterly divided over the prohibition of the trade in alcoholic drinks. Prohibition had been enforced in wartime by the German and Russian governments, and even in liberty-loving Britain the pubs had been forced to close in the afternoon. In 1917 America went further – Congress wrote into the Constitution a ban on making and selling all alcoholic drinks.

So started 13 years of prohibition. This was a triumph

for the American temperance movement, which for years had tried to build up a 'dry' party in Congress. Who supported prohibition? Mostly the old-established country dwellers who loathed America's fast-growing cities with their crooked politicians who used the saloons (pubs) as bases for organising the votes of the more recent immigrants; and thousands of respectable women and churchgoers were persuaded that drink was the root of most crime, disease, and sinful living. During the war, the 'drys' could also argue that crops used for alcohol would be better used for feeding starving Europe; and that German immigrants were powerful in the American liquor trade. It was in wartime that prohibition became law. It lasted so long because it was part of a rearguard action of the established Americans against the massive immigration of the last 50 years, and all that the immigrants seemed to stand for. The prohibition years were also the time of new controls of immigration aimed at preserving the commanding position of the white Anglo-Saxon protestants, and especially at keeping out the Japanese (see Chapter 5, p. 91; of the revival of the Ku Klux Klan, a secret society for haters of negroes, Roman Catholics (who were usually recent immigrants from Ireland, Italy, or Poland) and Jews (supposed by country people to be the secret bosses of the big cities). Al Smith's bid for the Presidency in 1928 was defeated; Al was of Irish descent, a New Yorker, a Catholic, a 'wet', a city politician. He lost to the Republican Hoover who had grown up on a farm where even the soap was home-made, then made a fortune in engineering. Before two Italians, Sacco and Vanzetti, were electrocuted on a dubious murder charge, Vanzetti claimed: 'I am suffering because I am a Radical; I have suffered because I am an Italian and indeed I am an Italian.'

These events show the strength of the conservative forces in American life, but at the same time it was Americans who were inventing modern times as we know them. Radio sets appeared in most American homes and millions 'tuned in'. Hollywood films met little competition during the war years and dominated entertainment far beyond the US. The automobile became part of the family; garages sprouted along the roads; the first mass-produced car, the Ford Model T, was launched in 1908.

Henry Ford copied the idea of the assembly line from the

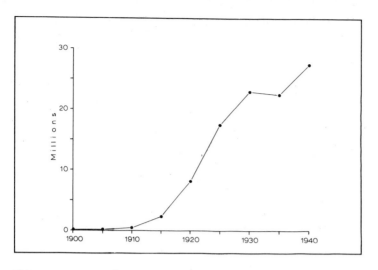

*Privately-owned cars in the U.S.A. 1900–1940*
Note the steep rise in the 'boom' years after 1915, and the fall in the 'slump' years after 1930

Chicago meat packers. Instead of the cars being stationary while the workers moved round them, the cars travelled past an avenue of workers who each had one simple task to do to each car as it went past him. This mass production did not cater for the individual tastes of the buyers, and it made the work monotonous, but it cut costs so much that cars were now within the budget of the average family instead of being a rich man's luxury. And Ford could cut the working day to 8 hours. For good or ill, the family car changed life more than most politicians ever could.

American politicians of the early 1920's were not impressive. The Democrats were still championing the League of Nations, and lost the 1920 Presidential election to Warren Harding, who was handsome but had nothing else to recommend him – or so his own party managers said; he let his colleagues make crooked fortunes. Some took bribes for allowing illegal liquor sales; one was sent to prison for selling off the navy's oil reserves kept at Teapot Dome, in return for a fortune in bribes. After Harding's sudden death, Calvin Coolidge took over and won the 1924 election for the Republicans. His slogan was, 'Keep cool with Coolidge'. He did not overheat himself in enforcing the impossible prohibition of alcohol, though he was teetotal himself. Strictly honest, he tidied up the mess of 'graft' left by Harding. He believed the government's task was to keep taxes as low as possible and leave business as free as possible. This seemed to be what people wanted.

So, he said, it must be what God wanted.

During these years of growing wealth and harsh controversy in the US, their government still took a lively interest in world affairs. Harding's administration worked to cut down the world's navies, and reached an agreement with the chief naval powers which was dangerously favourable to the Japanese. All American governments wrestled with the reparations problems (see Chapter 7, p. 108); they had to, since Britain and France could not pay their debts to America unless Germany paid them reparations. America lent the money needed to put Germany back on its feet, and reached two complicated agreements with the German republic on reparations payments. The Americans joined in the unsuccessful efforts at agreeing on international disarmament, which lasted until the Germans walked out in 1933 (see Chapter 7, p. 113; Chapter 8, p. 125). It was the Americans who launched the Kellogg Pact, a fine-sounding agreement to outlaw war, which 62 governments insincerely signed.

# Chapter 4
# Africa, Asia and
# Latin America

Apart from the United States of America and Turkey, the First World War and its outcome was an affair mostly of concern to Europe.

Some parts of the world, like Latin America and South East Asia, were hardly involved at all. Others were fought over, used as a source of supplies and manpower, and taken from the losers by the winners, as happened in Africa and the Middle East. It is to these that we now turn.

## 1  Africa's earlier history

The continent of Africa makes up one-fifth of the entire land surface of the earth. At the start of the twentieth century, between 100 and 150 million people lived there, not many for so great an area.

Before the Europeans came, Africa was not divided up into nations in the way that Europe was. Most of the continent was cut off from Europe by the great Sahara desert. On the northern fringes of the desert, by the Mediterranean Sea, lived nomadic Arabs and others. South of the desert, along the rivers emptying into the Gulf of Guinea, lived the tribes of the West African negroes. South of them, in the dense tropical forest of Central Africa, these tribes were in contact with primitive pigmy forest peoples. Yet further to the south, equally primitive groups survived in the Kalahari desert. To the east, around the great lakes and on the grasslands of the south dwelled the other great network of negro tribes, the Bantu-speaking peoples.

The people of Africa, like everyone else, lived by the crops they grew and the animals they herded. But the difficulties created by the soil and climate had kept most of them trapped at the simplest level, the struggle to survive. In Europe, food surpluses and contact with other parts of the world led to trade, and so to the growth of cities. None of this happened in Africa. Even if there were surpluses or contacts, jungles, deserts and waterfall-punctuated rivers hindered transport and communication. Of course, this cannot be said of the northern Arab area, where the Nile and the Mediterranean made transport and contact easier; but for the rest, we know too little of Africa's past, for no towns meant no written records.

The picture we have is of an Africa thinly populated by farming tribes, living in villages under local chiefs and kings of varying power. As one would expect, there were often wars between the tribes, and sometimes the wars led to the creation of big empires by the most warlike peoples, such as the Bantu Zulus and the West African Ashanti, both of whom had well-organised armies capable of giving a bad time of it to better armed European soldiers.

When Europeans came to Africa, most of them supposed that because the Africans were still tribal farmers, they were less intelligent than Europeans. This was a mistake. In fact the Europeans themselves helped to hold Africa back by encouraging the tribes to fight. They offered to buy the captives of African wars as slaves, and managed to remove something like ten million negroes from Africa in this way. Europe's first contribution to Africa was to encourage war and depopulation.

## 2   The European take-over

Beneath Africa's soil lies great mineral wealth, but the Europeans who conquered Africa did not know this at first. What took them to Africa was the wealth of Asia; the route to Asia lay round the coast of Africa, and so several European countries built harbours along that coast. From these harbours the slave trade operated.

Christian missionaries and adventurers had been exploring the interior, and discovering on their way the suffering that the slave trade was causing. They made such an outcry that most European countries set about stamping it out. Most of the work was done at sea by the British navy, but in some cases armies penetrated deep inland from the harbours in pursuit of slave-trading African tribes.

What started the real 'scramble for Africa' at the end of the nineteenth century, however, was the competition

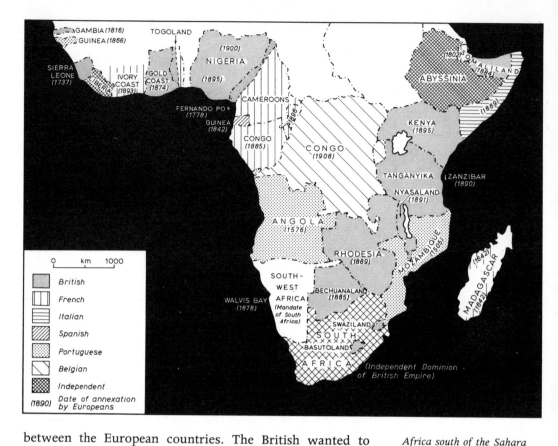

between the European countries. The British wanted to be certain that no one could cut them off from the wealth of their Indian Empire (see pp. 62–65) by seizing the Suez Canal, so they stationed an army in Egypt, 'to support the Egyptian government', so they said, but really to control it. The French were not to be left behind, and sent soldiers to take over large areas of north Africa from the west.

Others followed suit, and before long maps had to be drawn to show who claimed what. Along with the armies, sometimes before them, came the missionaries and traders. Often enough the European soldiers occupied parts of Africa in order to rescue or support them. The result was that by 1919 a map of Africa had been drawn which you can see above. It looked fine on European walls, but it was made by European statesmen with little idea of what it meant in terms of nations or geography.

If their claims to ownership were to mean anything, each of the imperial nations had to send officers to rule their territories, meeting the Africans and keeping order among

*Africa south of the Sahara between the two World Wars*

them. Soldiers had to be kept handy to back up the officers. Sometimes railways were built, both to help this administration and to encourage trade. The tribes could no longer fight each other, nor could they continue their free wanderings in search of better land. They could still move about, but now had to take work in the cities, factories and mines which the Europeans were building. Missionary schools brought European learning to Africa, but only very slowly, for few Africans saw these schools. Equally slowly, the introduction of European medical science caused the population to rise.

It still did not occur to the Europeans that these backward farmers would be anything different for hundreds of years. It cost a good deal of money to govern the African colonies. To meet this cost, Africa had to be made profitable, and white men were sent to do it – the farmer, the trader, and the industrialist, bold men ready to take risks seeking a fortune in an unknown land.

## 3  South Africa

Europeans settled in South Africa in greater numbers than elsewhere in Africa. The Boers, descended from Dutchmen, had farmed there for three hundred years, and developed their own language, Afrikaans. Moving north, they had fought and beaten Bantus moving south. Side by side with the Boers were the British settlers who had come in the great diamond rush at the end of the nineteenth century. The two peoples had fought over the country in the Boer War (1899–1902), but now lived uneasily together in the Union of South Africa, part of the British Empire, but a self-governing nation with its own Parliament and armed services.

They could afford self-government because of the fabulous wealth of minerals below the country's soil. In 1926 £42,000,000 worth of gold was mined, as well as diamonds, coal, copper, tin, asbestos, silver and platinum. South Africa was the continent's first industrialised nation.

The $1\frac{1}{2}$ million Europeans still found plenty to quarrel about among themselves. Should the official language be English or Afrikaans? Should the Union Jack be part of the national flag? In 1914 and again in 1939 there were Boers who wanted to join the war – but against Britain!

These quarrels also extended to the treatment of South Africa's 5 million Africans.

The Boers believed that the country belonged to the whites, and that the Africans should only be allowed there as servants, farm workers, or labourers. They had fought the Bantu too often to be able to think of sharing the country with Africans. Already they had restricted African farmers to small areas and the worst land. Many of the British were in favour of educating the Africans and giving them full equality. The British miners, however, who earned about £5 a week, were afraid of losing their jobs to Africans who would do the same job for £1 a week. They sided with the Boer farmers. In 1926 Parliament passed a law which reserved the best jobs for whites only. From then on the Africans who flocked into the mining towns were to have only the lowliest jobs and to live in separate compounds. To move about they needed to get special permission and passes. In 1936, those few Africans who had the vote because they lived in areas of British influence were told that they might elect only three special representatives, and those must be Europeans.

These colour bar laws were the work of the Nationalist Party, led by Jan Hertzog, representing most of the Boer farmers and the working-class whites of the towns. These groups both despised and feared the Africans, and had little love for Great Britain. They were opposed by a moderate Boer, Jan Smuts, a hero of the Boer War. He had fought in the First World War, served in the British government, and helped found the League of Nations (see p. 34). His fame and prestige brought him much political support, and he was able to hold the nationalists in check for many years. He was Prime Minister of South Africa from 1919 to 1924, and again from 1939 to 1948.


## 4   Tribal Africa under the Europeans

To the homelands of the Negro tribes, the vast regions of East, Central and West Africa, Europeans came later and in smaller numbers than to South Africa. In West Africa the climate was unhealthy for the whites – the Gold Coast was known as 'the white man's grave' – and so they developed the coastal cities for trading with the negroes, and encouraged them to grow crops which were in demand in Europe; vegetable oils, cocoa, cotton and rubber. The Europeans usually ruled indirectly through the chiefs. The Belgian Congo contained in the Katanga copper belt mineral riches second only to South Africa's.

This area, the basin of tropical Africa's greatest river, was run as a private estate by the Belgian king until 1908. He forced the Africans to collect rubber for him, which made him a fortune. If they did not deliver enough rubber, their hands and feet were cut off. Scandal over this forced the king to surrender control to his parliament in 1908, and he burned all the documents which told the full story of his rule. Within 40 years the Belgians had probably halved the Congo's population.

After 1908 the Belgians continued, less brutally, to exploit the Congo. In the up-river province of Katanga they found rich copper mines. Copper replaced rubber as the chief export; duties on copper gave the Congo government a large income. The Belgians did some good. They stopped the slave trade and attacked tropical diseases. They checked leprosy. Roman Catholic priests established primary schools. But the Congolese Africans were allowed neither the smallest say in their country's government nor the chance to qualify for any really responsible job. An African might be a brilliant medical student but he could not rise higher than assistant to a Belgian doctor.

South of the Congo lay the British territories of the Rhodesias. Northern Rhodesia contained the fringes of the Katanga copperbelt. In Southern Rhodesia by 1923 there were 35,000 Britons and enough wealth for them to be given self-government within the British Empire after the Britons had turned down the chance of entering the Union of South Africa. The million Africans of the territory were not asked for an opinion.

If we turn to East Africa and the colony of Kenya, where the whites were interested in the farming opportunities, and there was little mineral wealth to affect the story, we shall get a good idea of how white farmers affected Africa.

The coast of this area was long used to the settlements of Arab and Indian traders. Mombasa, an important and well-developed port, was about the only item of any value in the British colony, and from it was built a railway in 1900 to open up trade in cotton with the tribes of Uganda. The railway passed through promising agricultural areas, and by 1914 5,000 white farmers had come to the White Highlands, by far the best farming land in Kenya. By 1940 their numbers had swollen to 20,000. The White Highlands were forbidden to the Kikuyu, the dominant African people who farmed less productive reserves.

After the Europeans brought peace and their medical knowledge, the Kikuyu population began to increase. Naturally, they resented the restrictions placed on their farming. The Europeans, living in a strange land, were both afraid and contemptuous of the Africans. The basis of hatred between the races was laid.

Matters were complicated by the successful Asians who dominated the shops and trade of the coastal towns. These people could not be passed off as children, as the settlers liked to think of the Africans, and they caused the British

*Empires in North Africa and the Middle East*
The large map shows the situation in 1914. The small one shows the post-war map after the defeat of Turkey

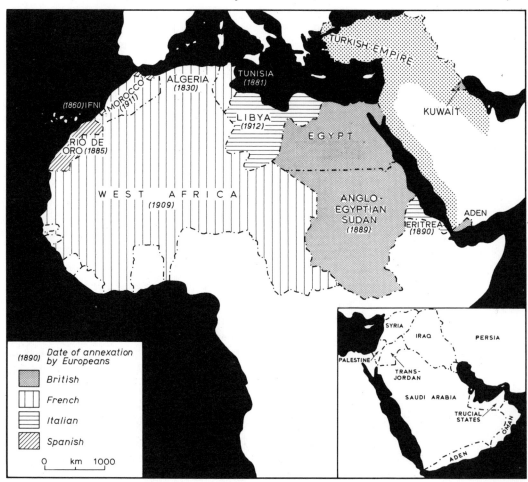

Government to think twice about granting self-government to the settlers. In 1923 Britain announced that Kenya would be ruled in the long term interest of the African majority. No one expected this to mean very much. But already in 1922 a Kikuyu Association had been formed, with the object of getting the White Highlands back for Kikuyu farmers. In 1928, a thirty-two year old Kikuyu, educated at a mission school and now a clerk to the Nairobi town council, became its General Secretary. His name was Jomo Kenyatta. By 1933 he had gone to a British university and written a book about his people. Any European who thought all Africans backward simpletons might have guessed, if he had thought about it, that Africa was not to remain uncomplaining under the white man for long. Through the 1930's unknown Africans in all parts were finding their way to school. Their names, Kwame Nkrumah, Hastings Banda, Kenneth Kaunda, Julius Nyerere, would be well enough known in time.

As always, it was towns and missionary education which had most effect on the Africans, by introducing them to European ways of life and ideas. Outside the towns and the few schools, most of them remained undisturbed in their tribal, farming life. Those who did come into the towns were, as in South Africa, kept firmly on the lowest rungs of the ladder.

## 5   The Arab lands of North Africa and the Middle East

Africa north of the Sahara has a different history from the rest of the continent. It has always been a poor relation of the Mediterranean civilisations; the Phoenicians colonised there; the ancient Romans had business in Egypt. Egypt itself had been one of the first centres of civilisation. Now these lands, along with their eastern neighbours, though inhabited by peoples of very mixed origins, were dominated by the Arabic language and the Moslem religion, established in the days of the Arab empire founded by the prophet Mahomet.

The map shows how the French, Italian and Turkish empires dominated the Arab lands in 1914.

In the French area there had been large scale settlement by Europeans and direct government from Paris. Algeria, for instance, took its name from the busy port of Algiers, for centuries the only place really controlled by the Spaniards, Turks, pirates, and French who claimed to rule the hinterland at one time or another. The unruly, warlike Arab desert tribes of the interior respected no authority in distant Algiers. It took the French army thirty years to establish command over them, and even then there was rebellion from time to time. By 1914 there were 750,000 Europeans trading and farming in Algeria, mostly from Spain and Italy, but all with the rights of a French citizen. The richest were the great estate owners, often wine-growers; in the towns of the coast there were rich and poor, very like any town in France, except that the very poorest were the Arabs who came into the towns to find work. The farming Arabs, of course, were left the second best land, away from the fertile coast. About one Arab child in fifteen found a place in the French-provided schools. During the First World War, many Arabs worked in France, and 70,000 of them stayed on there after it.

The French declared that Algeria was no colony, but a full and equal part of France – the Mediterranean was no more than a river. Yet hardly any Arab had the right to vote, most Arabs were miserably poor, and the white settlers had no intention of altering the situation.

Naturally, those Arabs who for one reason or another came into contact with the higher living standards of the French questioned this poverty among their own people. In the 1920's a society called the North African Star was created by the Arab workers in France, at first as a sort of trade union; but by the 1930's it was promoting the idea of an independent Arab state in Algeria. Ferhat Abbas, who had gone to a French school and came from a compara-tively wealthy family, took the French theory at its word and argued that as there was no real Arab nation, they should try to become Frenchmen. When he saw how this aroused the anger of the settlers he realised that France would spurn this policy herself if it was taken seriously, and after 1945 he too turned to nationalism. Others were starting Arab schools, where the first lesson was, 'My religion is Islam, my language Arabic, my country Algeria'. Before Algeria became a Second World War battleground, Arabs were beginning to reject the idea that their towns and deserts were part of France.

There were similar beginnings of nationalism in the

French controlled countries of Morocco and Tunisia, to the west and east of Algeria. The nationalist movement was strongest of all in Egypt, where the British army ruled the rulers of a real nation with a long history. Here there were few settlers. The British were in Egypt to command the Suez Canal, the route to India and the Far East. Foreign control of the Canal had already inspired a nationalist revolt in the 1880's against the Khedives, traditional rulers of Egypt whose title dated from the Turkish empire's rule.

British guns now kept the Khedive in power and dictated how he should govern Egypt. Not surprisingly, this unashamed dictation by force bred a lasting hatred among Egyptians. The First World War caused prices to rise, and many of the poor peasants were conscripted into forced labour for the British army. Between 1919 and 1923 there were repeated outbreaks of anti-British violence, growing to a full-scale terrorist murder campaign directed against British soldiers and civilians, and those Egyptians who co-operated with them.

The violence brought results, in two stages. First, in 1923, the British recognised the independence of Egypt under a King and Parliament, but reserving the Canal itself and the Sudan for the British, who also had the right to protect all foreign residents. Independent Egypt was not to make alliances with any other country but Britain.

The nationalists continued their terrorism against Britons and those Egyptians who were ready to accept the 1923 arrangements, and in 1936, the year in which the sixteen year old Farouk became King, a new Anglo-Egyptian treaty promised full independence by stages over twenty years, with the British army keeping the Canal Zone during that time.

In the First World War, Egypt had been the base for British operations against the Turks. The Turkish rule over Arabian deserts and ancient trade centres was all that remained of what had once been a mighty empire. Among the sheiks of the poor nomad Bedouin tribes of Arabia were those who dreamed of creating a great Arab nation. In 1916, beguiled by misleading promises, they led an Arab revolt against the Turks which assisted the advance of the British and French armies (see p. 26). Their reward was poor. An Arab state was indeed created – the useless inner desert we now know as Saudi Arabia. The British retained their protectorate over the petty sheiks of the coasts and the Persian Gulf. The fertile north of Arabia, with its cities and access to the Mediterranean, was shared between the French and British.

The French created two republics, Syria and the Lebanon, drove out the Arab leaders, and attempted to combine repression of nationalists with French education. For their pains they earned hatred and several attempts at rebellion. Twice they lost control of the capital, Damascus, completely.

In the peace settlement with Turkey, Britain gained mandates (see p. 35) over three new territories, Transjordan, Iraq and Palestine. The last of these was a focus of nationalist ambition for a people without a country, the Jews. In response to Jewish pressure, Britain agreed to regard Palestine as a Jewish 'national home'.

Even if the Allies had thus betrayed the hopes for an Arab state, their new patchwork of subject nations provided a framework in which separate nationalisms and independence movements could flourish. The dream of Arab unity was never forgotten either, although its leadership was disputed among the creations of the European powers and the Egyptians.


## 6   British India

India was like Africa, a land of many languages and peoples, ruled by European conquerors. In this case there was only one European nation, Britain, and the peoples it ruled belonged to a highly civilised society, whose art, wisdom and religions were as old as any in Europe.

Like all the countries which had not yet experienced the industrial revolution, India was a country of peasant farmers living in villages. Once the land had been divided into many states, ruled by princes of enormous wealth and power, but at the beginning of the twentieth century two-thirds of India had been taken over by the British and was governed directly by British civil servants and soldiers headed by the Viceroy of India. The other third was still ruled by its princes, Maharajahs and Nizams, but even they recognised the British sovereign as their Emperor, and the Viceroy in Delhi as his representative. Thus the Viceroy, appointed by the British government, ruled nearly

At the base of the human pyramid in British India – victims of famine before 1914

one-fifth of all the people in the world.

To bind this multitude together there was the English language, adopted as a common tongue by all who could learn it, there was British justice (outside the princely states), and there were two great religions, Hinduism and Islam; Hinduism a religion native to India, Islam the religion of the followers of Mahomet, called Moslems.

Although India was not industrialised, handicrafts were highly developed. Indian cloth, for example, produced on hand-looms, was world famous. Trade flourished in India. It was a land of great cities, splendid palaces and temples, and ancient learning. The peasants of India might

63

be among the poorest people in the world, but her princes were the richest, and between the two was a large, well-to-do middle class of landlords, merchants, lawyers, and others. Among the Hindus the 'caste' into which a person was born decided his life for him. The people who did the most menial jobs, such as street sweeping, were 'outcastes', untouchables. Members of some of the very highest born castes considered themselves contaminated if they even saw an untouchable.

Among the British officials and soldiers who ruled India, there were some who looked forward to the day when the peoples of India would be united and self-governing. A small number of Indians had been admitted to the Civil Service, and experiments had been made with local councils which were invited to comment on the government's actions. In 1885 some of the British civil servants, with the Viceroy's encouragement, had helped to start a society called the Indian National Congress to press the case for self-government by the Indians.

Of course, a great many of the British were opposed to this idea, and attempted to weaken the Congress party. It was partly due to them that the Moslems left Congress in 1906 and started the All-India Moslem League, to protect the interests of the Moslems against being swamped by the Hindu majority in the Congress.

By the time of the First World War, to which India sent a million men for Britain, many of the younger members of both Congress and the League were growing impatient with peaceful methods and their elders' policy of co-operation with the British authorities. Talk of violence, boycott and murder began to be heard. Even so, Britain was still moving, very slowly, in the direction of self-government. In 1919 schemes were introduced for bringing Indians and elections into the government; but in the same year there was a disastrous massacre at Amritsar when a nervous British general had his soldiers fire on an angry mass meeting of impatient Indians. 379 Indians were killed and 1,200 injured.

In the middle of this worsening situation, a new leader was coming to the notice of India and the world. His name was Mohandas Karamchand Gandhi.

Gandhi had trained to be a lawyer in England, and at the age of 23, in 1893, he had been called to South Africa on a case. In South Africa many Indians were feeling the effect of the first of the racialist laws which were to make that country into a fortress of European supremacy (see pp. 55–56), and Gandhi stayed there to fight and become an Indian hero, inventing a new style for fighting injustice – passive resistance. It was 1915 before he returned to India, world famous. He now insisted on living a life of poverty, eating only one meal a day, wearing only a loin-cloth, owning nothing. By his saintly example he could command the support of thousands, discouraging them from committing any violence, urging them to suffer patiently whatever the exasperated authorities did when they refused to obey unjust laws, went on strike, or blocked roads and railways with their bodies. In South Africa he went to prison four times, meekly asking the judge to impose the maximum sentence. His patience, kindness and saintliness made even his enemies admit their admiration of this remarkable man.

The strength that Gandhi found in himself through poverty and meekness he believed was also his country's strength. Like all nationalists, he wanted India ruled by Indians; but he also believed that India should ignore the industrial revolution, which he said had brought only unhappiness. India should lead the world back to the simple life of handicrafts and farming.

Led by Gandhi, Congress left its policy of friendship with the British and took up resistance by every possible form of disobedience except violence. But once law and order began to break down, the more fanatical nationalists turned to terrorism and violence, whatever their leaders did to prevent it. Worse still, there were outbreaks of mob murder between Hindus and Moslems. The British imprisoned the Indian leaders, only to be forced to release them whenever they wanted to reach some agreement. Four more times Gandhi went to prison; in 1922, 1930, 1933, and 1942.

## 7   South East Asia

East of India and south of China lies a peninsula of jungles and rivers, breaking into a tangle of islands; the peninsula and islands are occupied by peasant farmers growing their staple rice crops, and the area is also a source of oil, tin and rubber, as well as the spices which had made it the target of European traders as long ago as the sixteenth century.

The history of South East Asia is as long and complicated as the history of Europe, a story of wars, empires, the rise and fall of great men and great civilisations. But it too had fallen easy victim to the empire-building nations of Europe when they came first to trade and then to conquer.

The ancient kingdom of Burma had fallen foul of the British by warring against India, and had been conquered and incorporated into British India in 1886. Siam survived only because the British and French agreed to leave it as a neutral zone between their conquests. Laos, a remote and mysterious land to this day, the Kingdom of Cambodia, and the old Empire of Annam had been colonised by France under the collective name of Indo-China. Further south a dozen independent sultans of the Malay peninsula, troubled by ruling a people half their own, half Chinese immigrants come to work the tin-mines, were glad to let the British help them run their lands. At the tip of the peninsula lay the British island colony of Singapore, a vital naval base and a port which controlled the rich trade of the whole area. Between the mainland and Australia, thousands of islands made up the Dutch East Indies (though here too some British possessions were to be found), and the Philippine Islands, Spanish until 1898, then conquered by the United States of America.

The peoples of these lands had at first been inclined to accept their European rulers. For most of them it made little difference, and the native rulers often thought themselves better off under the protection of the Europeans, and worked with them quite willingly. But there were those who saw how it was that the white men were so rich and powerful, and dreamed of making their own people rich and powerful by the same methods. The first step in achieving that dream, of course, was to get rid of the westerners. So nationalism was born here too.

It started even before the twentieth century. In 1896 a Filipino hero, Jose Rizal, was executed by the Spaniards, and shortly after his followers fought a heroic guerilla war against their new conquerors, the USA. While they were still fighting, unconquered Japan stirred the whole of Asia by showing that an Asiatic nation could not only master the secrets of western technology, but could beat the

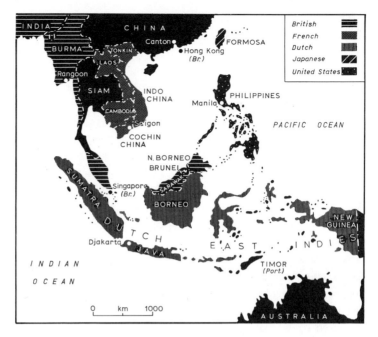

Europeans at their own game. In 1905, Japan won a war against Russia (see p. 90). Six years later, Chinese revolutionaries overthrew their Emperor and started on the enormous task of modernising China (see p. 81).

Nationalism and industrialisation had been made in Europe by long struggle and slow growth. For Asians it was bound to be even harder. They were learning alien ideas, and hoping to plant them in lands quite unprepared for them, where for centuries tradition and belief had been against change of any sort, and religion had encouraged respect for the old. For an Asian, to rebel, to demand changes, to modernise, was a frightening new departure. He needed a strong faith and certainty of success to encourage him.

This was exactly what the doctrines of communism provided (see p. 19). The example of the Russian revolution of 1917 and the Russian success in speeding up industrialisation in a backward country fired the hopes of Asian nationalists, and many of them became communists as well. Their argument was that democracy would not be efficient enough in a land of peasant farmers to achieve modernisation. Like the Russians, they would first need a long period of ruthless dictatorship to drag their people into the new age.

Thus, between the two world wars there came into being all over South East Asia both Nationalist and Communist Parties. They had different ideas about how their countries should be run after they were free, but they both had the same immediate object – to get rid of their foreign rulers.

The parties existed in the towns, among the students, the teachers, the doctors and lawyers. The great majority, the peasants, were too concerned, as always, with their struggle to make a living out of their tiny rice-paddies to have much time for politics. The revolutionaries were for their part not much interested in the peasants. As long as this went on, their chances of success were limited, for the peasants were the masses of Asia, and only on them could a revolution be built.

Several armed risings were attempted by both the revolutionary groups in the 1930's, and all of them failed. Their numbers were too few, the European police and soldiers too good for them. Most of the Asian leaders who were not executed spent many years in gaol or exile.

Only in the Philippine Islands was there real progress. In the USA many people remembered that once America had fought for its freedom from the British empire, and thought it wrong that they should now be building empires themselves. After the First World War the Americans were busy working with the nationalists of the Philippines to create a Filipino government which could take over the country again. By 1936 they had the island being run by Filipinos under a Filipino President, Manuel Quezon, and complete independence within ten years was promised.


## 8   Latin America

'Gold is most excellent . . .' wrote Columbus, and while Henry VII and his son tightened the Tudor grip on England, while Martin Luther parted company with the Pope, Spanish and Portuguese adventurers were following Columbus' sea-route to seek their fortunes across the Atlantic. Here they found the treasures which had tempted them to brave unknown seas, naked cannibals, poisoned arrows, and the splendid armies of the Aztec and Inca emperors. 'Gold is most excellent . . . with gold, the possessor of it does all that he desires in the world, and may even send souls to paradise.'

From the lush tropical islands which Columbus found, thousands of greedy Spaniards spread through Central and South America. Speedily they conquered all the native peoples, who had no wheeled transport, mounted troops, iron and steel, or firearms – all but those of the remotest areas like the Brazilian jungles, where to this day a few hold out. Indians the invaders called them all, even after they understood that America was a new world, not China or India as Columbus supposed. The Indians were forced to become Christians and to work for the white men, mining precious metals or growing crops. Back to Spain and Portugal the new American empires sent mountains of gold and silver; Indians toiled as slaves in their own homelands, growing sugar, coffee, bananas, tobacco, maize, for Europe's proud landlords. Where there were too few Indians, or they died in misery, millions of negro slaves were brought from West Africa, often sold by British merchants. Hence the large negro element in the peoples of Brazil and the West Indies.

The British and French colonies in America developed into the United States of America and Canada – for 300 years all the rest was part of the Spanish and Portuguese empires. The kings and queens sent out royal officials to govern them. The land was owned by pure-European 'creoles'; the Spanish sovereigns granted it to them, on condition that they cared for the Christian well-being of their Indian tenants. The royal government tried, without much success, to make the creoles on their *haciendas* (estates) treat the Indians decently. New creoles often left their wives in Europe and lived with Indian women. The half-caste children were called *mestizos* (mixed). In Latin America, then, were royal officials, creoles, *mestizos,* Indians and negroes – the darker your skin, the worse off you were likely to be.

In 1776 the 13 founding colonies of the United States started their successful rebellion against Britain. In 1789 the French revolutionaries destroyed upper-class privileges in Church and State: sovereignty in France and all other lands, they claimed, belonged to the people (see Chapter 1). These examples excited Latin American creoles and *mestizos*. Why should they not be sovereign in their own lands? Revolutionary wars raged for twenty years. Only in Brazil was self-government established peacefully.

Map labels: Panama Canal Zone, VENEZUELA, British, Dutch, French, GUIANA, COLOMBIA, ECUADOR, R. Amazon, PERU, UNITED STATES OF BRAZIL, BOLIVIA, PARAGUAY, CHILE, ARGENTINA, URUGUAY, Rio Plate

Legend:
Portuguese empire until early 19th century
Spanish empire until early 19th century
0 km 1000

Spain fought back, but could keep only a few islands, of
which Cuba was the most important. In 1824 Spain's last
army in America was beaten.

The rebel army leaders set up a chain of new republics,
from Mexico to Chile, each with a fine-sounding constitution modelled on the USA. The new republics were unready
for the liberties they had claimed – and Simon Bolivar, the
greatest hero of the wars against Spain, saw this. In
America, he wrote – 'treaties are scraps of paper; constitutions, printed matter; elections, battles; freedom, anarchy,
life, a torment.' 'America is ungovernable. He who serves
a revolution, ploughs the sand.'

Bitter words – and the 19th century seemed to prove

70

Bolivar right. Amongst the new republics there were fierce frontier wars; within each, the central government had little control: many countries were too large, too divided by mountains, deserts or jungles, for strong central authority. Real power stayed with the creoles, unchallenged dictators inside their *haciendas*; or with the revolutionary generals and their successors warring against each other for the presidency.

In those republics where orderly political life did develop, the big issue was the power of the Roman Catholic church – its right to control schools and sanction marriages. Liberals attacked the Church, conservatives defended it – but the issue was decided within the ruling classes. The Church generally lost, but this often did not help the masses – the poor miners and country workers. Like the old royal government the Church had recognised their human dignity and often protected them from the creoles.

Often the conservative creoles faced liberals led by *mestizos*, who grew rich through confiscating church lands and, after civil wars, conservatives' lands. So the once-despised *mestizos* grew in power and dignity. The nineteenth century was giving new and often harder masters to the negroes and Indians – their misery could be ended only by breaking up the estates and giving over the land to those who worked it.

Take Mexico, for example. The first rising there against the Spaniards was Indian, led by an Indian priest, Miguel Hidalgo, in 1810. He had worked with the Indians to start co-operative enterprises – for them the natural way of living; they knew nothing of private property in food-growing land. Before the Spaniards came, tribes owned land and shared it among heads of families. The Spanish government cut down Hidalgo's co-operative grape orchard. He tolled his church bell to summon the Indians to war; marching behind the images of Mexico's patron saint, the Virgin of Guadalupe, but with no firearms, the Indians were soon defeated by the Spaniards. Hidalgo was assassinated.

Mexico won its independence, but after Hidalgo only one leading 19th century Mexican stood for the rights of the Indians. This man, Benito Juarez, after whom Mussolini was named (see Chapter 3), was Indian himself. He fought his way to the presidency in 1860; but he found bandits and ex-soldiers roaming everywhere, he could not keep order without using violence himself, elections were battles – and Juarez the liberal ended by setting up as a dictator.

One of Juarez's generals, a *mestizo* named Porfirio Diaz, took over Juarez's position in 1876 soon after he died. During Diaz's thirty years of brutal rule, the hardships of the masses increased. Diaz did stamp out the bandits; indeed he enrolled many of them in his dreaded police force. Diaz did hold elections; but he made sure his men always won. Diaz did protect the Church, and its bishops returned the compliment by teaching the poor to serve God, in the person of their bosses, to love their humble state and work, and turn their hopes to Heaven where there was true wealth.

Mexico was as quiet as a harshly-run gaol. This encouraged foreigners to invest money there. Huge British and American firms exploited Mexico's oil; foreign investors built mines and railroads, and within 10 years bought up one-fifth of the land. By 1910, the Indian villages had lost almost all their land – only one in ten had any left at all. It was 'no entry for Indians' in Mexico City's chief park – Diaz did not want foreign visitors to be reminded whose homeland Mexico was.

Mexico's story was not much different from many other Latin American countries: civil wars, dictators, the native peoples worse and worse off, foreigners muscling in to profit from the mineral wealth. There were exceptions; Brazil's history was much more peaceful, and Argentine and Uruguay had only small Indian populations – these lands, peopled by European emigrants, soon grew wealthy through European investment and the sale of beef and grain.

## 9   The Mexican Revolution

Mexicans feel that their country deserves the credit for beginning the series of revolutions which have tried to deal with the basic problems of Latin American people's lives. In 1910 President Diaz planned to have himself elected for yet another term as President. The people of Mexico City had had enough of him. When they demonstrated in the streets, he fled. The leader of the opposition, a *hacienda*-owner, cared more for political freedom than for social justice – but he had started more than he knew!

In the countryside the Indians rose in arms against their landlords. Their brave and unselfish leader, Zapata, said: 'I want the land taken from the *hacendados* (hacienda-owners) and given to the poor . . . I want the land to be for the people, not for the rich'.

Land confiscation was a bit too much for the more cautious revolutionary leaders. They delayed it. Zapata kept his Indians in arms and urged them to seize the land, and defend it by force, rather than wait for the law's permission. Zapata was shot, but his memory lived. The Indians' demand for land could not be ignored.

For years after 1910 the revolutionary leaders fought amongst themselves; there was a lull in 1917, when they agreed on a constitution, written before the Russian revolution started. This constitution declared war against the privileges of the old order. The three crucial articles made State primary education compulsory (a body-blow at the Church's power over minds); declared that the people were owners of all Mexico's land and mineral resources (a warning to *hacendados* and foreign visitors); and guaranteed to workers the right to organise in unions and to strike. The constitution also promised minimum wages, an 8-hour day, the end of child labour, and employers' responsibility for accidents and illness caused by work.

Fifty years later the articles on education and working conditions were far from being fully operational – but Mexico was the first country in the world to write such ideas into its constitution. As for the third article above, in the 1920's the revolutionary government helped to organise unions of city workers – and this co-operation of government and unions was a feature copied in many other countries.

The government began returning *hacienda* land to the Indian villages. The conservatives were alarmed. They tried to use the army to overthrow the president – but he armed the town workers and called out the peasants to support him. In face of this solid resistance the army revolt collapsed. The Mexicans showed how to overcome an army attempt to throw out a popular government – a common threat in Latin America. Since then, there have been no serious revolts in Mexico.

To establish a system of popular education was one of

the most urgent tasks of the revolutionaries: it still confronts most Latin American countries, and is made harder by a rising child population. Before 1910 most Mexican children had no schooling at all.

The revolutionaries could not afford to build a school in each of the thousands of villages where most of the people lived. Instead they sent out men to persuade the people to build their own schools. The villagers built schools. The teachers taught what the villagers wanted and needed to know. Gardens, baseball pitches, barbers' shops, kitchens, chemists – all these assets, unknown before in the villages, were built on to the schools by the people. These schools did not operate from 9 to 4 but stayed open at all hours; they were not run by headmasters, but by committees of villagers.

About 2,000 schools like this were built – but 40 years after the Revolution began, half Mexico's children still had no schools; as cities grew and people moved from the villages to the city slums, school dodging and child labour were hard to control.

The revolutionaries ran into trouble when they closed down the Catholic primary schools. The clergy answered with a strike. For three years there were no church services. Some Catholic supporters set fire to the new State schools – but the strike failed to restore the Catholic schools. The government patched up its quarrel with the Church – but Mexico City did not control all that happened in Mexico's thirty states. Persecution of the church continued in states where the left-wing 'redshirts' were in power: occasionally priests – traitors according to the redshirts – were martyred. Another headache for the revolutionaries was how to arrange a peaceful transfer of power when a new president was elected. As in other Latin American countries, elections were often dishonestly run, and beaten candidates for the presidency often raised rebel armies rather than accept defeat; also such presidents as Diaz wangled extra, illegal terms of office.

To remove these dangers the organisations which backed the revolution – business firms, trade unions, political parties, peasants' unions – combined to set up one organisation, the National Revolutionary Party, which should plan new laws and agree beforehand who was to be the next president. Thus there would be less chance of a president

Nine human problems for
the Mexican revolutionaries:
slum children in Mexico City

setting up as a dictator, or of a rival trying to split the revolutionary movement. So far this has worked. The Party stayed in power but did not prevent other parties from working. Mexico, then, was an unusual country – one party always in power, yet allowing free speech and action to its opponents.

In the 1930's Mexico's revolution seemed to be losing pace. The land reform lagged – many landlords gave the Indians none of their land, or gave only barren, worthless land where nothing would grow. Then in 1934 came a new, determined President, Lazaro Cardenas – himself an Indian. In his term of office he distributed twice as much land to the Indian villages as all the other presidents since 1911; but he saw that the villages could not make good use of the land without technical help, and credit to buy stock and equipment. He therefore started a new credit organisation to lend money only to villages which worked out serious plans for improving their land. The same organisation stored the crops and provided expert advisers.

These were great steps forward. More than anyone else Cardenas gave the Indians new hope and dignity. Still, at the end of his 6-year term, more than half the villages were getting no credit – they were too backward to be likely to repay it. The land reform was still unfinished. In some areas, the best land was still privately owned. In any case there was not enough land to go round. Mexico needed more industries to give work to the surplus population of the villages.

In 1940 Cardenas ended his term as President. He had become a national hero by handing over Mexico's railways to the railwaymen, and nationalising the British and American oil companies. This bid for Mexican control over Mexican transport and mineral wealth set an example to the rest of Latin America. Cardenas was so tremendously popular that he could easily have had himself re-elected, but he refused to break the constitution.

It was his firm handling of foreign interference in Mexico that especially made Cardenas a hero to Mexicans. They were delighted to find their country treated as an equal, particularly by the US government which had an unpleasant record of interference in Mexican affairs. President Wilson (see Chapters 2 and 3) had intervened in the troubles of Zapata's time, sending US forces to bombard the Mexican port of Vera Cruz in 1916. Just before war broke out in Europe, Wilson sent an army into Mexico in reprisal for border incidents, and all-out war between Mexico and the US might have followed, if Wilson's attention had not been distracted by events in Europe. What a contrast with 1938, when the US government agreed that Mexico had every right to nationalise its oil, provided compensation was paid.

## 10  The United States and Latin America

By 1900 the Americans of the US had explored and settled all their vast country and launched their industrial development. They had goods to sell, money to invest, and a need for Latin America's tropical raw materials. Already in the time of Bolivar their government had shown that it meant to be master of the continent – no European country was to increase its political power there, since according to the Monroe Doctrine the US would resist any outsider's interference in America. Later, in 1898, it was the US which polished off Spanish resistance in Cuba, and which set up the stooge Republic of Panama, building there a canal to link the Atlantic and Pacific Oceans.

The unsettled Latin American governments of the early 20th century were little inclined to pay their debts to foreigners; and foreign countries had the right to send in troops to collect the money. Not wanting any other feet in American doors, US President Theodore Roosevelt, in a corollary (addition) to the Monroe Doctrine, declared that the US would act as international police, to protect all foreign property rights in Latin America. Obviously the idea was to keep European governments out – but Roosevelt's policy, nicknamed the 'big stick', roused bitter hatred in Latin America, as it was used to justify repeated US interference, Wilson's bungling in Mexico being the worst example. In Cuba, Roosevelt actually made the Cubans write into their first constitution the Platt Amendment, giving the US the right to interfere in Cuba to protect 'life, property, and individual liberty'. Also Cuba was to allow the US naval bases in Cuba – and the Cuban government has still not got rid of one of these.

The Platt Amendment was no dead letter. The US regularly interfered in Cuba, and other Caribbean countries. Sometimes the Marines landed. Sometimes calling home the US ambassador was enough to topple a timid government or scare it into toeing the US line.

After 1918, the 'big stick' policy was on the way out. The time of European empire-building was over – that danger need no longer worry the US, whose investments now gave them overwhelming economic power in Latin America. Also, Latin American states, now more self-conscious as members of the League of Nations as well as of their own Organisation of American States, reacted strongly against 'big stick' treatment. This might threaten US exports.

Late in the 1920's President Coolidge dropped the 'big stick' and launched what President F. D. Roosevelt was to christen the 'good neighbour' policy. Coolidge referred all the US's outstanding quarrels with Latin American countries to arbitration. F. D. Roosevelt cancelled the Platt Amendment. This was good news for Latin American nationalists. But the US still had colossal investments in Cuba, and the rest of Latin America. During the Second World War it was obvious that the USA would still try to control Latin American governments. For instance the Argentine government, which showed sympathy to the Axis alliance, found the US trying to isolate or even overthrow it.

# Chapter 5
# China and Japan

## 1 China

'The night was long and the crimson dawn cracked slowly'. This is a line from one of Mao Tse-Tung's poems. Why start a chapter with it? Because Mao is no ordinary poet but chairman of the Chinese Communist party; and because his poem is about China's history. The crimson dawn means the Communist revolution in China. The long night means the time when the Chinese masses were the victims of the old way of life; the hundreds of millions of peasants, and the small but growing number of town workers, ruled and exploited by the upper class of landlords, bankers and army officers, in league with foreign businessmen. The red dawn filled China's (and the world's) sky in 1949, when after thirty years Mao and the communists expelled the last government which wanted night's darkness, not the dawn. As you can't understand day unless you know night, the night of China and the slow dawn is what this chapter is chiefly about.

What of the ordinary Chinese, then, during the night? Most were peasants. The median size of their farms was 1.3 hectares, and landlords usually took about half their crop for rent. This left them barely enough to keep them alive. Most had to borrow money to live on between springtime and harvest; interest was at least 30 per cent. Most were governed by 'warlords', army generals who used their troops to rule and paid them by squeezing taxes out of the peasants. One warlord had already in 1926 collected the taxes due for every year until 1957! So – crushing rents, interest and taxes forced more and more peasants to sell up their farms (if they owned them) or leave home and look for work in the towns, or in some warlord's army.

Why did they put up with all this? There is no easy answer. There had been many bitter peasant rebellions – and once, hundreds of years back, their leader had made himself emperor. For most of the nineteenth century, some-where in China the peasants were in arms against the government; until in 1900 came the Boxer Rising whose chief slogans were: 'Protect the Ching Dynasty' (this means the Chinese royal family, usually called the Manchus, who had seized power in the seventeenth century, after invading from Manchuria) and 'Exterminate the foreigners.'

The rising was led by a secret society, the Harmonious Fists – nicknamed Boxers by foreigners. Note that the Boxers still did not blame the royal family for the people's hardships; they blamed the foreigners who had been interfering more and more since 1842.

1842 – not a famous date to us, but a fatal year for China. For 100 years before it, Europeans were not allowed in China at all, except for merchants, who in winter could visit part of the waterfront at Canton. But Europeans were keen to visit China – to do more business, and to spread their religion. British merchants smuggled opium into China. The Chinese government's efforts to wipe out drug addiction thus led to war between China and the British government, backing up their merchants; the Chinese lost, and after 1842 they could not keep the foreigners out.

British, American, French, Germans, and others, they came: preaching Christianity, attacking the Chinese customs of ancestor-worship and spirit-worship; opening orphanages for the unwanted baby girls whom the Chinese left to die; building railways, whose engines defiled the graveyards and angered the spirits of the dead (so the Chinese thought); sending steamships hundreds of miles up China's huge rivers; building banks and factories; taking over whole Chinese ports like Hong Kong; bringing in their own police to protect them. The Manchu government, with its antique, wasteful procedures, rocked by peasant revolts, granted ever more privileges to the foreigners, losing ever more authority itself. Of course, some Chinese made great profits from their European contacts. Some became Christians. Many saw how much China could learn from Europe about science, medicine and efficient government; but the ignorant peasant simply blamed the 'foreign devils' for every disaster: when there was a drought, the Boxers said it would not rain until all the foreigners had been killed or expelled.

While the Boxers were murdering missionaries and their

converts and besieging for fifty-five days the walled foreign quarter of China's capital, Peking – while European troops looted Peking in revenge, and bullied the Manchus into surrendering yet more privileges – Mao was only a boy working on his father's farm. He started work when he was five, for his father, who was a typical well-off peasant. With his profits from dealing in pigs and rice, the father had bought a small farm, and did well out of lending his savings at high interest to poorer peasants; a hard man – but his wife was gentle. She brought Mao up in the old religion, spirit-worship, but the boy soon stopped believing it. Some temples had been converted into schools, and the spirit-idols destroyed – they did not seem to protect themselves! Mao was not superstitious like his mother, nor grasping like his father; once, in a storm at harvest-time, he helped his father's poor tenants to get their rice under shelter, instead of helping his father. When he was seventeen, Mao decided to go to school; and there he was, when there was the first grey gleam of China's dawn, the revolution of 1911.

Mao, the grown-up schoolboy, was thrilled to see how the Manchu dynasty was in 1911 overthrown by China's one modern organisation – the army. It had always obediently dealt with rebels for the Manchus, but now it deserted them; many officers had transferred their loyalty to a new organisation, the Kuomintang, led by a Chinese Christian doctor, Sun Yat Sen. Kuomintang means roughly nationalist party: (Kuo = country, min = people). The KMT wanted:

(i) to make China a state where the Chinese people were in full control, not the Manchus (who were Tartars or Mongols) and not the Europeans;

(ii) to replace the empire of a royal family by a government freely chosen by the people as in France or the USA (but Dr Sun came to realise that China could not at once become a democracy after 4,000 solid years of empire; the people would have to be trained to rule themselves. Training would be the KMT's job. They would be like the stake for a rose tree. It needs the stake to grow up. When it has grown up, you can take the stake away);

(iii) to secure the people's livelihood by sharing out the landlords' estates among the peasants.

Compare this programme with that of Lenin in 1917. First, the KMT were nationalists, believing in a Chinese race which should govern itself, regarding foreigners as the enemy; whereas to Lenin the only real enemies were class enemies. Second, the KMT and the communists agreed on the need for a period of one-party rule before real democracy could work. Third, 'people's livelihood', if taken seriously, meant ruin for the landlords, as did Lenin's cry 'land to the tillers.'

The KMT's founder, Sun Yat Sen, was another peasant's son, a travelled man, a convert to Christianity, trained as a doctor in Hong Kong, a British colony. Working through secret societies, he plotted again and again to overthrow the Manchus, who outlawed him, and once kidnapped him in London. At last, in 1911, came success; the Manchus abdicated, for even the army was against them. China became a republic – but the KMT's three principles were not carried out. The new government in Peking fell under the influence of the greedy, ambitious Japanese. It could not control the warlords, who seized control of whole provinces and set up their own governments, and were quite happy to curry favour with foreigners in return for loans. The people did not rule themselves; instead they had a new tyrant – the local warlord. The peasants did not get the landlords' estates; as we saw, the warlords' taxes forced even more to sell what land they had, or surrender it to landlords or money-lenders. In 1918 50 per cent of the peasants were landowners; in 1926–7 only 25 per cent.

Dr Sun, who had hoped to be the first President of the Chinese Republic, had not enough organised supporters to stand against the warlords. He never controlled more than a small fraction of China, around Canton. In 1925 he died of cancer, on a journey to Peking to meet North China's chief warlord. The peasants had known and cared nothing about him or his KMT. Their enemy was the local landlord – KMT army or warlord army was equally a menace. One peasant said: 'The landlords and the KMT plundered and hit and swore, and took the people for forced labour, and one army was worse than the next; that was all we farmers knew.' Before dying Sun had made a fateful decision – he agreed with the Russian Bolsheviks and the new, tiny Chinese Communist Party (CCP) to remodel the KMT on communist lines and accept communists as members.

How was the CCP born? Like the KMT, out of the Chinese desire to throw out the foreigners. The 1911 revolutionaries, the KMT, had failed in this; indeed, in 1919 came the news that the victors in the World War had decided that Germany's assets in China should be handed not to China but to Japan! This news infuriated the thousands of Chinese university students who were learning to challenge all the old ways of thinking. Their hero was a brilliant professor at Peking, Chen Tu-Hsu, who wanted to set his country free from the grasping foreigners and grabbing landlords. He thought the real reason for China's weakness was the people's clinging to out-of-date ideas; like the peasants who tried chemical fertilisers on their cabbages but threw the crop away – they were so large the peasants thought they must be poisonous. Chen summed up: 'The universal laws of science must take the place of the Chinese heaven.' It was no use trying to make a democracy, because the old way of thinking (called Confucianism, after Confucius the ancient Chinese teacher) taught people to be obedient, not to decide for themselves.

*Five Relations* (according to Confucianism)
[ 1 Government must be kind
[ 2 People must be loyal
[ 3 Father must be kind
[ 4 Children must be obedient
  5 Brothers and Friends must help each other

Chen said the people in the bottom line were taught to be loyal, and so on, however much those on top ill-treated them; thus 'the meek die in grief; the rebellious resort to violence.' In a famous speech he went on to appeal to China's young men and women; he urged them to cast off the antique ideas which were ruining their country.

'O young men of China! Will you be able to understand me? Five out of every ten whom I see are young in age, but old in spirit; nine out of every ten are young in health, but they also are old in spirit. When this happens to a body, the body is dying. When it happens to a society, the society is perishing. Such a sickness cannot be cured by sighing; it can only be cured by those who are young and also courageous. We must have youth if we are to survive, we must have youth if we are to get rid of corruption. Here lies the only hope for our society.'

In 1919 Chen and his students scored a great political victory which marks the start of the communist movement in China. When the news of the peace treaty arrived, the students staged demonstrations – then went on strike – then called a general strike! There was a big response from railway and factory workers; and the government gave way, refusing to sign the treaty. The three most pro-Japanese ministers resigned and fled to Japan.

The May 4th movement, named after the day of the first student demonstrations, owed a lot to the example of the Russian Revolution, and the Bolsheviks increased their popularity by giving up all the special privileges which Russia had ever extracted from the Manchus. This contrasted with the behaviour of Britain and the USA who hung on to their privileges, and helped Japan to get more. So even Dr Sun came to feel that Russia was China's only friend.

Some leaders of May 4th, including Mao, started the Chinese Communist Party in 1921. Sun made a 'United Front' with them. 'People's livelihood', he explained, 'meant socialism.' He welcomed Russian advisers, especially to train an army for dealing with warlords. One young officer, Chiang Kai-Shek, was sent to Moscow to study the Red Army. Forty years experience had taught Sun, so he wrote in his will, that China could be independent and equal only if the masses (to whom the communists alone tried to appeal) were awakened.

Were they awakening at last? – it seemed so in 1925, when the workers in a Japanese owned factory in Shanghai went on strike, and were fired on by police commanded by English officers. Anti-foreign fury swept China's cities: British and Japanese goods were boycotted, and strikes nearly ruined Hong Kong. Support for the KMT and CCP soared. Next year Chiang launched his army on an expedition north from Canton, to clear out the warlords and the Peking government. In the cities on his way, the middle classes and workers flocked to help him – in Shanghai they seized control before he arrived, whilst in the countryside communists such as Mao urged the peasants to rise against the warlords. At last it seemed as if China would have one government, the foreigners would be expelled, and the landlords crushed.

Another false dawn! China still faced more than twenty

years of civil war, and war with Japan. Chiang had no intention of allowing the KMT to turn into a tool of the communists. Many KMT supporters, bankers, businessmen, landlords, hated communism more than they hated the Japanese. Chiang's own wife belonged to a millionaire banking family. Chiang had to choose – his wife's friends, or the communists. He chose to turn against the communists. One night in Shanghai his men rounded up all the left-wing leaders they could find, and tortured and killed them. Eliminating rivals, Chiang's men soon controlled the KMT, sent the Russian advisers packing, and banned the CCP. The Reds had taken Stalin's orders, to co-operate with the KMT and give no excuse for a break. Too late, Stalin changed his tune and ordered the Reds to stage revolutions in industrial towns; they tried, but Chiang's army crushed them with heavy losses. Mao led a peasant rising in his own province, but the KMT troops beat them. Mao was taken prisoner, escaped and fled to a lonely mountain area in south west China. Here, against Stalin's orders but out of Chiang's reach, he began to organise village soviets. He pointed out that as 70 per cent of the people were poor illiterate peasants, the men who organised and led them would be the masters of China. This clashed with Marx's teaching that the town working class were the natural revolutionary leaders. Mao made a start. He talked the peasants into combining against their landlords, paying no more rent or interest, and seizing the land for themselves. Two thousand KMT soldiers, led by the communist Chu Teh, deserted and joined Mao, to form the nucleus of the Red Army.

Chiang went on to defeat the North Chinese warlords, but he had two new enemies now, the soviets and the Japanese. First the Chinese soviets went from strength to strength, and four army campaigns against them failed disastrously. The Red Army fought a new kind of war, following Mao's four rules: the enemy advances, we retreat; the enemy halts, we harass; the enemy tires, we attack; the enemy retreats, we pursue. Heavily outnumbered though they were, they could fight like this now that the peasants supported them. The Red Army were strictly trained to keep the peasants' goodwill. These eight rules were learned by heart by every soldier, and, set to music, became a popular army song!

1 Speak politely.
2 Pay fairly for what you buy.
3 Return everything you borrow.
4 Pay for anything you damage.
5 Don't hit or swear at people.
6 Don't damage crops.
7 Don't take liberties with women.
8 Don't ill-treat prisoners.

As for Chiang's second enemy – the Japanese government aimed at building an empire at China's expense. Japan had helped to pay for and organise the railways and industries and mines of Manchuria (see p. 90) thus putting Manchuria far ahead of the rest of China in this respect – and Japan had no intention of letting the KMT get the benefit of this. What is more, the Japanese now had an excuse for invading China: Chiang's failure to crush the communists. (In 1936 Japan joined Nazi Germany and Fascist Italy in the Anti-Comintern Pact: see Chapter 8, p. 132.) In 1931 the Japanese army seized control of Manchuria from the local warlord. Chiang appealed to the League of Nations, which condemned Japan as an aggressor but did nothing to stop the Japanese from advancing southwards. Nor did Chiang try to stop them. His plan was to beat the Reds first, then turn against the Japanese.

To find out how to beat the Reds, Chiang hired German experts. On their advice, the KMT army surrounded the soviets with roads and railways, evacuated the villages, and built blockhouses to garrison each area, pressing in from the edge like a nutcracker. The Reds suffered terrible losses. At last they decided to break out, leave south west China, and set up a new base in the far north, near Manchuria, where they could be safe from the KMT. The Red Army, 100,000 strong, broke out of the KMT trap and began the 'long march' of over 9,000 kilometres across snowy mountains, deserts and swamps, harassed by the KMT, warlords and savage tribesmen. Only 30,000 survived, to form the veteran core of the communist movement. But these set up a new soviet, and following Mao's lead, they appealed not just to the poor peasants, but to all Chinese patriots, by not killing landlords or confiscating land, and calling for a second United Front, against the Japanese. (This fitted in with Stalin's policy of the United Front against imperialism, see Chapter 8, p. 130).

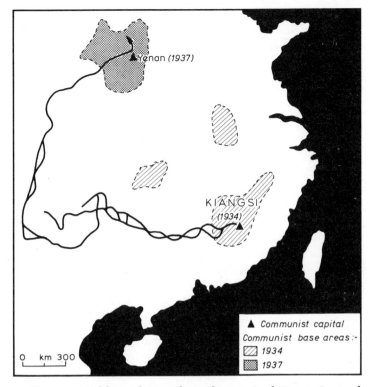

Chiang would not hear of another United Front. Instead he rushed to Sian in North China, to see why his local general was not being more energetic in fighting the Reds. This man, and his troops, agreed with the Reds' propaganda that Chinese should fight Japanese, not each other. He arrested Chiang, and by threatening to kill him, forced the KMT to accept a United Front. The CCP and KMT would work together, fighting the Japanese, and guided by Dr Sun's three principles (see p. 81) in return Mao accepted that the Red Army would become the 8th Route Army, under Chiang's orders, and the soviet would become just a local border administration.

In 1937–8 heavy fighting with Japan developed; China was alone against a far better trained and equipped enemy. The Japanese quickly seized all China's coast, almost cutting China off from outside help. The US and other countries sold oil and other vital raw materials to Japan. The KMT fought fiercely for a short time, then retreated to the mountainous, roadless, railwayless interior. Chiang settled down there, waiting for Japan to involve itself in war with the USA, France, or Britain. He knew he could not win without allies. Mao and his generals organised guerrilla fighting against the Japanese, just as, before the Sian Agreement, they had tackled the KMT. Soon, in some parts of China, though the Japanese might control the towns, the countryside was in the hands of the CCP. Mao prepared for a complete communist take-over of China to follow Japan's final defeat. What could Chiang do to stop this?

## 2 Japan

East of mainland Asia the map shows a chain of islands sweeping in a grand curve for over a thousand miles. In the north they are near the Siberian coast, in the south near Korea. Their people call them Nippon (meaning, where the sun comes from); we know them as Japan.

These people still revere as their emperor a man whose family can be traced back for more than 2,000 years, and according to the old official religion of Japan (Shinto, or the Way of the Gods) further still, to the Goddess of the Sun. The emperor is to his people a human god, an intersection of the two worlds of gods and men; so no one has ever dared to try to turn his family off the throne: on the other hand, his position could be sacred only if he never took the responsibility for controversial decisions; so his power has generally been used by advisers. And yet in the last resort, in desperate emergency, the emperor is obeyed. Only he could make the Japanese armed forces accept defeat in 1945 (see p. 150).

Japan and China could be compared to two brothers who have entirely different personalities and yet you can tell that they have the same parents. China is the elder brother, and the Japanese learned much of their way of life from the Chinese empire, in the years when on the other side of the world the Roman empire was disintegrating.

It is easy to see how Japanese writing is like Chinese (although the spoken languages are entirely different). The sacred emperor was an idea taken from China, and like the Chinese, the Japanese were brought up to respect the five relations of Confucius. As Japan developed, it grew away from the Chinese model. At the base of the social pyramid were the millions of rice-growing peasants, struggling to survive in spite of land shortage, earthquake, flood and famine. This was as in China; but higher up the pyramid, all was different. In China the emperors governed through a civil service of mandarins chosen by written examination. In Japan, the emperors did not govern at all. They carried out religious and ceremonial duties, leaving the government to the *shogun* or supreme general. The *shogun* and his family depended on their control of land for their strength, since land not money was the basis of wealth. They had about 40 per cent of the land in Japan, and another 20 per cent was held by lords who had done homage to them. But outside these areas the *shogun* had very little control. A *daimyo* (great-name) or lord could run his own lands as he liked. The *daimyo* in turn granted their land to *samurai* (warriors) who must fight for their lord and were paid wages in rice. The *samurai* were highly trained soldiers who left the work of growing food to the peasant farmers. Manufactured goods were made by the craftsmen, who lived chiefly in a few large towns. Their goods were sold by merchants. Thus there were four ranks; highest the *samurai*, who were allowed to wear two swords, and use them on the other classes whenever they pleased; next, the farmers; next the craftsmen; next, the merchants. (The *samurai* could not agree on whether merchants were just parasites or not; but most *samurai* depended on borrowing money from them.) It was illegal to marry outside your own rank, or do the work of a different rank from that of your parents. Also the *shoguns* did not allow foreigners into Japan, except for one port for Dutch and Chinese merchants; and the penalty for a Japanese who tried to emigrate, or who left the country and came back, was death.

So for hundreds of years Japan was even more cut off from the outside world than China. Then came a great change. In the middle of the nineteenth century, the system was breaking up, as the ruling class of *samurai* fell into debt to the merchants, as the towns and the use of money grew more important, and as the *daimyo* outside the *shogun's* clan grew more rebellious. A crisis came when the Japanese saw how the European countries were breaking into China, and how the Chinese were powerless against them. Japan profited from China's experience. In China the British punched the first holes in the 'bamboo curtain'; in Japan it was the US and Russia whose steamships in the 1850's were demanding admission to Japanese ports as they opened the Pacific Ocean to their trade. The Japanese could not hope to resist squadrons of ironclad steamships, power-fully armed; they agreed to admit Christian missionaries and foreign consuls and traders. But they kept a deep national pride which determined them not to allow a foreign take-over of their country – instead they would beat the foreigners at their own game by copying all their modern techniques.

So Japan went to school again; not with China this time but with the European nations. A group of brilliant men emerged from the *samurai* and merchant classes; within a generation they scrapped the *shogun's* control of Japan, scrapped the independent power of the *daimyo*, scrapped the rice wages of the *samurai*, and the 4-rank system, forbade the *samurai* to wear swords, started primary schools for almost all Japan's children, trained all the young men to fight, built fine networks of roads, railways, and telegraphs, reformed the Navy on British lines, the army on German, and worked out a constitution to give Japan cabinet government and a parliament. The emperor's court even copied European clothing and haircuts.

Many *samurai* hated all this copying of Europe, and Japan's new rulers had to face one serious rebellion, led by a hero of Japanese history, Saigo Takamori, huge, powerful, a hunter and fisherman, a brilliant swordsman; but Saigo and his *samurai* army were soundly beaten by the govern-ment's newly trained peasants; wounded in the battle, Saigo was beheaded at his own request by a friend. His memory inspired countless Japanese who turned to rebellion or assassination in later years against govern-ments that did not seem patriotic enough.

While China fell apart, Japan built itself up; and by the 1890's was ready to claim a share of the Chinese empire. In a short and successful war, Japan turned the Chinese out of Formosa and Korea. The next step was Manchuria: but the Russians were interested in this area. Before taking on the Russians, the Japanese strengthened themselves by an alliance with Britain (1902). What a triumph for them, to deal as equals with the British! The war with Russia which followed brought greater triumphs; the defeat or surrender of Russia's armies in the Far East; the almost complete destruction of Russia's navies. The Asians had beaten the white men – the news resounded across the world! Japan's control of Manchuria was strengthened, and the Japanese government encouraged the Chinese revolutionaries who wanted to copy Japan's example. (The Japanese soon learned that the Chinese had no intention of swapping European for Japanese control.)

It was the First World War which made Japan into far and away the strongest country in the Far East. While the other great powers were locked in battle in Europe, Japan, fighting as Britain's ally, had little to do, and could interfere more and more in Chinese affairs; while Japanese industries flourished, securing valuable new markets which war-torn Europe could not supply. After the war, Japan was treated as a Great Power and given a permanent seat on the League of Nations Council (see Chapter 3, p. 35); agreements with Britain and the USA left the Japanese fleet as far and away the strongest in the Far East (see p. 51). How would Japan's strength be used? There were danger signs. Popular opinion in Japan was bitterly anti-European, with some reason, for after 1918 the British obeyed US prompting and insultingly dropped their alliance. The British empire prevented a declaration on racial equality from being included in the League Covenant, and the Americans and Australians refused to take any of Japan's overcrowded population. The US sent troops to Siberia after the Bolshevik revolution to make sure Japan did not fish in these troubled waters.

Socialism spread among the intellectuals and factory workers, but its ideas of international brotherhood had little appeal and in any case it was roughly suppressed by the government who used brutal police methods to deal with dangerous thoughts. Opposition to big business was expressed also in movements which aimed at strengthening the emperor's power compared with the businessmen, who had strong connections with the political parties. The Japanese parliament was not much respected, and was often the scene of fights between members. Once there was a panic when a visitor threw a snake among the MPs. He had been bribed to do so by one of the parties, but found it difficult to direct the missile which fell among his own side. The army and navy had more control over the government than parliament had; and in the army there were many pupils of Saigo who wanted less copying of foreigners and more active empire-building in Manchuria and China.

The Great Slump (see Chapter 7) hit Japan hard. Millions

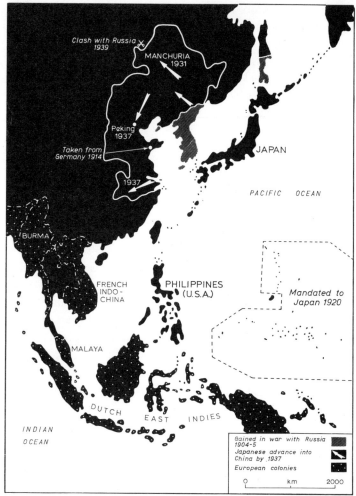

Clash with Russia
1939

MANCHURIA
1931

Peking
1937

Taken from
Germany 1914

1937

JAPAN

PACIFIC   OCEAN

BURMA

FRENCH
INDO-
CHINA

PHILIPPINES
(U.S.A.)

Mandated to
Japan 1920

MALAYA

D U T C H   E A S T   I N D I E S

INDIAN
OCEAN

Gained in war with Russia
1904-5
Japanese advance into
China by 1937
European colonies

0          km          2000

*The rising Japanese Empire*
Russian and Chinese weakness, and the opportunity of the First World War, gave Japan's ambitious rulers their chance to launch a fierce empire-building drive, chiefly at China's expense

of Japan's farmers made ends meet by rearing silkworms; the silk was mostly sold to the US. Japan's cotton industry had made giant strides since 1914; with the development of rayon and similar synthetic goods, the demand for silk and cotton dropped. Japan's farmers depended on selling rice: now there was a world glut of rice and prices fell away. Many farmers had to sell daughters to work in brothels. The army, which was mainly manned by peasants, was near mutiny. The government reacted like most governments; aiming to balance the budget, it slashed civil service pay – teachers often got nothing – and returned the currency to the gold standard (see Chapter 7). Japan's extremist nationalists took violent measures. One of them shot the Prime Minister who died months later of the wound. Some senior army officers were caught in a plot [March 1931] to overthrow the government by force; they were lightly punished, the government did not dare to tackle them seriously.

To the army commanders, the right course of action was obvious, to push on with the Japanese conquest of Manchuria, while China and the other great powers were in no state to resist: in Manchuria Japan could find room for her surplus population, and employment in building up a new industrial area. This would mean war with China, and the risk of trouble with the rest of the world. China, a member of the League of Nations, could appeal for the League's help. Hearing reports of what the army was up to, Japan's chief ministers ordered the war minister to cancel any plans for action against the Chinese in Manchuria. The war minister gave this message to an officer who had been involved in the March Plot. He took care not to deliver it until Japanese forces were already in action around Mukden, Manchuria's capital.

The Chinese soon lost control of Manchuria; Japanese forces pressed on into northern China; the government did not dare to stop them, although it promised the rest of the world that it would do so. The League of Nations condemned Japan as an aggressor but no one was willing to take a lead in starting sanctions. Manchuria now provided a base for Japanese pressure on the rest of China. The army had fooled the government and shown up the weakness of the League. Meanwhile, another prime minister was murdered, for not being patriotic enough; the assassins were sent to prison but most of them were freed after a few years.

From now on, the civilians lost all control of Japanese policy – different factions of the army struggled for power. Japan became entangled in a full scale war with China, and grew more and more like the fascist states of Europe. By 1938 the armed forces took 70 per cent of the budget; in 1938 military training was made a compulsory part of school timetables. A National Mobilisation Law gave the government power to direct labour and fix wages and prices. In 1940 all the political parties united to form one party, the Imperial Rule Assistance Association. By a different path Japan had ended in the same prison as her Axis allies – the one-party state.

# Chapter 6
# Stalin's Russia

Meet Stalin, speaking to a meeting of Russian factory managers; a pleasant-looking man in a grey tunic with seven buttons down the front, no tie, baggy sleeves; his face squarish with hair brushed back from a low forehead, very different from Lenin's egghead dome; moustache but no beard; narrow heavy-lidded eyes. More than once you hear the name of Lenin mentioned with reverence, and perhaps one or two of the listeners know some words of Lenin which he never quotes . . . 'Stalin is too rough . . . I propose to the comrades to find some way of removing Stalin from his position . . .' All know that their country is ravaged by famine and disease, its communist masters struggling, against the will of millions, to end private farming and build inside five years industries which in other lands needed a century. The managers are doubtful; could the new factories not wait until there is more food for their builders, could the pace not be slackened? Stalin is sure: 'No, comrades, it is not possible! . . . to slacken the pace would be to lag behind, and those who lag behind are beaten. We do not want to be beaten, . . . No, we don't want to. Russia was ceaselessly beaten for her backwardness . . . for military backwardness, for cultural backwardness, for political backwardness, for industrial backwardness, for agricultural backwardness . . . You remember the words of the pre-revolutionary poet: "Thou art poor and thou art powerful, thou art mighty and thou art helpless, Mother Russia!".'

## 1 How Russia built her industrial strength

Stalin was sure that sooner or later the capitalist countries would again try to overthrow Russian communism by force. The Russians would be crazy to trust in communist revolution in the rest of the world. They should accept that they were on their own; they should build, whatever the sacrifices, 'socialism in one country' – Stalin's favourite slogan. As Russia was, in the 1920's, she would be an easy prey, lagging at fifth place in world industrial output. The rich countries were getting richer, more powerful. Only a tremendous spurt could close the gap and make Russia safe. Until 1928 the gap was not being narrowed. By then Russia's factories were producing only as much as back in 1913! And so far Stalin had shown no zeal for forcing the pace. He understood that new factories were possible only at the expense of the peasants, who would have to hand over their crops at very low prices so that the cost of feeding factory workers would be kept down. Russia was so poor! While Stalin was crushing his rivals for Lenin's authority he posed as the peasants' friend and laughed at the 'super industrialists' such as Trotsky, who in 1923 had sketched a 5-year plan to electrify Russia. Early in 1929 Stalin banished Trotsky from Russia, the other leading communists were eating out of Stalin's hand, and he could risk a brutal acceleration of the industrial build-up.

For new industries there are two essentials: plans and capital. Any business must plan ahead, and the Bolsheviks were involved in this as soon as they took over Russian large scale industry. During the NEP (see Chapter 3) each concern used 'control figures' of the coming year's output, based on results so far. These figures indicated the profits expected and the new investment needed for each separate concern. Stalin's spurt would need plans like this, not just for separate concerns but for the whole country. By 1925 the planners, prodded by Lenin, who was specially anxious to get electricity in every Russian house, had worked out control figures for the whole country. In 1928 they were looking further ahead; they hatched a plan to make Russia a great industrial country in five years. Now Trotsky was gone, Stalin himself turned super industrialist – he set fantastic targets for the plan and insisted that they would be reached a year early.

How about capital? Before 1917 Russian industries had relied on foreign loans. The communists refused to pay these back, and confiscated all bank deposits in Russia – so their credit was bad. They hoped to squeeze bigger grain surpluses out of the peasants, for sale abroad, but during the Great Depression (see p. 108) no foreigners would buy

Russian grain. If no capital came from abroad, no loans, no grain payments, how could Russia pay for the foreign experts and machinery and the millions of new industrial workers? It could be done only by keeping the wages bill as low as possible.

If the workers were made to accept a wretched standard of living, most of the wealth created by their work would be available to pay for more experts, more machinery, more workers.

People accept hardships more willingly in wartime than in peace, and Russian life during the Plan had a wartime feeling. Stalin and the communists presented the plan as a declaration of war – on Russian backwardness. They used a wartime vocabulary: workers were grouped in troops and brigades and sent to the iron, steel, or coal fronts. The iron industry cost more casualties than the battle of the Marne, said an American engineer working for the Russians. As in wartime, appeals to national pride spurred on the workers. As in wartime, defeats were claimed as victories, and the people were kept in the dark about the country's situation. A year ahead of time, Stalin declared the plan a success. This was half true. For instance, Stalin's target for pig-iron output was not approached for another ten years. Yet we cannot call the plan a failure. The planners had not claimed to forecast its results exactly. Their chief aim had been to gear the people to a swift build-up of state-controlled productive power. In this, the plan succeeded. In steel-making, for instance, Russia had overtaken Britain, France, and Germany, where millions were out of work; and only the USA was still ahead.

A second plan, with more reasonable targets, was launched at once, and also declared achieved a year ahead of schedule. By 1939 Germany had regained its lead in steel production, but in oil and electricity Russia was second only to the USA. This was a great achievement, won at a grim price in human suffering. The pity was that most of the work was ruined in the Second World War.

What was life like for the workers? The government struggled to hold wages down; in any case there was nothing to buy but food and clothing: sometimes not even those. The empty shops were no accident. The planners gave priority to heavy industry which was allowed four times as much money as consumer goods. Such goods for

*Results of the first two five-year plans, as claimed by the Russians*
Russian output of electricity, coal and steel

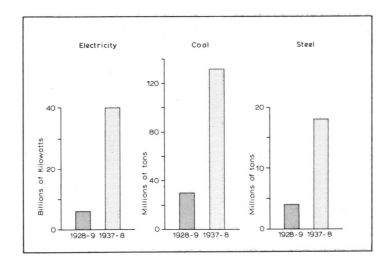

sale as were made were mostly sent to Moscow and Leningrad to impress foreign visitors.

Why did the workers put up with a falling standard of living? Many believed what the communists told them: that sacrifices were necessary for future wealth. Many did well out of Stalin's policy of rewarding lavishly those who earned privileges. It was dangerous to resist the falling standard of living. Strikes were illegal. Trade unions did not defend workers against management; their job was to administer welfare benefits and encourage working efficiency. As in fascist countries, unions included managers as well as workers. Managers fixed wages: there was no bargaining with workers' representatives. Labour discipline was strict. From 1932 you could be sacked, and lose your ration cards and lodgings, for missing one day's work without good reason. Russian courts treated being twenty minutes late as equal to absence; in 1939 foremen were given power to sack on the spot for being over twenty minutes late or for idling or leaving before time. Every worker employed by the State or by co-operatives must have a 'work book'. If he lost his job the reason was written in this, and no employer could sign him on unless he produced his 'work book'. There was no unemployment pay except for illness confirmed by a hospital certificate. Once you lost your job you could not refuse the next one offered, even it if was not your trade and was in some distant, disagreeable part of Russia. Loss of a job cost a worker his sick pay, paid holidays and pension. In 1940 it was made a criminal offence, carrying a penalty of up to four months' gaol, to leave a job without special permission.

Output per worker was low in Russia. To raise it the communists used piece rates and bonuses of up to seven times basic pay. Party members were expected to lead 'shock brigades' which set an example by always being punctual; never absent, caring for tools, working on rest days (every sixth day),nagging slack comrades and so on. Factories were expected to join in socialist competition, trying to beat the output of other factories in their branch of industry.

Shock brigades got extra food and other privileges but not extra pay. Stakhanovites got extra of everything. Stakhanov was a coal miner who beat all records for coal hewing, and earned a month's wages on one shift just by introducing division of labour in his team. Hitherto they had all cut the coal, and all joined in cleaning and loading it, all getting in each other's way. Now he cut all the time: the others cleared and loaded. Workers who did such wonders were named Stakhanovites. They toured factories to show how output could be raised; they had dinner in separate rooms from other workers and could earn up to twenty times the normal wage. Sometimes their indignant mates sabotaged or even murdered the Stakhanovites; but the idea succeeded in spreading more efficient techniques and higher production rates. For outstanding workers a system of medals was introduced. The highest honour was to be named a Hero of Socialist Toil and granted the Order of Lenin.

Stakhanovites lived well – ordinary workers were no better off than before 1914, and much more strictly controlled. Yet they were lucky compared to the uncounted millions of forced labourers who had to work on the toughest projects. The first labour camps had been started in 1918, for making enemies of communism useful, and teaching them the joys of honest work instead of killing or imprisoning them. During the 5-year plans, the political police were in charge of many large projects, and to supply these with labour the courts sentenced lawbreakers to at least three years in labour camps – short gaol sentences almost dropped out of use. In 1932 ten years' forced labour became the lowest punishment for damaging State property. When the Stalin Canal, linking the Baltic to the White Sea, was finished, 72,000 prisoners who had survived working on it were set free as cured of their anti-social tendencies. We do not know how many forced labourers there were – 7 million is a low estimate – or how many of them were casualties.

## 2 How the peasants lost their land

In the 1920's the growing towns of Russia lived in fear of famine. The wretchedly backward farms did not produce enough food to feed them. Thanks to the events of 1917, the land was divided into nearly 26 million farms, mostly very small. Modern techniques were out of the question on most farms, where the land was shared out each year among the members of the village commune, and one-third left fallow, as in the English Midlands 500 years ago. The food supply was getting worse: firstly, because the peasants were having more children and keeping more food for themselves; secondly, because there was nothing to encourage the peasants to sell food to the towns, which produced scarce, expensive and shoddy goods to exchange for food from the country. Most peasants were very poor. In 1926 one-quarter of all their families were described by the government as being in the category of absolute poverty. Five million farms used wooden ploughs.

The only way to feed the towns was to force large scale modern farming on the countryside, so' that food output would rise, while the new methods would release more people from the land to work in factories; and if the new, large farms were State controlled, the government could make sure that food was cheap in the towns. So the first 5-year plan aimed to bring one-fifth of all peasant households into large scale collective farms, meaning that each village would club together its land and stock, forming a new unit in which the peasants would be shareholders. The poor and 'middle' peasants were to be tempted to join collectives by the promise of interest-free loans, and free technical help. These would be paid for by crushing taxes on the *kulaks*, the richer peasants.

Nearly a million households agreed to join collectives; but mostly they kept their land separate and agreed only to work together. So the land units were still small and there was no advantage gained through large scale working after all. Worse, the *kulaks*, the most progressive farmers with the largest surpluses for sale, now deliberately grew less food. Why should they sell, if taxes wiped out their profits? In 1929 there was a menacing food shortage which faced the communists with their worst danger since the civil war. They had to confiscate the peasants' food stocks. This set the countryside against them. Stalin decided to wipe out the *kulaks* and bring almost all the peasants into collectives as fast as possible. The *kulaks'* wealth would be used to set up collectives. Peasants in collectives must stop keeping their own land separate (except for small plots, for each family's food supply). Local soviets could turn *kulaks* off their land; *kulaks* must not rent land or hire workers. To equip the collectives with tractors, Russia would build the world's largest tractor factory and set up a network of garages (Motor Tractor Stations) to service them.

Stalin's new slogan, 'war against the *kulaks*,' gave the poor peasants a wonderful chance to work off their grievances against the richer ones. Local communist parties reinforced by shock brigades from towns joined in ruining the *kulaks*. All peasants who did not wish to join collectives (that is – the vast majority) were lumped together with the *kulaks*. Over huge areas order broke down. Town soviets invaded villages, looted *kulak* property, feasted on *kulak* food and drink, and evicted *kulaks* from their homes. So-called *kulaks* were liable to arrest and deportation; they were allotted new lands in scrub and swamp areas, with enough tools and seed to make a new start, and output quotas to meet on pain of being evicted again. The peasants answered violence with violence. Murder and arson spread. Communists were ordered to stay indoors after dark and to keep away from windows. Prisons were full, often with peasants who had merely shouted some anti-communist slogan. The secret police reported that in many villages the communists had stripped their victims of clothes, shoes and underwear. There were mass desertions from the villages, and countless suicides of whole *kulak* families. Animals died in millions; the *kulaks* destroyed them, and had a last orgy of meat-eating, rather than surrender them to collectives. Many villages were solidly against collectivisation, even down to the landless labourers; the communists 'persuaded' them by billeting troops on them. The Party claimed that the poor and middle-class peasants joined collectives voluntarily. They wrote to local newspapers denying this: 'If anyone spoke against it he was frightened with arrest and forced labour . . . I beg you not to reveal my name because the Party people will be angry . . . Every day they send us lecturers asking us to sign up for such and such a collective for eternal slavery but we don't want to leave our good homes. It may be a poor little hut but it's mine.'

Stalin saw that his rule was in peril and in March 1930 he backed down. He had been misunderstood, he said; force must not be used to set up collective farms. Within them, peasants must be free to farm for themselves on the side, and to leave altogether. Promptly more than eight million families left the collectives. Disasters were still to come; in the next two years perhaps three million people died in famines.

The government continued the drive for collective farming, offering tractors, tax relief, and expert help to the collectives, putting ferocious taxes on private farmers. The peasants dragged their feet; sabotage of collective property was common, though shooting was the maximum penalty for this. In the end the communists won. By 1939 more than nine-tenths of all farming households belonged to collective farms. The government could be sure of feeding the towns.

The State food tax was the first call on collective farms' output. This, with another 20 per cent as fees for use of tractors, was collected by the Motor Tractor Stations. Then each collective farm had to set aside enough to cover payments on loans, compulsory insurance, and reserves for next year's planting. If there was anything left, the shareholders took their share, graded according to workdays contributed – this was to discourage peasants from giving too much time to their own smallholdings. One day's actual work counted as five workdays for a tractor driver, but only half a workday for an unskilled hand. Town or country, Stalin's version of socialism did not mean equal shares.

## 3 Was the Revolution betrayed?

Neither Marx nor Lenin had supposed that a communist country might be ruled by one man, a dictator who had exiled or executed all possible rivals; but Lenin, as builder of the Party, planner of the Revolution, and organiser of Soviet Russia, had a unique position which Stalin inherited. Posing as Lenin's humble pupil, Stalin created a religion of Lenin-worship with himself as high priest. This began with Lenin's funeral, stage-managed by Stalin: the embalmed corpse was put on permanent show in Red Square after a pompous ceremony in which Stalin led the crowd in homage to the dead leader. 'In leaving us, Comrade Lenin ordained us to guard the unity of the party like the apple of our eye. We vow to thee, Comrade Lenin, that we will fulfil honourably this thy commandment. . . .'

The other leading communists suspected Trotsky of casting himself as dictator. They backed the humble General Secretary against the brilliant Commissar for War. The Party condemned Trotsky's ideas; in 1925 he resigned his job. He made no fight for the leadership – he was too convinced of the necessity of accepting Party decisions. 'I know that one must not be right against the Party. One can be right only with the Party . . .' Now Trotsky could not use the Red Army against him, Stalin could turn against the other communists who had backed him against Trotsky.

For two years Trotsky was quiet. He even pretended that Lenin's will was a forgery! But then, horrified by the communist failure in China (see p. 85), for which Stalin was responsible, he said that he would try to replace Stalin if Russia should be involved in war. This speech, setting himself up again as an alternative to Stalin, was Trotsky's own death sentence. The Party refused to print his writings. He was expelled from the Party, exiled from the capital, banished from the country.

The disasters of the collectivisation period drove Stalin to label all his possible rivals as traitors in league with foreign capitalists: he dared not admit that there could be any alternative to himself. The rise of the German Nazis, who made no secret of their plans to loot and enslave Russia, gave Stalin a bogey to frighten the masses so that they mistrusted all opposition to Stalin as possibly linked with the Nazis. Lenin had taught communists to scorn patriotism and be loyal to the international working class movement. Stalin played on Russian patriotism, claiming that Trotsky was plotting a foreign invasion and that foreign sabotage was behind any undeniable failure. Contact with Trotsky or his supporters was counted as treason. Thus you could be punished for not informing the police of a traitor in your family. Trotsky did indeed try to organise a world anti-Stalin communist movement. He was sentenced to death by a Russian court, and his skull smashed with an ice-axe by a Stalinist agent in Mexico in 1940. Thousands of his Russian supporters were sent to labour camps, where they tried to organise resistance and were shot in hundreds.

Stalin's terror did not stop short here. In 1934 a young communist penetrated the office of Stalin's right hand man in Leningrad, Kirov, and shot him. The killer and his gang of young supporters were shot after secret trials, and an interrogation by Stalin himself; forty of Stalin's own bodyguard were gaoled or executed after secret trials. Tens of thousands of suspects were sent from Leningrad to Siberia. Stalin admitted: 'We had to handle some of these comrades roughly. But that cannot be helped. I must confess that I, too, had a hand in this.' The murder led to a strict purge of the party, and a chain reaction of accusations against leading communists. In the years 1936–7 all the surviving members of Lenin's cabinet except Stalin himself were charged with being spies for Britain, France, Japan and Germany, and plotting to kill Stalin, wreck the country, and restore capitalism. After organising the trials, two police chiefs themselves were charged and shot. Most of the trials were secret, but in a few public trials the prisoners made full confessions extracted by torture and blackmail. In 1937 the police claimed to have discovered a plot by some leading Red Army generals to kill Stalin and seize the Moscow HQ of the political police. In fact, the political police themselves had framed the generals, by working with the German Secret Service to forge evidence of treason. This evidence could have been based on documents dating from the time of the Red Army's co-operation with the German Army (see p. 45).

A drastic purge of the Army followed. Several thousand officers were shot (according to the German Intelligence, between 60 per cent and 70 per cent of those with war experience). Within the Party, nine-tenths of those who had been members in 1918 seem to have disappeared in the purges.

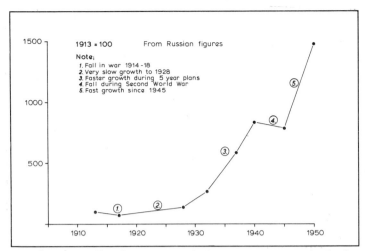

Only the official version of these events reached the public. In each town there were only two newspapers, run by the government and the Party. As the Communist Party alone was legal, and controlled the Government, there was not much choice for readers. These papers reprinted the leading articles from Moscow, and the news all came from the official agency. Thus when one winter the people of Kharkov were without electricity, trams ran at rush hours only, stations were lined with beggars, and typhoid was raging, the local press had news only of the triumphs of the 5-year plan. Control of travel hindered the spread of news. Special permission was needed to visit a large town, and all absences from home of over twenty-four hours had to be reported to the police. Any contacts with the world outside Russia was dangerous.

The country's growing wealth, the ruin of the *kulaks*, Stalinist wage scales, and the replacement of purge victims with Stalin's supporters, created a new ruling class. The core of this was the Party. In spite of repeated purges the Party sheltered many time-servers and hypocrites such as one secretary of the League of Militant Atheists, who had ikons at home and baptised his children! It can be argued that in Russia the rich were richer and the poor poorer than in the USA. Families could build up fortunes again after 1936, when the right to dispose of property by will was given back; and if a high ranking man died his family could collect grants giving them an income up to 100 times that of an average Russian working family. Was this the workers' state?

While Russia was struggling out of its ancient poverty, and menaced by foes perhaps imaginary, but terrifying, the injustices and tyrannies could be defended on grounds of security and of the need to play on human fears and greed as sources of unity and wealth. So it might be hoped that these evils of Stalinism were temporary, fated by Stalin's very achievements. Any such hopes were doomed for twenty years by the Second World War.

# Chapter 7
# World Crisis 1929–33

One country will be left out of this chapter. That is Russia, which was on its own (see Chapter 6). The rest of the world was joined together in the capitalist system. The movement of money ignored frontiers. Thus, an American business man might lend money to a German city council, or buy English pounds with his dollars: then if he was short of money he could sell his English pounds or call back his loan from Germany.

After the war, the chief countries in Europe owed money to America. The allies had bought American goods on credit, and were still paying the instalments. America was lending money to Germany, and the Germans used it to pay reparations to the allies and to build their new factories, roads, railways, airports, sports stadia, and health centres, in the 1920's the most advanced in the world.

It all depended on America. If the Americans called back their money from Germany, the German recovery would collapse. If the Germans could not afford to trade with Britain and France, these countries would lose business, and could not pay for their imports from America except by sending their gold reserves to America. If these gold reserves fell too low, people who held their money in pounds or francs would be afraid that it would lose its value in gold, and would exchange them for a safer currency.

This international money system had made possible the credit which paid for Europe's recovery after 1918. (Russia, left outside, recovered very slowly.) But – it all depended on American loans. In 1929 the time came for Russia to show the world the advantage of having money which foreigners could not buy or sell.

Until October 1929 all seemed to be well. America had its headaches: the prohibition laws (see pp. 48–49) had led to a huge illegal trade in alcohol, run by gangsters such as Al

*The 'boom' of the late 1920's as shown by the production of cars in the USA, 1919–29. Note that the value more than doubled within ten years*

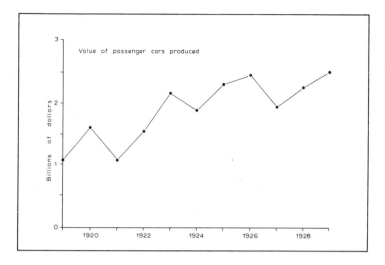

Capone, who in a city like Chicago were more powerful than the elected government. Yet the country had never been so rich or optimistic. A record number of cars was built in the year: 5 million. President Coolidge claimed (December 1928) that America had never shown so fair a prospect: due, he thought, to the strength of the American character.

Britain had recovered from the scare of 1926. In that year the Trade Union leadership called for a strike of all workers to stop a cut in coal-miners' wages. The 'general strike' failed: the miners' wages were cut; thousands of miners were out of work, since Britain's coal exports had fallen, so the mine owners had the whip hand. Yet the unions succeeded in a way. Other employers preferred to agree with them on wages rather than risk strikes. So the ordinary British family, outside the mining and other depressed areas, had never been so comfortably off.

In Germany, the bitterness of the early '20's seemed to be dying as the country blossomed out in the sunshine of the dollar. In the parliament of the Republic, the peace-loving Catholics and Socialists were the largest parties. Wages were rising, unemployment was less than a million. True, Mussolini (see Chapter 3) had his German imitators – Hitler's Nazi Party, sworn to bring all Germans under one dictatorship, revive the Germany army, and take vengeance on the supporters of the 1918 revolution and peace treaty: but the Nazis, the party of ignorant and vicious hatred, could win only 12 out of 491 parliamentary seats in 1928.

True, Germany's foreign secretary, Stresemann, was keeping secret contact with the Russians so that the Germans could train soldiers, and test aircraft, tanks, guns and gas illegally on Russian soil; but he was working peacefully with the British and French. Germany was now a member of the League of Nations; the government had freely accepted the 1918 frontiers in the west, and the unarmed Rhineland (Locarno Treaty 1925); the French army had left the Ruhr coalfield (seized in 1923 to bully the Germans into making overdue reparations payments); the Americans had co-operated in slashing the reparations bill to a comfortable level. It seemed that the wounds of 1919 might heal in peace.

## 1   The onset of the slump

1928 was a year of hope; but the hopes were soon to fade. Experts still argue about what went wrong, and like a doctor on the telephone, we can only make our best guess at the patient's illness. The good times of the '20's rested on two doubtful bases. One was American credit, the other was hard-up primary producers: that is, the farmers and fishermen who supplied the world with food and the miners who dug out its minerals. These were getting a poor reward for their work. Competing against each other, they kept their profits low, so they had little cash to spend on manufactured goods. Manufacturers depended for most of their sales on the rich (those who could afford to own shares in industries) and on those who worked for comfortable wages in manufacturing. The profits of the '20's were not being widely shared. The rich got very rich, but in every country there were millions of poor who just survived. In Britain the coalminers were on the dole, in the US growers left their cotton to rot as there were no customers, in Brazil the coffee crop was burned on the plantations.

There came a time, then, when the new industries were making more goods than they could sell. This problem was multiplied by the New York Stock Exchange boom of the late 1920's which collapsed into a slump in October 1929. As thousands of people got the idea that they could make easy fortunes by buying shares in businesses and selling them again at a higher price, the prices of the shares soared.

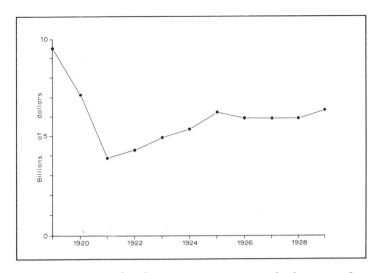

*Income of US farmers, 1919–29*
This graph shows how primary producers suffered a severe loss in income after 1918 and did not recover throughout the 1920's. Probably this helps to explain the depression in the 1930's

Loans to Europe dried up as Americans rushed to transfer their money to American shares and from all over the world money was sucked to New York to be loaned to the share purchasers, who paid 12 per cent interest on this money which they borrowed to pay deposits on their shares. Everywhere men of means told themselves that 12 per cent was 12 per cent. Like a soap bubble, the boom expanded. The bubble would burst once speculators feared that they could not sell their shares at a profit because the shares were over-valued.

In summer 1929 American business seemed to take a turn for the worse, and speculators' confidence began to fail. One or two exposures of frauds on speculators, and warnings by financial experts, led to a panic in October, when on one day 16 million shares were sold. The result was a collapse of credit in America. Many banks had invested money in shares at fantastically high prices. They were ruined when these became practically worthless. The million or so Americans who had put money into the boom lost heavily. So the demand for goods, and also for workers to make them, fell sharply into a terrible slump – wages fell by more than half, but those who had work at all were lucky – at one time there were more than 16 million unemployed.

In Europe, America's slump had bad results. The end of American credit crippled German business – a chain of bank failures ruined thousands, and millions were turned off work. As wages fell, so did the sale of goods, and falling demand led to yet more cuts in employment. Governments tried to pay their own way by cutting wages and increasing taxes. This made things worse.

The trouble was that the governments had the wrong ideas about how to deal with the slump. 'Sooner or later it is ideas, not vested interests, which are dangerous for good or evil.' So wrote the British economist J. M. Keynes, who was busy working out other ideas. The men in power believed that it was dangerous for governments to interfere with the economic system. Their main idea was that the free initiative of individuals would serve the community through market competition. Competition led to over-production, which caused slumps, but slumps were bound to end naturally. Government interference would make the situation worse by delaying the natural cure.

Keynes argued that the slump was not natural and un-avoidable, but was an unnecessary muddle which the governments were making worse. By trying to save money they were increasing unemployment. 'Whenever you save 5s you put a man out of work for a day,' he said in a broad-cast. Governments could, and should, prevent unemploy-ment by controlling credit and government spending. If a slump was likely, a government should use its credit to raise money and lend it cheaply thus setting more men to work. Taxes should be cut so that money would circulate more freely. The government itself should start more projects such as road and bridge building. If necessary the government should go into the red on purpose. Debts could be paid off later. To stop a boom from getting out of hand, a government should use the opposite of these three policies. Alas, most governments were busy making borrowing harder, increasing taxes, and slashing their expenditure – correct for a boom, all wrong for a slump.

All Europe was in debt to America. Now America would lend no more, how were the debts to be paid? In gold? – Most of that was already in Fort Knox; and it was dangerous to lose too much gold. In exports? To protect America's collapsing industries from competition, President Hoover clapped heavy tariffs on imports. Other countries did the same. Exports shrank, so did wages, so did employment, in a vicious circle – mass unemployment, the post-war menace was back. Meanwhile, in Russia during the 5-year plan, there was a shortage of workers! No wonder that many looked to the Russian example with new respect – while others saw with fear how the slump helped international communism.

On each side of the North Atlantic, governments faced with disaster interfered, more energetically than ever before in peace time, with their countries' economic life; in France and Britain, old rivals in politics shelved their differences and tackled the problems together. In Germany the old parties faded out before the Nazi extremists who promised drastic remedies. In America the Democratic party swept to victory over the discredited Republicans, and stayed in power for over twenty years.

## 2 Britain in the 1930's

The slump hit Britain hard, but instead of driving out the men who had run the government in thé 1920's, it strengthened their position.

In 1929 there were three important political parties in Britain. The newest was the Labour party, which relied chiefly on Trade Union support. The party's policy was settled by an annual conference of local Labour parties and trade unions – and the unions had the chief weight in the voting since their representatives had block votes according to the number of their members. Labour had never yet won a majority in Parliament. (This first happened in 1945.) But they controlled many local councils, and gave working-class people their best chance of becoming councillors, mayors, magistrates, or school governors.

In local and national politics, Labour's chief rivals were the Conservatives or Tories. Millions of working-class people supported the Conservative Party but it was really run by the upper and middle classes – landowners, businessmen, and professional people who saw socialism as a danger. They looked to the Conservative Party to protect (conserve) the free enterprise or capitalist system, and the traditional British pattern of Royal Family, Church of England, Lords and Commons. Conservative party members and business firms paid to keep the party going. It was richer than the Labour Party, and seven out of ten national daily newspapers supported it.

Before 1918 the Tories' chief rivals had been the Liberal

Party, now on its way out. Once its strongest supporters had been the Nonconformists (members of churches other than the Church of England or Roman Catholic Church). Now, most people had lost interest in religion; what is more, the Liberals were split between the followers of Lloyd George and of Asquith since their quarrel over the Prime Ministership in 1916. In local councils, the other two parties were squeezing the Liberals out. The national government was increasingly pulling the strings of local government – for instance by preventing them from paying more than the official rate of unemployment pay; so local governments had little initiative and could only side roughly with the ratepayers (who owned houses or businesses) or the rest (few working class people owned such things, so they did not pay rates directly). So the Liberals, who generally supported the ratepayers, did not seem much different from the Conservatives.

The Labour and Conservative parties had reliable supplies of money and local organisations kept in action by the annual local elections – in both respects the Liberals were much weaker. Lloyd George tried to strengthen them by claiming: 'We can conquer unemployment' – the other parties obviously could not since throughout the 1920's there were at least a million out of work. His solution was for the government to borrow money, instead of cutting its expenses, and to set men to work on transport, communications, and housing; giving work and pay to the unemployed would raise the demand for goods as they spent their wages and the economy would come out of its stall. This argument got the Liberals nowhere in 1929. Most people still blamed the government for spending too much rather than not enough. When Sir Oswald Mosley made similar suggestions in the Labour Party, he found little support there; and as he would not drop his ideas, he was expelled. He developed into an admirer of Hitler and Mussolini.

Labour were in power at the time of the Wall Street Crash. This was their second government. The first, in 1924, had Britain's first-ever Cabinet with a working-class majority. It achieved little, beyond a Housing Act which made possible a great increase in the number of council houses built for rent, and an Education Report which laid down the principle of change from primary to secondary schools at eleven plus, and suggested that there should be two kinds of secondary school; Grammar and Modern. At this time, most working-class children stayed all their school lives in elementary schools where only the simplest work was taught. The promised 'secondary education for all' was slow in coming; the slump and the Second World War delayed it, and in 1958 the Minister of Education was still promising to get rid of these 'all-age' schools.

The 1924 and 1929 Labour governments were both out-numbered in the House of Commons by Conservatives and Liberals; this made them weak, but at first the 1929 government seemed to do well. It sorted out the reparations question with France and Germany; it reached agreement with the US about the size of navies; it organised an International Disarmament Conference which tried to make a reality of the promise to disarm made by the victors in 1918. At home, it gave farmers the right to work together on fixing prices for their products instead of beating each other down; and planned the Transport Board to take London's public transport out of private control. (Londoners will know a smaller success of this government: the Serpentine Lido in Hyde Park.)

Then came the slump. Within two years British exports fell by almost half, and unemployment doubled. The German banks which collapsed in 1931 owed money to London banks. Losing this money, the London banks could not pay their own debts abroad. Foreign holders of sterling (money in pounds) were afraid that the British government would cut the value of the pound in gold, so that it would be easier to pay British debts in paper money. So the foreigners sold their sterling as fast as they could. The London bankers told the government that the only way to save the pound, that is, to stop it from falling in value through a glut of sales, was to balance the budget by making stiff cuts in government spending. This would prove that the government meant to pay its way without falling back on printing more paper money that could not be exchanged for gold.

It seemed that the only way to balance the budget was to cut unemployment pay (the dole) by 10 per cent. The Conservatives and Liberals, whose backers did not have to live on the dole, supported this. The trade unions did not. The Labour Cabinet split on the issue, and the Prime

Minister. Ramsay MacDonald, formed a new 'national' government backed by the Liberals and Conservatives but by only a handful of Labour MPs. The so-called 'national' government lasted until 1940.

The National Government brought in an emergency budget, with heavier taxation and cuts of 10 per cent in all wages and salaries paid by the government – whether to cabinet ministers, to unemployed workers, or to anyone else. Teachers were honoured with a 15 per cent cut. This tough budget failed to save the pound. Foreign bankers still had two reasons for not trusting the pound. First, the Labour Party attacked the new budget, so British support for it was not unanimous; second, there were mutinies in the Royal Navy. The sailors got the harshest cuts softened, but their mutiny prompted more selling of sterling. The government went off the gold standard, and the pound lost one-quarter of its value in gold.

Yet in the 1931 election it won a huge majority. Neville Chamberlain, the new Chancellor of the Exchequer, put import duties on all foreign goods except food and raw materials, and he saved money by cutting arms expenditure to the lowest figure of any year between the wars. Road, school and house building was slashed – in the worst years of the depression the government provided as little work as it could. It helped industries which could find no market for their goods to cut down production – for instance all cotton factory owners paid into a fund for destroying six million spindles and compensating their owners. After this the small number of surviving firms hoped for better prices. Labour's system of farmers' marketing boards was spread, and the government gave cash subsidies to the farmers, to make sure they got a fair return for their work.

After 1933 the world was pulling out of the slump. Only certain areas did not revive: those which depended on industries such as coal and cotton which had permanently lost their markets – these continued to have as many as two out of three men unemployed. The government labelled them 'special areas,' gave them a little extra money, and tried feebly to provide jobs in them. Those who had been out of work for years were kept alive with benefit money, but from 1931 they had to take a 'means test' before they got any benefit; if a man had savings or children at work he might not qualify. People hated the means test and

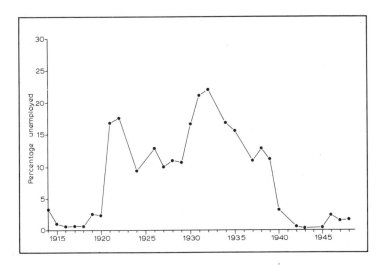

*Unemployment in Britain between the World Wars* The graph shows how unemployment was chronic in Britain until the Second World War. The slump after 1929 more than doubled unemployment, and the National Government made no improvement, but after 1932 there was a recovery

some Labour councils would not run it. In 1934 Chamberlain scrapped it.

Faced with the slump, Britain's government did little that was any use, and struck hardest at those who were already worst off – the unemployed. The Conservatives, who were supposed to believe in free competition, supported policies like price-fixing which strangled competition. Life got better after 1933 – except in the special areas – but not thanks to government action.

## 3 Germany: the Nazis take over

Meanwhile the slump hit Germany harder than any other country in Europe. The settlement of 1918 was altogether destroyed. This settlement had installed a Republican system. All adults could vote for the President. He chose the ministers, led by a Chancellor: they had to work with the parliament (*Reichstag*) elected by the adult population every four years. The Republic never looked really healthy. There were too many political parties, which had to combine to form a *Reichstag* majority; and only one party, the Social Democrats, was really loyal to the Republic. The powerful Communists would not work with the Social Democrats, whilst millions of votes went to nationalist parties which denounced the whole 1919 set-up – Republic and Treaty alike. The ex-Kaiser's most successful general, Hindenburg, was the most widely respected man in Germany; as president from 1925 to 1934, he regarded his job as to keep the seat warm for the Kaiser or his son.

One of the nationalist parties was Hitler's, the National Socialists. In the early twenties, Hitler was famous in Germany – there was popular support for his extremist programme as post-war disasters made people feel that mild remedies could not help. Hitler tried, once, to seize power by force. This landed him in gaol, where he wrote the first part of *Mein Kampf* (My Struggle) – his life story. He resolved to become Chancellor by legal methods. For years, while little was heard of him, he worked away, building a hard core of paying Party members, highly organised all over Germany with special branches for boys and girls, and a private army, the *Sturm Abteilung*, which beat up anyone who tried to challenge Hitler at public meetings. The SA, a home from home for ex-servicemen, was larger than the legal German army.

Hitler was waiting and hoping for some new disaster which would make the German masses listen to him. The slump did this for him. In the 1930 election the Nazis, promising drastic action to deal with unemployment, became the second largest party in the *Reichstag*. It was still three years before Hindenburg asked Hitler to be Chancellor – meanwhile he preferred Brüning, the 'hunger chancellor' who tried the same nasty medicine as Britain's national government: wage cuts and balanced budgets. Brüning aimed at bringing back the royal family, but Hindenburg would have no other king but William II or

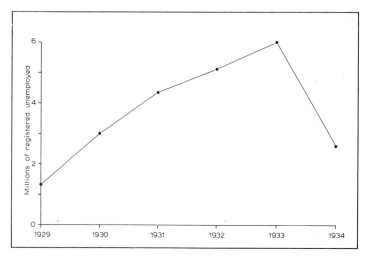

*Unemployment in Germany 1929 to December 1934* Note the steady climb until the year of Hitler's take-over; then there is an improvement for which the Nazis claimed credit. But Britain and the US were also recovering in these years with no Hitlers to help them

his eldest son, and Brüning's left-wing supporters would not stand for this. While Brüning's schemes failed, Hitler tightened his links with the German army, promising to give them back their old power and glory, to keep the SA in second place, and to seek revenge on the traitor peace-makers of 1918 – their heads, he said, would roll in the sand.

Hitler was now soft-pedalling the socialist parts of the Nazi programme and getting friendly with rich bankers and businessmen who cast him as their saviour from communism. These friends paid the SA's wages and the bills for his election campaigns. In 1932 Hitler stood for president against Hindenburg. He lost, but the Nazi vote was rising fast, and Hitler was watching for the right moment to take over as Chancellor. Hindenburg disliked him, foreseeing that he meant to establish a Nazi dictatorship, and knowing that he either could or would not stop the SA from street fights with the left-wing parties and assaults on Jews. Yet only Hitler, with his temporary friends the other nation-alists, could turn out a working *Reichstag* majority, so at last he got his invitation (January 30th 1933) and formed a government with 3 key Nazi ministers and 8 nationalists.

Now he pressed on towards dictatorship. Seeking an all-Nazi majority he called for new *Reichstag* elections and raised a fortune from German businessmen to pay for his campaign, promising them in return the ruin of the communists and the rebirth of a great German army. To stampede the voters, he claimed that the communists were planning immediate revolution: no evidence of this could be found until a Dutch communist, a lone wolf, set fire to the *Reichstag* building in Berlin.* Now the Nazis had the excuse they wanted. Publicly they blamed the German communists for the fire, arrested thousands of suspects of all kinds, and interfered violently with all the election campaigns except those of the Nazis and their allies. This was the biggest taste yet of Nazi terror; but in the election they still got less than half the votes! Arresting the communists wholesale made Hitler's majority more comfortable, and when he asked the newly elected *Reichstag* to surrender all its powers to him for four years, only the Social Democrats voted against him. Soon, he had closed down every non-Nazi party. There was no resistance. The setting-up of Nazi dictatorship was a victory without enemies. In May

*In 1969 it was proved that the Nazis themselves planned the fire

1933, Hitler paid his debts to the bosses. He closed down all the Trade Unions and restored leadership in the factories to their owners. No more collective bargaining: quarrels between leaders and led would be settled by Nazi 'labour trustees'.

The Nazis had always blamed the Jews for Germany's troubles. They now banned Jews from working in schools, universities, the civil service, law and medicine, and the SA launched a boycott of Jewish shops. In 1935 the Nuremberg Laws banned Jews from German citizenship and from marrying German citizens. Jews found life in Germany ever more difficult and dangerous, as their neighbours were officially encouraged to hate and persecute them. Many committed suicide. Many emigrated. They were the lucky ones.

Until 1934 Hitler was not really secure. He was only Chancellor and the President could sack him. But in spring 1934 Hindenburg was obviously dying. Hitler meant to be the next Head of State himself. This would make him Commander-in-Chief of the armed forces. Would the army tolerate this? To buy their support Hitler decided on a break with the SA whose leaders still hoped that the SA would replace the army. Pretending that the SA were planning a socialist 'second revolution', Hitler dismissed them all and had their commanders shot without trial. When Hindenburg died Hitler scrapped the title President, and proclaimed himself Germany's *Führer* (leader); all the forces had to take an oath of personal loyalty to him. The army raised no objection – but Hitler won both ways: the SA's job as his personal army was filled by the vicious, black-uniformed SS (*Schutz Staffel*).

After March 1933 there were no more free elections, but Hitler got tremendous majorities in several plebiscites. Nazism was popular. Almost everyone was delighted with Hitler's attacks on the Versailles treaty, and with the fall in unemployment – from 6 to 1 million in three years. No one could deny that Hitler got thousands of men back to work, for instance building roads and making war weapons. Few cared to think about the ugly side of Nazism, though more and more suspects disappeared into concentration camps.

Hitler, now secure in power, claimed that the Third *Reich* which he had founded would last a thousand years. He could not hope to convert all adult Germans to Nazism,

*Was Hitler popular in Germany?*
The line shows the Nazi vote in elections up to 1933. Note that their popularity declined between July and November 1932. It seemed to have passed its peak when Hitler became Chancellor. In the election of March 1933 the Nazi vote climbed again, but Hitler still needed the Nationalists' support to give him a majority.

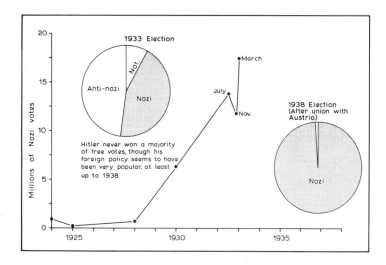

but this did not bother him if he could be sure of the German citizens of the future. Hence his attacks on the Christian churches (which taught a way of thinking absolutely contrary to Nazism – a way of love, not hate), and on the enemies of Nazism in art and literature. Hence the enormous attention the Nazis gave to education and youth organisations.

The Roman Catholic Church soon made a concordat (agreement) with Hitler, who could not afford at first to annoy the most powerful church in Germany. He promised to let the Catholics run their own affairs, their own churches and youth clubs; but soon he mounted a nasty campaign against church schools, accusing the monks and nuns on their staffs of homosexuality; and he closed the youth clubs. The concordat was strained, but the Pope never denounced it. At least, though, he never pretended that Christians and Nazis had anything in common. The Protestants gave Hitler more trouble. They were used to taking orders from the government and most of their clergy willingly swore loyalty to Hitler, but a brave minority formed the Confessional Church which openly condemned the Nazi persecution of the Jews. Hundreds of Confessional Church supporters were sent to concentration camps. During·the war some joined in plots against Hitler.

Given time, Hitler would probably have banned all forms of Christianity; Nazi plans for a national church involved replacing the Cross on church altars with Hitler's book *Mein Kampf* ('to the German nation' they said, 'and

Ganz Deutschland hört den Führer mit dem Volksempfänger

The Nazis used radio to bring their message to Germany's millions. 'All Germany hears the Führer on the People's Receiver'.

therefore to God, the most sacred book.')

As for art and literature, Hitler had a vulgar prejudice against modern art, and hated anti-nationalist, socialist or democratic literature. Modern-style works of art were banned from museums. Hitler's propaganda minister, Goebbels, organised burnings of anti-Nazi books. Germany's best living authors left the country. Teachers had to take an oath of loyalty to Hitler, and to put over Nazi ideas in all lessons. After they left school young people's education in Nazism continued with a year of compulsory work on roads, farms, etc., and then with National Service in the armed forces. Outside school hours, children spent their time in Nazi youth organisations catering for all ages from six to eighteen. At ten years of age, boys took tests in camping, athletics, and the Nazi version of history, and then swore to give their lives to Hitler. The 'Hitler Youth' was made compulsory in 1939.

## 4 Mussolini heads for trouble

The slump affected Italy less than Germany or Britain. Italy was a poorer country with fewer industries and less tied to world markets. In 1929, Mussolini was at the summit of his career. To the tune of world-wide praise, he made a pact with the Pope, recognising the Pope as sovereign of the Vatican City and giving millions of pounds to the Catholic Church. Mussolini had striven to make his country self-supporting in food and raw materials; the 'battle for wheat', to save Italy from importing grain, came near success at the cost of growing wheat on much unsuitable soil – but the armaments build-up left Italy even more dependent upon foreign iron and steel.

The Fascist Party's original left-wing purposes had been neglected. Mussolini made a great display of the draining of marsh lands for farming, but it was chiefly the big landlords who profited from this. He sacrificed the factory workers to the bosses. The workers heard no more of the eight-hour day he had promised them: strikes were illegal and the workers could organise only in the Fascist-controlled syndicates. Prices soared in the 1930's and wages lagged behind – they were fixed by corporations in which workers and bosses were supposed to co-operate, but Fascists had the last word.

During Hitler's hard times in the 1920's Mussolini helped him out, and Hitler cribbed Mussolini's ideas – the black shirts, the Roman salute. When the two met, in 1934, Mussolini disliked Hitler but he ended as Hitler's pupil. He forced the Italian army to learn the German goose-step, and copied Hitler's anti-Jewish laws, banning marriages between Jews and 'Aryan' Italians, and banning the Jews from professions. To show he was in earnest he dropped his own Jewish dentist, but he did not really bother to enforce these unpopular laws. Italian enthusiasm for Mussolini declined, as he made Italy more and more a cheap imitation of Nazi Germany.

## 5   The United States: Roosevelt's New Deal

For the US, as for Germany, the late 1920's were prosperous, and the Republican party took credit for this, but when the slump came, they were at a loss how to cope. President Hoover, successor to Coolidge, had himself pioneered the use of increased government spending to smooth out the business cycle of booms and slumps. He also came to the rescue of America's farmers by trying to keep up food prices: the Federal government supported marketing boards and bought crops at a loss. He lent money to banks and businesses, trying to save them from collapse. But all this was not enough. Faced with the largest-ever budget deficit in 1931, he called for economy. A balanced budget was essential, he said. He vetoed a Congress relief programme, and tried wage cuts and heavy tariffs. He refused to start a dole for the unemployed, who were thus worse off than their European fellows. He insisted that individuals, or the separate States, must see to the relief of hardship. The slump would last for years, he thought, and government interference would be medicine for the wrong disease – it would make things worse; the patient must be left alone, to recover naturally.

This point of view did not go down well with the unemployed. In 1932, 30,000 ex-servicemen met in Washington, camping in shacks nearby, to demonstrate for immediate payment of a bonus due in 1945. (All over America, evicted families were living in such shacks, nicknamed Hoovervilles.) Hoover ordered the army to turn out

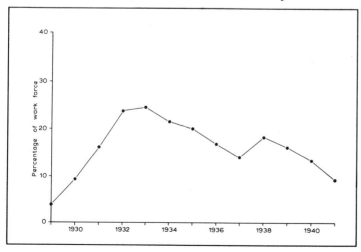

*Unemployment in the USA 1929–41*
Note the steep rise before 1932, and the improvement during the New Deal; but one worker out of ten still had no job in 1941

the squatters' 'bonus army'. There was fighting, 3 deaths, 1,000 injuries – the shacks were burned down. Small wonder that in the same year the Democrats won a huge electoral victory, and their new President, F. D. Roosevelt, carried forty-two out of forty-eight states.

Roosevelt's career was unspectacular before 1932 except for his courage in sticking to his work after infantile paralysis left him a cripple in a wheel chair. Now he urged that unless the Government tackled the slump, people would lose all confidence in the political and social system, and turn to fascism or communism. He did not aim to get in the way of free competition, only to give it state assistance, and to spread this to the small man as well as the huge banks and combines favoured by the Republicans – it was time, he declared, for a 'new deal' for the American people. The State should act to give them this, where private initiative broke down – the Republicans called this Bolshevism but Roosevelt said he was only a Christian and a democrat. The people of the US in this desperate time were looking to the central government to free them from their fear that the depression was incurable. Perhaps the government could show a way to avoid for ever the collapse of boom into slump. Roosevelt believed that 'the only thing we have to fear is fear itself' – the country's resources were rich and unharmed. On these the people must be set to work.

In Roosevelt's famous 'first hundred days' he closed all the banks, and reopened only reliable ones; scrapped

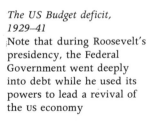

*The US Budget deficit, 1929–41*
Note that during Roosevelt's presidency, the Federal Government went deeply into debt while he used its powers to lead a revival of the US economy

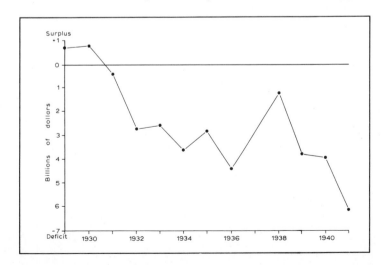

prohibition – the sale of taxed alcoholic drinks would give the government useful income; slashed government salaries and pensions (this was old-fashioned); scrapped the gold standard for the dollar, so that more money would circulate; launched the Civilian Conservation Corps to employ young people on such projects as reafforestation; lent 500 million dollars to the States for emergency relief; helped small farmers to avoid eviction by giving them easy credit – and all farmers to make a living by fixing how much they could sell and at what price; started a public authority to develop the hydro-electric and land resources of the Tennessee Valley; and lastly, signed the National Industrial Recovery Act which financed huge road and ship-building programmes, fixed maximum working hours and minimum wages, established trade unions as legally entitled to bargain with employers, and set out to persuade each industry to take on more workers, and pay them more, instead of competing with each other in reducing costs.

Not all these projects succeeded. Until 1940, there were always at least 7 million Americans out of work. Yet Roosevelt's 'new deal' was resoundingly approved by the voters in 1936 when they gave Roosevelt the biggest election victory in American history up to that time. It brought new hopes to millions and saved them from homelessness or starvation, and it showed that not only a dictatorship could tackle social disaster on a grand scale and with courage, nor need social disaster necessarily lead to the establishment of a dictatorship as had happened in Germany.

# Chapter 8
# The Road to Global War

No Air Force at all; a miniature Army and Navy; no sub-marines; the Rhineland defenceless – so that the French army, the most powerful in Europe, could march in unopposed; an Allied Control Commission on German soil to watch out for treaty-breaking; – this was Germany's situation in the 1920's, when Hitler was writing *Mein Kampf* and building the Nazi Party, pledged by its 'unalterable' programme to snap out of these handcuffs fastened on Germany by the 1919 Treaty. Already in 1927 Stresemann (see p. 108) got rid of the Control Commission, and even it had not prevented secret treaty-breaking – the training of extra ('black') troops, and of air force pilots in the commercial airlines; the building of submarines, the testing of weapons in Russia. Yet when Hitler took office as Chancellor, German armed forces were painfully weak, and he felt that for years to come Germany's neighbours would be able to throw him out, if he gave them the excuse and if they had the nerve.

That is why Hitler presented himself as a peace-lover. To the Germans he was a patriot who would not see Germany treated as second-rate, so they adored him and voted for him – even most of the prisoners in his concentration camps voted approval when he took Germany out of the Disarmament Conference and the League of Nations. (The League, Germans thought, was a racket to keep the Versailles treaty alive, and at the Conference the French would not stand for Germany being treated as an equal.) To foreigners Hitler posed as an ex-serviceman who knew at first hand the horrors of war (he had been wounded and gassed on the Western Front) and who was anxious to settle all quarrels in a friendly way. The British and Italian governments sympathised with him over disarmament, and blamed the French for provoking him!

In Germany Hitler was so popular that he dared to make

an agreement with Poland, promising for ten years not to use force to satisfy German grievances over Danzig and the Polish Corridor – the most hateful parts of the 1919 treaty. The agreement cost Hitler nothing as he would not be ready to tackle Poland for years, and anyway he had no respect for promises; but it was a blow to the French, who had counted on Poland as an ally against Germany.

Not until 1935 was Hitler ready for more action in foreign affairs. Meanwhile he was busy, crushing his Nazi rivals, organising the Nazi dictatorship, and pushing on with re-armament. He dared not even help his friends the Nazis in Austria, his home country, who wanted to add Austria to the Reich – in 1934 they murdered Austria's Chancellor and tried to take over, but Mussolini, wanting Austria independent, promised to help the Austrian government against Hitler, whom he considered a mad little clown. He sent some troops to the Austrian frontier. Hitler kept out of the row.

Next year, he startled Europe by announcing that Germany was starting to call up young men for National Service and to build an Air Force – indeed he claimed to have already an Air Force as big as Britain's. This was Hitler's first open defiance of the Treaty of Versailles. What would the Allies do about it?

Nothing, it seemed, but organise a conference at Stresa, in Italy, where the British, French, and Italian governments warned Hitler not to do anything so wicked as breaking a

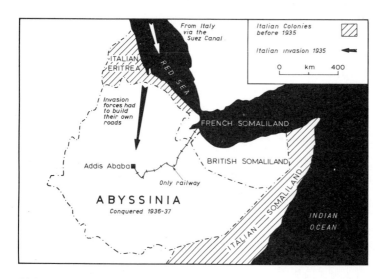

*Abyssinia and the Italian invasion*

1935: The Abyssinian emperor's cavalry ride out to meet Mussolini's machine-guns

treaty; the next time they would punish him. Hitler's actions were answered with words.

Mussolini had other fish to fry! He was planning an attack on Abyssinia, to round off Italy's African empire, and he expected Britain and France not to interfere with this, since he had so kindly backed them up at Stresa. The French were naturally more upset about Hitler's moves; they hunted for more supporters against the Nazi threat. They and the Russians agreed to help each other if attacked. There was only one country likely to attack them!

If the Stresa Front had held firm and carried out its threat, Hitler could have got no further – but it collapsed almost at once. Britain banged a hole in it, by privately agreeing with Hitler, without telling France or Italy, that he could build as many submarines as Britain and have a fleet one-third as big. Mussolini flattened it by attacking a League member country, Abyssinia.

This was the last fully independent country in Africa. It was only ten years since slavery had been abolished there, the slave trade had not been rooted out, and the Emperor, struggling to modernise, still could not keep order after dark even in the capital city. A few years earlier the British had argued that Abyssinia was not civilised enough to join the League of Nations. Mussolini promised to civilise the country, at the same time linking up Italy's other colonies and showing off Italy's armed strength.

Since 1919 supporters of the League of Nations argued that the League could stop wars, if its members worked together in applying sanctions (see ch. 3, p. 35). They should first stop all trade with a country which attacked a League member, and second, if necessary, combine their armed forces against the attackers. In Britain most of the voters seemed to agree with this argument in the summer of 1935, while Mussolini was arranging his armies, and in the autumn there was to be a British general election.

## 1  Abyssinia and sanctions

There was disagreement within the National Government (see pp. 114–115) over using sanctions against Italy. Some thought it unwise to drive Mussolini on to Hitler's side when Italy's support against Hitler might be precious; but the Foreign Secretary, Anthony Eden, urged a tough line on sanctions, as a way to end the run of dictators' successes. In public the government said they would support sanctions against Italy. They won the election. While Italian troops were already advancing into Abyssinia, Britain, France, and other League countries cut off their trade with Italy – but not all of it! Oil was the only import which Mussolini really needed; and Britain and France still let him buy it. On this question, the French government agreed with the anti-Eden men in the British government.

Mussolini threatened war against countries which stopped him from getting oil. Britain and France spinelessly stalled the oil sanction, hoping that Mussolini would take so long in conquering Abyssinia that the other sanctions would force him to give up the idea.

In fact, his army soon beat the Abyssinians. He had poison gas, motorised troops, machine guns, bombers – and the sanctions only helped him by making the Italians more patriotic. Why should their country be picked on in this way? Other European nations had already grabbed most of Africa. Women sent Mussolini their wedding rings to help pay for the war.

With the Stresa countries still squabbling about Abyssinia Hitler seized his chance. In 1935 he had sworn to respect the Locarno Pact (see p. 108); now, in March 1936, using as his excuse the French agreement with Russia (communism and the Jews being his twin bogeys) he sent German troops into the Rhineland. The army was weak. The trained professionals had their hands full drilling the new conscripts. Hitler had ordered immediate retreat if the French advanced into the Rhineland. France would not act without British support, and most British people felt that Hitler was only marching into his own backyard. So Hitler got away with it. He offered his usual tranquilliser, saying there was nothing more he wanted, and he was ready to make 25-year non-aggression pacts (as with Poland) with any country that asked.

The march into the Rhineland was a triumph for Hitler. Now he could plan seriously for German attacks to the East, against France's allies, Czechoslovakia and Poland; and for the addition of Austria to the Reich. The only way the French could stop him was by invading Germany, and now he could build such heavy defences on Germany's frontier with France that this would be impossible. In 1936, then, Hitler ordered serious preparation for war to begin. Attack would be in the East. Germany must be ready to fight Britain and France within four years, in case they tried to interfere. Hitler's ex-fighter pilot friend, Göring, was put in charge of a 4-year plan to make Germany self-supporting in raw materials. Faster and faster, weapons were made, fortifications built, servicemen trained. But Hitler needed another year of quiet – he could not risk war against France until the Rhineland defences were ready. So he did not get tough with Czechoslovakia or Austria until 1938.

Meanwhile, all things seemed to work together for him. He gained useful allies – Italy and Japan – and his future enemies, Britain, France and Russia, showed they could not stand by each other, nor protect their friends.

Those friends needed protection, since Hitler and Mussolini claimed that Nazism and Fascism were international movements, and supported such movements in other countries. No European country lacked parties which copied fascist ideas; some of these parties were feeble like the Irish Blueshirts or British Blackshirts – but some were dangerous. In France, for instance, they started riots in 1934 which looked like a plot to overthrow the Republic. Left-wing and Liberal parties saw that they had better sink their differences, and work together against the fascist menace.

## 2   Stalin and popular fronts

Stalin ordered Communist parties to co-operate in 'popular fronts' of anti-fascist parties. He foresaw another war in which Russia would be worse off than in 1914. Then, Russia had only one serious enemy – Germany. Now, Russia had two possible enemies, Germany and Japan. He could make difficulties for both by supporting popular fronts. In China (see Chapter 5) this would unite the Chinese in resistance against Japan. In Europe it might dam the flood of fascist success. In 1936, the French and Spanish general elections returned popular front governments. Was the spread of fascism slowing down?

The new Spanish government was unfriendly to the tremendously wealthy Roman Catholic Church with its stranglehold on education; and to the great landlords whose huge estates had made democracy a sham. The popular front took some steps towards sharing out these estates among the workers, and towards trimming the ridiculously large and expensive Spanish army which had a habit of interfering in politics.

These moves prompted a rebellion of the army, supported by most of the upper classes and by those who wanted the church to keep its social power – and by the Spanish Fascist Party which reckoned it needed to save Spain from communism.

## 3   Mussolini, Hitler and Spain

Mussolini and Hitler were alarmed at the Spanish situation. They thought popular front governments were communist puppets, and concluded that communism would soon be established in Western Europe. This would be a threat to them. Mussolini had encouraged the rebels. He sent them aircraft, guns and men. He was keen to export fascism to

Spain, smash the popular front there and knock the French in the eye.

The Spanish rebels expected quick success, but the popular front fought hard, and a 3-year struggle began. At the Battle of the Guadalajara, Italian troops ran away from the popular front armies. Mussolini could not face a defeat for fascism in Spain and sent more and more help to the rebels, who threw up a crafty leader, General Franco. Hitler was delighted to see the Italian army involved in Spain. This would make it easy for him to take over Austria (where Mussolini had frustrated him in 1934) and would make Mussolini less likely to co-operate with the French government. They, naturally, sympathised with the Spanish popular front. Hitler wanted Franco to win, but not too fast. German fighter planes and bombers punished Spanish towns and troops severely, the pilots got useful practice in bombing and strafing, but Hitler left most of the work to Italy.

It is against international law for a government to help rebels in another country, but a government facing rebellion has the right to buy equipment, or seek help, from other governments. If the British and French had stood by these rules, and sold war material to the Spanish government, Franco's rebellion would probably have failed in spite of his Italian and German friends. But the French government was afraid of stirring up civil war in France by helping one side in Spain's civil war; and the British Conservatives, not fancying the popular front anyway, were still anxious not to quarrel with Mussolini.

So Britain and France refused to help the Spanish government – though they could not stop thousands of volunteers from joining the International Brigades which fought nobly against Franco. Instead of helping, they got all the chief countries to promise not to help either side. Hitler and Mussolini of course would promise anything. At first the Russians promised too; when they saw Germany and Italy still helping Franco, they sent help to their friends in Spain. Stalin wondered why the British and French turned a blind eye to German and Italian treachery, and decided these governments were not really serious in wanting to check the spread of fascism.

While war raged in Spain, Mussolini spoke of the 'axis' which united Italy and Germany in their struggle for peace, and Hitler announced that Germany and Japan had agreed to work together against international communism. Thus, in autumn 1936, the line-up of Hitler's allies in the Second World War had already emerged.

## 4  Austria & Czechoslovakia: Hitler wins without war

By the end of the next year, 1937, Hitler felt that Germany was strong enough to risk war against Britain and France. These countries, he thought, would be certain to resist his plan to conquer living-space for Germany in Eastern Europe. Germany must smash them, and not later than 1943–5 – after that, Germany's lead in armaments would be lost, as Britain and France were now rearming. These two countries might also interfere with Hitler's immediate plans to add Austria and the German-speaking parts of Czechoslovakia to the Reich in 1938. Hitler would risk this. The German army and air force got new orders – to plan invasions of Austria and Czechoslovakia.

1938 might have seen war in Europe – but no, instead of resisting Hitler, the British and French governments did their best to help him. Chamberlain, now Prime Minister in Britain, thought it was no use fighting nationalism. He had seen the English forced to pull out of Ireland after years of war against the Irish nationalists and forced by Indian nationalists to let the Indians take over a big share of the authority in their own country (see Chapter 4). To appease (i.e. to satisfy) the Germans, by giving way to their demands – as far as these could be supported by the argument that one nationality should not rule another – that was what Chamberlain aimed at; if Hitler's demands went beyond this, then maybe Britain must fight him; but not until she was strong enough to win! Chamberlain pressed on with Britain's rearmament, meanwhile trying for peaceful agreements with Hitler. The French government were sure of one thing – no war against Hitler unless Britain was at France's side. So Hitler found that he was welcome to help himself to Austria, and break up Czechoslovakia – Britain and France would not interfere, at least so long as all was done peacefully, without any actual invasion.

This he proceeded to arrange. Austria first; he ordered Austria's Chancellor to admit the Austrian Nazi Party into the government. The alternative was German invasion. It was no use looking to Mussolini for help this time, Hitler said; Mussolini was his friend now. Nor would Britain and France rescue Austria. The Chancellor gave way, and then to block the path to Nazi take-over, rashly announced a plebiscite in which the Austrians would be able to vote for or against union with Germany. Such a plebiscite, not supervised by the Nazis, did not suit Hitler at all. He ordered the Chancellor to resign or the Germans would march. The Chancellor resigned, an Austrian Nazi took over, and doing what he was told by the Germans invited the German army to occupy Austria. Hitler entered Vienna in triumph with his troops – even though 70 per cent of the army vehicles broke down on the road. So he got his way, without use of force, and Austria got the full Nazi treatment. Mussolini said, 'What has happened was bound to happen.'

A glance at the map shows how the German occupation of Austria weakened Czechoslovakia's position – and Czechoslovakia was obviously next on Hitler's list. This would be a tougher job for him. Czechoslovakia had a powerful army supplied by East Europe's largest armaments works, a serious air force, a mountain frontier, and alliances with Russia and France. Hitler had a card to play, worth all these – all he wanted, he could claim, was self-determination for the German-speaking people of Czechoslovakia (generally known as the Sudetens). These people had little to complain of, but Hitler encouraged the Sudeten Nazi party to prod them into nationalist, anti-Czech frenzy.

*1938 Hitler strikes*
German nationalism, their own weakness and the failure of the other Powers to back them, left Austria and Czechoslovakia to fall before Hitler's assertion of German strength

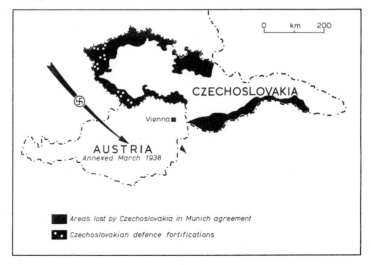

*Areas lost by Czechoslovakia in Munich agreement*

*Czechoslovakian defence fortifications*

Chamberlain felt Hitler's cause was just; he and his French opposite numbers dreaded a collision with Hitler – but treaties bound them to help the Czechs against Hitler, if the Czechs asked for this. So instead of working with the Czechs and the Russians, who insisted that they would help, the British and French did Hitler's work for him by persuading the Czech government to surrender the Sudeten lands to Germany.

Was this cowardly, or common sense? The French generals feared they could not break through Hitler's Siegfried Line (the not yet finished defences in the Rhineland) – nor even hold off a German attack through Belgium. The British Cabinet followed Chamberlain's lead – he said he did 'not care two hoots' if the Sudeten Germans joined Germany, and he thought that there was no point in backing up the Czechs as Britain and France 'could not possibly save Czechoslovakia from being overrun by the Germans' if war came.

Yet war nearly did come, over Czechoslovakia, in September 1938. Hitler was hoping for the complete collapse of Czechoslovakia, not just the peaceful handing-over to him of the German-speaking areas. Chamberlain flew to see him, and twisted the arms of the Czechs till they gave up the Sudetenland; then he flew to see Hitler again and found this was not enough! Now Hitler was demanding that within three days the German army must be marching into Czechoslovakia.

This was too bitter a dose for Britain and France. They refused to bully the Czechs any more and prepared to fight. The British got their anti-aircraft guns out, all forty-four of them, and planned to evacuate children from the cities; trenches were dug in parks for shelter, and the Royal Navy alerted.

Hitler's generals were frightened. The Czech army alone was almost as big as the German (and better trained); if the French dared attack in the west there could be little resistance. Hitler was swearing that he would not fight the Czechs unless they were on their own – but the generals doubted him, and some plotted to arrest him if he landed Germany in war with Britain and France.

Hitler did not know this, but he could see that the ordinary people of Germany dreaded war. Rightly guessing that the British and French would lose their nerve, he was content, for the sake of peace, to tone down his demands slightly.

So came the Munich conference. Mussolini persuaded Hitler to agree to another meeting, with himself, Chamberlain, and Daladier, the French Prime Minister. At Munich, Mussolini put forward, as a compromise, a plan which had actually been drafted by the Germans. Hitler graciously accepted this – so did Chamberlain and Daladier. Now within a fortnight the Germans were to march into the Sudeten areas. The Czechs and Russians were not consulted. Chamberlain persuaded Hitler to sign a declaration that in future Britain and Germany would co-operate to settle disagreements peacefully. This he waved to the cheering crowd at London airport, and he claimed to have brought back 'peace with honour', and 'peace in our time'!

Winston Churchill, Chamberlain's most powerful critic, saw it differently. Throwing away the chance to ally with Russia, Britain had betrayed East Europe's only democratic country, strongly defended 'with an army only two or three times as large as ours . . . a munitions supply only three times as great as that of Italy.' In the September crisis he said '£1 was demanded at the pistol's point. When it was given, £2 was demanded at the pistol's point. Finally the Dictator consented to take £1.17.6, and the rest in promises of goodwill for the future.'

## 5   Hitler turns against Poland

On one thing Churchill and Chamberlain were agreed. British rearmament must hurry up – and indeed 'peace in our time' lasted less than a year. In March 1939 Hitler engineered the collapse of Czechoslovakia. He bullied the President into inviting German troops to occupy half of his country, although he had promised, at Munich, to respect the new frontiers. So had Britain, France, and Italy – but the British and French governments said they were let out, since Czechoslovakia had collapsed by itself; and Mussolini merely had a tantrum because Hitler had done this without warning him beforehand: 'Every time Hitler occupies a country he sends me a message.' The plain fact that Italy was the weaker partner in the Axis exasperated Mussolini, who answered Hitler by sending troops into Albania, whence he could threaten Greece, Yugoslavia, and

Labels within the map:
Leningrad
ESTONIA
*Possible German invasion route*
LATVIA
LITHUANIA
RUSSIA
Danzig
GERMANY
GERMANY
POLAND
*Mainly German speaking*
0 km 400

Turkey. But, at the same time, he refused to drop his friendship with Hitler and, in May 1939, agreed to the so-called Pact of Steel between Germany and Italy.

The German march into Bohemia convinced Chamberlain, at last, that Hitler's fair words could not be trusted. Now he must show Hitler, clearly, what Britain would fight for. The British government gave guarantees of help to the countries now threatened by the Axis: Greece, Romania, and – Poland.

In Germany, Hitler launched a propaganda campaign, demanding that Danzig (see Chapter 3, p. 36) be handed back to Germany and that the split between East Prussia and the rest of Germany be ended. The British and French governments did not particularly quarrel with these demands; but this time they were not prepared to bully an ally into surrender. As for the Polish government, they thought it was a mistake to talk to Hitler. They refused flatly to discuss Danzig, or the Polish corridor. Summer 1939 – and war evidently approaching.

Churchill and his parliamentary followers, and the French government, now urged Chamberlain to mend fences and seek alliance with Russia. The threat of war on two fronts, which would then face Hitler, would trump all his aces. It would either prevent war, or make sure Germany lost it. The Germans saw this as well, and tried to persuade Stalin of the advantages of Russian neutrality.

Stalin suspected all these new courtiers. He had decided that the popular fronts would not be strong enough to check Hitler. He did not intend to drag Russia into a war against Germany. There is no proof that he would have supported the Czechs against Hitler. So far, the British and French had let down all their allies, and had avoided dealing as equals with Russia. He thought they would be quite happy to see German tanks roll east – against Russia. How about Hitler? For years he had labelled communism the great enemy of civilisation and announced that Germany must expand eastwards. Stalin could not trust him, and dreaded Russia being left alone to face the Nazis, with her army weakened by the purges (see Chapter 6, p. 103). Probably he would have preferred an alliance with Britain and France, if they had shown him that they meant business.

The French were keen to ally with Russia. They really would be at war with Germany, if Hitler attacked Poland. But Chamberlain did not trust the Russians and doubted if their army was any use. Also Poland's fascist-type government, ruling large areas conquered from Russia after 1918, had no intention of letting Russian troops on its territory. What was more, the Baltic republics (see Chapter 3, p. 35), felt the same. While empty of Russian troops, they offered an easy route to Leningrad for the German army. Britain refused either to push the Poles or the Baltic states around, or to make an alliance with Russia until this matter was cleared up. Stalin decided the British did not mean business. Their Prime Minister had made three flights to see Hitler, but only unimportant juniors came to see Stalin, and the British military mission took the slowest boat to Russia, instead of a plane. At Munich, Britain and France had bought time from Hitler by ditching Czechoslovakia. Now, Stalin would buy time from Hitler by ditching Poland.

Stalin decided: and inside a week, Ribbentrop and Molotov, the German and Russian foreign ministers, had signed a neutrality agreement and drunk toasts to Nazi-Soviet friendship. The agreement had a secret section: the two new friends would carve up Poland between them.

Hitler had sworn to spare Germany another war on two fronts. This was one promise he could now keep. Six months before, he had told his army to prepare Case White, plans for the invasion of Poland and the bombing of Warsaw. Now Case White went into operation.

Britain and France dithered for a day or two, hoping to fix up more talks. Then they declared war. The British Empire followed suit.

Italy stayed out. Mussolini knew how weak the Italian armed forces were. (In 1946, his police chief revealed that the police used to lend vehicles to the army to make a better show at parades.) At the time of the Pact of Steel, he had thought that Hitler would settle the Polish problem peacefully and that war would not come for three years. When he found Hitler was determined to conquer Poland, even if this meant war with Britain and France, he made his excuses to Hitler and waited to see how the war went.

Japan, Hitler's other ally, also stood aside. By 1939, the Japanese were far ahead in creating a new East Asian empire of Japan, China and Manchuria. They had headaches: Chiang and Mao still held out, and the Japanese army in Manchuria had serious border clashes with the Russians. When in August 1939, the Russians and the Germans suddenly seemed to be the best of friends, Japan did not warm towards Hitler.

## 6  Germany victorious, 1940-41

The German attack on Poland was a complete success, and the next stage of the war concerned the Baltic area. Russia, with Hitler's blessing, was busily recovering some of the losses of 1917, taking a share of Polish territory and waging war against Finland in the winter of 1939–40 to extend her frontiers at that country's expense. To Germany, the Norwegian port of Narvik was vital, for through it came her iron ore from neutral Sweden. With the Russians advancing, and the chance of a British or French move against Narvik, Hitler felt he could take no chances. In April 1940, his armies moved with crushing speed and effectiveness to occupy both Denmark and Norway.

The following month, France became the centre of the stage. Even as Britain's new Prime Minister, Winston Churchill, was taking office, the German armies swept

Effects of a German bombing raid on London

through neutral Holland and Belgium, hurled the British
army back across the Channel from Dunkirk, overwhelmed
the French and entered Paris on June 12th. Thinking the
war was nearly over and that he could obtain some booty
on the cheap, Mussolini now brought Italy into the war on
Germany's side. France accepted defeat and German occupation on June 22nd. Only a few Frenchmen refused to
accept the surrender. One of them, General Charles de
Gaulle, went to England to set up a rival French government – the 'Free French'.

Hitler now wanted to close down this part of the war. When Britain refused to discuss peace, Hitler launched an air attack across the Channel. Through the late summer and early autumn of 1940 a great air battle – the Battle of Britain – raged over southern England. Three things combined to prevent a German victory: the newly developed British radar system; the skill and heroism of the R.A.F.; and too much chopping and changing of targets by the Germans between airfields and the civilian population. At the end of 1940, therefore, Britain was still very much in the war.

But Hitler was in a hurry to launch a more important project: the destruction of communist Russia. He was concerned about the advances of his supposed friend Stalin, who had taken advantage of Hitler's commitment in the West to occupy the helpless little Baltic states of Lithuania, Latvia and Estonia and lop off part of Romania. On June 22nd 1941, the Germans launched a three-pronged attack on Russia which, by December, had carried their tanks over and beyond the Crimea, to within thirty miles of Moscow, and into the suburbs of Leningrad. Stalin had hoped the Nazi-Soviet pact would last a little longer and his troops were ill-prepared to meet the German onslaught. 'We are being fired on', one Russian unit radioed its headquarters on the day the invasion began. 'What shall we do?'

## 7   Japan and the United States join in

The course of the war in Europe had a tremendous effect upon events in the Far East. As we have seen, Japan was trying to create an empire in that part of the world. Broadly speaking, Japan could move either north – into Russia – or south – towards the European empires (pp. 92–93). The Nazi-Soviet pact of August 1939 seemed to close off the road to the north because it gave Russia a powerful friend who was also Japan's ally. The collapse of France and Holland in the summer of 1940 gave the Japanese another reason for moving south: these countries were no longer strong enough to protect their Asian possessions. Japan began to put the squeeze on the French, to allow Japanese troops into French Indochina, and the Dutch, to sell Japan much-needed oil from the Dutch East Indies on favourable

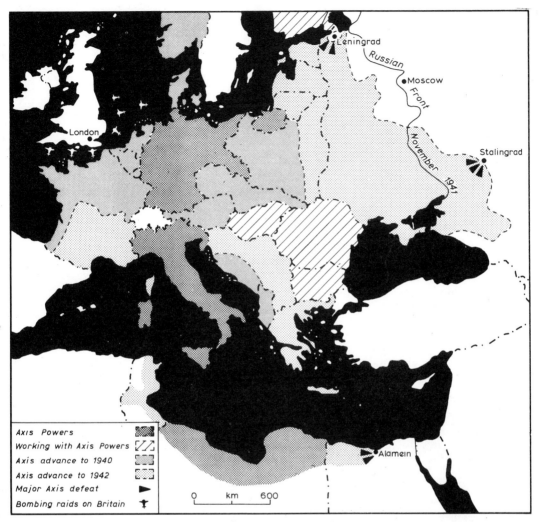

*Axis advance to 1942*

Legend:
Axis Powers
Working with Axis Powers
Axis advance to 1940
Axis advance to 1942
Major Axis defeat
Bombing raids on Britain

terms. If, as seemed very likely at the time, Hitler succeeded in knocking England out of the war, British colonies in the area (such as Malaya, Burma and North Borneo) would have been the next on the list.

But there was another power to be reckoned with: the US. President Roosevelt was worried about the Japanese threat to American possessions in the Far East, such as the Philippines. He also thought that Japan was acting in close agreement with Germany and Italy – which was not true – and that, once the war was over in Europe, all three countries would turn on the US. This was why he did his best to keep the British in the fight, supplying them with weapons and equipment on bargain terms known as 'lend lease.' At the same time, he warned the Japanese against further adventures in South East Asia.

In June 1941, the Japanese had one last chance to change their policy. When Hitler invaded Russia, he begged Japan to do the same, thus putting Russia in the nutcracker between Germany and Japan which Stalin had always dreaded. But Japan was now too deeply involved in the south. In any case, she did not see why she should help the Germans now when they had not bothered about her interests in reaching agreement with Russia in 1939. The Japanese therefore ignored the German pleas and, in July, got the French to agree to the stationing of Japanese troops in southern Indochina.

This was the last straw as far as Roosevelt was concerned. He got the British and Dutch to join with him in putting an embargo on the sale of oil to Japan. Without the vital fuel, Japan's war machine would grind to a halt, and Roosevelt would not lift the embargo unless the Japanese agreed to abandon many of their conquests. The Japanese commanders would not accept such a humiliating sacrifice; they preferred to fight, grabbing the sources of the oil and other raw materials they needed in the process.

They reckoned they could hold the US at arm's length on a 'defence perimeter' until the US government saw reason and agreed to a fair settlement. The Japanese navy and civilian government were worried about taking on the US, but the army had the last word. The prime minister resigned and General Tojo, nicknamed 'Razor', took over. Before Japan's declaration of war reached America, Japanese carrier-based aircraft smashed the US Pacific Fleet based at Pearl Harbour and attacked British and Dutch possessions at the same time. A few days later, Germany and Italy, who were angry at Roosevelt's continued support of the British, also declared war against America. There was now hardly a part of the globe which was not caught in the storm of war.

# Chapter 9
# The Second World War

## 1 About the war

Because Great Britain joined the war in 1939, people in Britain usually think of the war as starting in that year. If you have read Chapter 8 carefully, you may think that 1939 was simply the year that Britain came into it, after watching from the sidelines as the war took root in Abyssinia, Spain, China and elsewhere. This was a world war again, but it came like a thunderstorm, first drops here and there, then the full fury.

The First World War, you will remember, seemed to end in exhaustion, without having decided much. The Second was decisive in every way. Armies were commanded by men who had fought in the earlier war as junior officers, and who had learned the hopelessness of static trench warfare. The tank had made fast manoeuvres possible again, despite the machine-gun. Bomber aircraft were a fast and devastating weapon on the battlefield, and when they were used against the civilian population they were a new force in the battle of supplies and morale. This time the

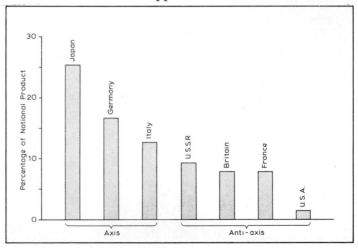

*The Axis economies geared for war*
Expenditure on armaments, 1933 to 1938, shown as percentages of the national product (total output of wealth)

battlefields were huge, the victories and defeats total. Instead of the 'battle of the Somme', it is the 'battle of France'; instead of the 'battle of Jutland', the 'battle of the Atlantic'.

The results of the war were more decisive, too. The great countries of Europe, Germany, France, Britain, Italy, were devastated and exhausted. Russia and America, conquerors of Europe in 1945, became the giants who dominate the world. The sudden change affected others beside Europe, Russia and the United States. So great was the power of Europe in Asia and Africa that their weakness was decisive there too. The Second World War is a turning point in world history of enormous importance.

## 2 The war from 1942 to 1945

But this was all in the future in the winter of 1941–2. Then the triumphs of the Axis powers in Europe were matched by their Japanese allies in the Pacific. After the attack on Pearl Harbour (see p. 142) Hong Kong, Malaya, Singapore, Burma, the Dutch East Indies and the Philippines fell in

Japan's advance to 1942

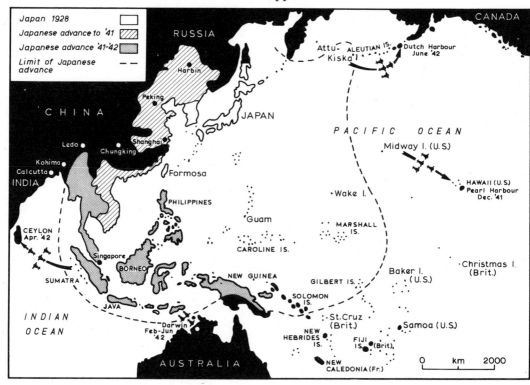

Russian artillery at
Stalingrad, 1942

swift order. By 1942, they had isolated Chiang Kai-Shek from Allied supplies, and their progress threatened both Australia and British India.

But later in the year, the tide turned in favour of the Allies. In the summer, the second stage of the German invasion of Russia was launched at the southern end of the front. A great thrust, made at the oilfields of Caucasia and the important industrial town of Stalingrad, was slowed by bitter Russian resistance, and it was September when the Germans arrived before Stalingrad.

In the ruins of the suburbs, in gruesome cold, all through the howling winter the Germans fought to take the city. Every factory, every house, the Russians defended to the last. Both dictators saw the 'city of Stalin' as a prize they must have; both gave the order 'no retreat'; but Stalin had the better reason. He was assembling armies which closed round the German rear. On February 1st 1943, twenty-three generals and 90,000 men, the survivors of the Stalingrad winter, surrendered to the encircling Russians. The whole German line began to move back.

Meanwhile, as Stalingrad developed, the armies of Britain and her empire advanced from the victory of El Alamein along the North African coast, the final change of tide in the fighting that had flooded back and forth there since the beginning of hostilities.

The third victory of 1942 was at sea, in the Pacific. Here it was the American fleet, recovering from Pearl Harbour, which won two battles; the battle of the Coral Sea in May, and the battle of Midway in June. The Japanese advance was held.

By the beginning of 1943 the fortunes of the Allies had passed their lowest point, and the might of America combined with the resistance of Russia to reverse the flood of battle. An Anglo-American force landed in Algeria and Morocco to take in the rear the Axis armies falling back before the British drive from El Alamein, and the North African coast was cleared. It was in North Africa that the Italians were interested, and in North Africa the Italian army had been committed. When Italy itself was invaded in July 1943, Mussolini was imprisoned by his disillusioned fellow-countrymen and the new Italian government deserted Hitler and joined the Allies. Mussolini was later rescued by the Germans and he organised his remaining supporters to continue the fight alongside the German armies. The fighting in Italy lasted until 1945. Shortly

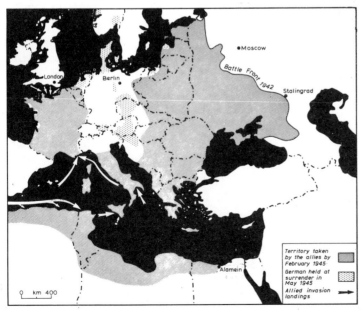

*Axis retreat 1942–5*

Effects of the atomic bomb
dropped on Hiroshima

before the end, Mussolini was captured and shot by Italian communists.

A massive air bombardment was mounted against the cities of Germany, and the German air force fell back onto the defensive. The last German air attacks on Britain were with a new weapon: rockets fired across the English Channel.

147

The mushroom cloud from the atomic bomb which destroyed Nagasaki just before Japan's surrender in 1945

By the spring of 1944, American and British troops were advancing through Italy; the Red Army pressed on into the Baltic states, the Balkans, and Poland. On June 6th, the western Allies invaded northern France, and by August they held Paris. By October, the Allied armies were poised on the frontiers of Germany. The end was near in Europe. On May 2nd, 1945, the Russians took Berlin. Two days earlier, to the sound of Russian guns, Hitler had killed himself rather than fall prisoner. On May 7th, the German armies surrendered.

The Allied plan had been to win the war in Europe first, then to defeat Japan. In 1944 the Japanese had tried to carry the war forward into India, but they had been held by the British 14th Army at the battle of Imphal. In the Pacific the Americans now had command of the sea, and were making a slow, bitter and costly advance from island to island. There was now no question that Japan could be beaten; the only question was how many Allied lives it would cost to overcome the loyal and courageous Japanese army. Even as the Japanese government was discussing the question of surrender, the Allies played a brutally decisive

*Japanese retreat 1942–5*

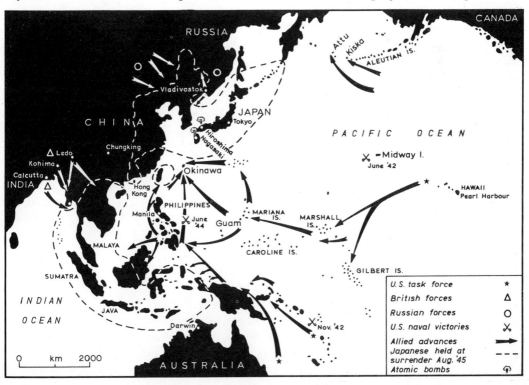

card. On August 6th, 1945, an atomic bomb was dropped on the city of Hiroshima. The power of this new scientific development was appalling. One bomb destroyed the whole heart of a city, killed and wounded more than 100,000 people, and left behind the lingering effects of poisonous radio-activity. Three days later it was Nagasaki's turn. On August 14th the Emperor of Japan broadcast to his people and his still widely spread armies. '. . . Should we continue to fight, it would not only result in an ultimate collapse and obliteration of the Japanese nation, but it would also lead to the total extinction of human civilisation.' He would pave the way to peace 'by enduring the unendurable and suffering the insufferable.' Japan had surrendered.

## 3 Europe and the politics of war

As the map on page 141 shows, the war brought German rule to most of Europe; this meant not only the presence of German soldiers, but also the application of Nazi methods and principles. In August 1941, Hitler and Mussolini announced their plans for Europe in these words: 'The new European order which will result from victory is to remove as far as possible the causes which in the past have given rise to European wars. The destruction of the Bolshevist danger and plutocratic exploitation will create the possibility of a peaceful, harmonious and fruitful collaboration of all the peoples of the continent . . .'

During the short wartime period in which the Nazi party controlled Europe, these words turned out to mean the enslavement of Europe to the German war effort. The food and resources of the conquered were taken. So were the men. In 1945 there were over 5 million foreigners conscripted from their homes and at work in Germany. Because of Nazi theories about race and breeding, all Europe was covered with concentration camps where forced labour was extracted from all sorts of people whom the Nazis found undesirable; Jews, Slavs, political enemies, intellectuals, criminals, gypsies. Many were classified 'to be worked to death', and in the later stages camps were built to exterminate entire races. The gassing and burning of over 6 million Jews in camps like Treblinka and Auschwitz by the ss is probably the lowest depth which cold, monstrous, organised cruelty has reached in the history of mankind.

Rounded-up for the concentration camps. A scene from the Jewish quarter of Warsaw in German-occupied Poland

Everywhere in Nazi-occupied Europe the deportations and the tyranny of the SS and the Gestapo produced underground resistance organisations which kept alive hopes of eventual liberation by their courage and daring. The Resistance played a part in the eventual defeat of Germany, especially by assisting the advance of the Allied armies when it came.

The nations which won the war did not do so in complete harmony. Each one was looking after itself, first in the struggle to survive in the period of disaster, and then in the plans for peace once it seemed that victory was certain.

More than the others, the United States added to this self-interest many plans for a better world for everyone. This had been the second time she had had to come in to a world war after hoping to stand aside. Now she hoped for a peace which would prevent world wars from starting. President Roosevelt wanted a new organisation to replace the League of Nations. He looked forward to getting his troops home from Europe within two years of the end of the war. He was hopeful of coming to satisfactory agreements with the Russians. As for Britain, the American leaders suspected that she only wanted to preserve her old empire. When Britain warned them not to trust the Russians they thought Britain was exaggerating in her own interest. Anyway, the United States was more interested in the Pacific, and hoped for Russian help against Japan. So in the middle years of the war Roosevelt listened with favour to Stalin's repeated demands for an early invasion of France, which the Russians argued would relieve them of carrying the main burden of the war alone and force Hitler to weaken his armies in Russia.

Churchill resisted this idea as long as he could, on the reasonable grounds that such an invasion would be a disaster unless it was properly and very carefully prepared. In truth, Churchill did not believe in seeking a head-on clash with the Germans by trying to breach their Atlantic Wall. His idea was to sap the enemy's strength by several landings in northern Italy and the Balkans, which he called the 'soft white underbelly'. Thus the second front was not opened until June 1944, although the Russians had been desperate for it in 1941, and the Americans had told them it could be managed in 1942. When it came, the tide in Russia had long been turned. Thoughtfully the Russians remembered those in Britain and America who had said in 1941 that the best thing was to sit back and let Russia and Germany destroy each other.

These differences in attitude affected the two big conferences between the three leaders in 1945. The first was held at Yalta, in the Crimea. There was little agreement. Stalin wanted to fine Germany heavily. The British thought his

Potsdam Conference, 1945
Seated: British Prime
Minister Attlee, US President
Truman, and Stalin

figure too high; Germany would starve. (Compare the reparations problem after the First World War, Chapter 3.) There was talk of reducing the power of Germany by carving the country up into smaller states, but all that was finally agreed was the zones of occupation for the victorious armies. The fate of Poland, already freed by the Red Army, caused long debates. The Red Army had established a government of communist Poles which already was hunting down prominent anti-communist and anti-Russian Poles, many of whom had been leaders of the Polish resistance against the Germans and supported a Polish government of leaders who had spent the war years in London. The British were particularly angry about this, because back in 1939 it was for Poland that they had finally gone to war. In the end, the Russians agreed to take some London Poles into the government and to hold free elections so that the people of Poland could take their own decision.

Before the second meeting at Potsdam in newly surrendered Germany, there was a change of leadership in the USA. Roosevelt died on April 12th, and was succeeded by Harry Truman. The new President was less inclined to sympathise with the Russian point of view. One of his first acts was an angry demand that the Russians honour their promises about Poland. In June, Poles from the West did enter the government. On the surrender of Germany, the US Army withdrew from its furthest lines of advance, back to the zones marked out at Yalta. But at the same time the flow of American aid to Russia was stopped so abruptly that ships already at sea were turned back to be unloaded.

At the Potsdam conference in July, and after, the disagreements grew. In Bulgaria and Romania the Red Army was assisting the advance of the Communist parties to power. Truman alleged that this was a breach of the agreement at Yalta to encourage free elections in liberated countries. Stalin was probably holding to an older agreement with Churchill about leaving Greece to British control if he could have Bulgaria and Romania, for he did allow free elections in Hungary, which the Communists lost. It was certainly true, as Stalin pointed out, that he was not interfering with the British in Greece, although the British army there was mirroring his Bulgarian and Romanian action by driving the communist heroes of the Resistance out of power at bayonet point.

## 4 The United Nations Organisation

The suspicion with which the wartime allies were beginning to watch each other endangered the birth and early years of their best project for preventing another world war. At the time of the turning point in the struggle, they had given themselves the title of the United Nations, and declared their intention of creating a world after their victory where people would enjoy security and justice free from the fear of aggression and the terrors of war.

What this meant in practice was that there was to be another attempt, despite the floundering of the League of Nations, to build an organisation through which the nations could work together to enforce the peace. The details were worked out by representatives of the USA, the USSR, Great Britain and China in 1944, and discussed the following year in San Francisco by the forty-eight governments now allied against the Axis. It seemed from the keen debates that the war-weary world had learned from the League's failure, and really wanted the United Nations Organisation to work.

On the face of it, the UN had a better chance than the League. To start with, the United States was in this time, and the USSR was a founder member. Outwardly, the organisation looked much the same. There would be a Security Council of the 'big five', the USA, the USSR, Great Britain, China and France, plus six changing representatives of the rest of the world. Every member country would have a place in the General Assembly, and there would be an international office staff called the Secretariat. It was not a world government, but an agreement between nations to settle quarrels without fighting, and to act together to crush any nation which might try to fight.

The fate of the League had shown how hard it was to put this simple theory into practice. No nation likes giving up its freedom to do what it likes, and no powerful nation likes to submit to the judgement of small ones which it could easily defeat in a war. This had made the League half-hearted. Then, every single member had had the right of veto; that is, a single vote against any idea put an end to it! The chances of getting anything done under that rule were always slim.

Fortunately, in 1945 the big powers were worrying about the little nations dragging the world into war, rather than conflict between themselves. They saw themselves as policemen of the world who would work together to keep the others in order. On these terms they were willing to build the United Nations Organisation, but very much to their own liking. The protests of the smaller nations at San Francisco were ignored; peace-keeping, and control of the UN's peace-keeping force, were reserved exclusively to the Security Council, where each of the big five, and no-one else, had the right of veto. In other words, the power of the UN to keep the peace could not possibly be used against any of the big powers. The cats would keep the mice in order, but the mice could not control the cats. Even if it was better than the League, when everybody had a veto, it weakened the UN badly in later years when it happened that quarrels between the cats became the most serious threat to world peace.

There were other improvements on the League. The Security Council was to be a permanent meeting, so there would be no fatal delays in calling it together. The top official, the Secretary-General, was made responsible for telling the Security Council about any threats to peace, and the first Secretary-General, Mr Trygve Lie, cleverly used this as a reason for setting up teams of independent UN Observers who could not only cut through false information to get to the truth of any trouble, but also came to act as on-the-spot peace-makers in many conflicts.

From its first meetings, the UN ran into trouble. The big powers fell to wrangling on the Security Council, and utterly failed to set up the international force which was to do the peace-keeping. The UN was saved by the enthusiasm of the small nations, rapidly growing in numbers as the European colonies became free nations. There were many advantages for them. In the UN they could stand together against the big powers, and they benefited from the many projects for social and economic assistance. In this way the UN did become in a sense the mouthpiece of world opinion, and it always seemed to the big powers that they could not afford to ignore it.

This, however, is looking a little ahead. About the UN at the end of the war, we must notice one very important fact. Not only was it established on American soil and supported by American money, but of its fifty or so original members, most were committed to supporting the US, either from choice or because they were living on American loans. It was therefore an American-controlled organisation, and Russia had every reason to treat it warily.

# Chapter 10
# Africa, Asia and the Second World War

The events of the two world wars were followed with interest by nationalists in those parts of the world which had been either colonised or bossed by the Europeans. The Japanese had shown during the second one that the all-conquering, industrialised, proud Europeans were not necessarily unbeatable. It might even be possible to take advantage of the Europeans' habit of tearing each other to pieces. Everywhere the pace of nationalism, the demand for independence, was accelerated by the Second World War.

## 1 Africa

In Africa the supreme power of the white man seemed undisturbed. Twelve years after the war, five European countries held sway over most of the continent. Yet the war did speed up Africa's journey towards freedom from Europe. Wartime wealth disturbed old habits of obedience. The war created a boom demand for Africa's raw materials, and cut Africa off from European-made imports, so more and more Africans were drawn into the mining industries and the factories built to supply their own continent with manufactures. Africans, uprooted from the tradition-bound country areas of jungle, plantation, desert or savannah, listened to the message of the young nationalist politicians. The Asian revolutionaries inspired these young men, who taught their audiences that Africans were being treated as third-class citizens in their own homelands – politically, they were dominated; economically, exploited to enrich the Europeans; socially, insulted by the colour bar. Only by establishing political control in their homelands could Africans recover their dignity, and use Africa's wealth to benefit Africa's people. As Kwame Nkrumah, one of these new-style politicians, said, 'Seek ye first the political kingdom, and all things shall be added unto you.'

In the Second World War, many Arabs naturally hoped to gain by the defeat of Britain and France, and favoured the Axis.

They were given little chance of action, however. Egypt was the base for the British armies in the desert fighting, and the British grip on the country was tightened. Even when France fell to the Germans, Syria and the Lebanon were quickly taken over by British and Free French soldiers. (The two countries were also given fresh promises of eventual freedom, just as misleading as earlier promises see pp. 61–62.) In Iraq there was a revolution which put a pro-German government in power in Baghdad, but this too was suppressed by British soldiers, in spite of assistance from the German and Italian air forces.

It was the exhaustion of their European masters in 1945, at the war's end, which gave the Arabs a chance. Britain and France were war-weary, and dependent on the USA, a country with little sympathy for empires. They were less haughty now, more inclined to talk to the Arab leaders as equals. When France tried to restore her rule over Syria and the Lebanon, there were serious riots in the two countries, and the French withdrew. The British were happy to settle for full independence for Iraq and Jordan in return for alliances and the right to keep military bases and airfields in these countries. By this means, they hoped to keep their control over the Suez Canal and the oilfields of the Middle East.

With the defeat of Italy, Libya became a free nation, but in the rest of north Africa and around the Persian Gulf, no nationalists of sufficient strength had yet appeared to disturb the Europeans.

One other decision in the share out of the Arab lands after the First World War caused serious trouble after the Second. To many of the scattered and persecuted Jewish peoples, the blessings of nationalism seemed to offer an answer to their problems, too. They persuaded the British to set aside the Arab land of Palestine as a future Jewish state (see p. 62). As Jews flooded into the area to escape the Nazi persecutions. Arab resentment against them grew. By 1945, a vicious three-way terrorist war was raging between Arabs, Jews, and the harassed British authorities.

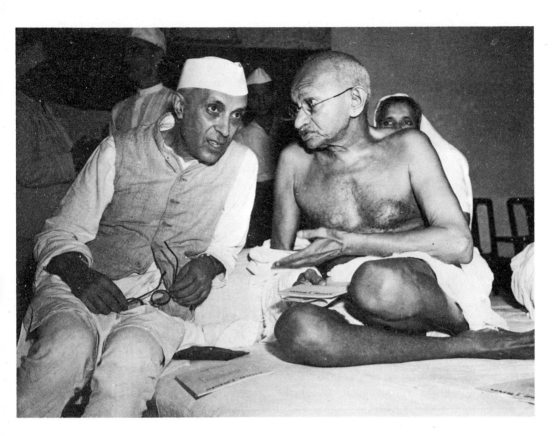

Nehru and Gandhi

Despairing of this muddle of their own making, too weak and poor at the war's end to take on the cost of maintaining law and order, the British quit the scene in 1948.

The armies of the surrounding Arab states immediately converged on the Jewish intruders, who in turn announced the existence of their new state, Israel. Their fight to defend it was successful. The fighting ended in stalemate; the new nation's frontiers were the ceasefire line patrolled by tiny detachments of UN forces; the Arabs and Israelis remained facing each other in hatred, a situation which was to continue to trouble the peace.

## 3  India

It was in 1942 that the invading Japanese armies arrived on the frontiers of British India (see p. 145). Those British leaders who had been against self-government for the Indians were now inclined to give way, to make sure of Indian support against the Japanese. Britain's American allies, traditional opponents of empires, pressed for concessions to the Indians. In India, a few Indians saw the Japanese as liberators from the white man, and went over to them, but most of the Indian units of the British armed forces remained loyal; Gandhi, Nehru (see p. 230) and the Congress party refused to listen to new British offers, convinced that the British would lose the war and be thrown out of India anyway.

They were wrong, and the Japanese were turned back, but the end of the war brought a new Labour government to power in Britain, men who were pledged and determined to set India free and quickly, whatever the dangers of religious war or the Indians' inexperience in governing.

1946 was a terrible year of argument and decision for the leaders of Congress and the Moslem League and the Viceroy Lord Wavell. The British were now ready to go, but to whom were they to hand over? Nehru and Gandhi, leaders of the Hindu majority, wanted the whole of British India kept intact, to become one great nation. The Moslems feared rule by Hindus and refused to co-operate unless India was divided up to create a separate state for Moslems, to be called Pakistan. The wealthy overlords of the princely states wanted a settlement which would keep them safe from the democratic plans of both parties.

The British feared that any plan would be so resented by one side or the other that civil war would be bound to follow. Already during 1946 mob violence between the two religious groups was flaring up again. Desperately Wavell hunted for agreement – but to the Moslems any agreement was a surrender of their demand to be separate.

At the beginning of 1947 the British government tried to force the issue by announcing that the British would leave India in June 1948, civil war or not. Admiral Lord Louis Mountbatten was sent out as the new Viceroy to supervise the withdrawal.

Mountbatten decided that the only way forward was to give the Moslems their Pakistan, and he persuaded the unwilling Hindus to give their grudging agreement. The Viceroy was gloomy about the future, but once the decision was made, the British got out at breakneck speed. In the space of three months a series of fast, difficult, and often unsatisfactory decisions were made. The boundaries of the two new states were drawn up, the Indian army divided

Calcutta 1946
Moslems armed with 'lathis' surround a dead Hindu

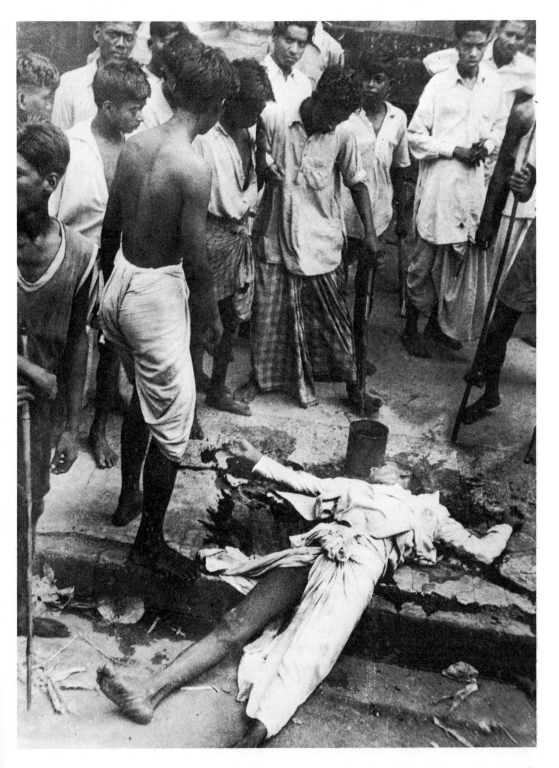

between them, and nationalists with no experience of government were catapulted into high office. The British marched out of India on 17th August, 1947.

Behind them they left many problems to be settled by force and bloodshed. 15 million people of both religions whose homes happened to be on the wrong side of the new frontier became refugees, fleeing from crazed mobs to the safety of Hindu India or Moslem Pakistan. Uncounted hundreds of thousands were murdered in riots and massacres.

The princes of the states either submitted to one or other of the new nations, or were brought to submission by force of arms. The state of Kashmir, with a Hindu Maharajah and a Moslem population, was left divided by a cease-fire line after the Indian army had seized most of it. The Kashmir problem remained to poison relations between the two countries.

Gandhi himself, the man of peace, was assassinated by a Hindu fanatic who blamed him for agreeing to the creation of Pakistan.


## 4   South East Asia

It would be hard to exaggerate the effect on Asian minds of the advance of the Japanese armies after Pearl Harbour. Filipinos watched an army of Asians dismiss the Americans. Malayans looked on in amazement as the might of the British Empire surrendered the great base at Singapore. The inhabitants of the East Indies saw their Dutch masters and their British and Australian allies marched off to captivity. Indo-Chinese saw Frenchmen take their orders from the conquerors. The entire myth of European superiority was shattered forever. Not only were the white men beaten; it was yellow men who were doing the beating.

Nationalism was already afoot in these areas. America had promised the Philippines their freedom, a promise they made good in 1946. Independence movements had made great progress in India and Burma. Among the Chinese half of the population of Malaya there were strong branches of their homeland's Nationalist and Communist parties (see Chapter 5). An underground nationalist resistance movement with a strong communist membership had troubled the French in Indo-China for many years before the war. The Dutch held in their East Indian prisons the leaders of a long active nationalist party, headed by Dr Sukarno.

At first, to many of these groups, the Japanese triumph seemed like an Asian liberation from the Europeans. The Japanese wanted to encourage this, but their hope was ended by their conquerors' ruthless use of the resources of the people they were liberating in the interests of their war effort. The arrogance of the Japanese officers, often worse than that of the whites they had expelled, did the rest, and before the war was over many nationalists were fighting as guerrillas against the Japanese. They were promptly supplied with guns by their old and future enemies, the British and their allies. Thus the Malayan Communist guerrilla leader, Ching Peng, marched in the victory parade in London in 1945, and a little later began a ten year war against the British army.

The way the war ended in the Pacific caused the beginning of the end of European rule over the countries of South East Asia. The Japanese armies still stood in possession of many of their conquests when the atomic bomb obliged their Emperor to order them to surrender. The armies of the victors were weeks away. The local nationalists did not miss this chance. Sukarno announced the independence of Indonesia, and made ready to defy the Dutch. Ho Chi Minh's Viet Minh came out of the mountains, took over the running of Vietnam, and awaited the French. The Kings of Laos and Cambodia bided their time.

The British were faced with a similar situation in Burma, and had promises of independence to make good to India, Ceylon and Malaya. British relations with her old colonies, although not completely free from violence, were able to develop more successfully than the others, partly because of the election in London of the traditionally anti-imperialist Labour Party at the end of the war, and partly because her victory in the war reduced the need to restore her national pride by winning back her old colonies.

## 5 China

China had been fighting a Japanese invasion long before the US and Britain had gone to war with Japan. Forced deep

inland, away from the cities and the populous areas, Mao
Tse-Tung's Communists in the north and Chiang Kai-Shek's
KMT in the south looked beyond the defeat of Japan to their
forthcoming battle for the control of China. The KMT were
particularly slack about fighting the Japanese, to the
despair of the American officers sent to encourage them.
The end of the war in 1945 brought on a race between the
two parties to take over from the Japanese armies of
occupation.

Chiang saw the end of the war as his chance to get the
whip hand over the communists. He tried to counter
Mao's support from the peasants with American help. Thus
he had KMT troops flown in US aircraft to the cities of
North China and Manchuria, where the communists controlled the countryside. The communists disobeyed his
orders by taking over from the beaten Japanese wherever
they could.

The communists got some support from Russia, though
less than the KMT got from the US; but the US and Russian
governments were both unsure what to do about China.

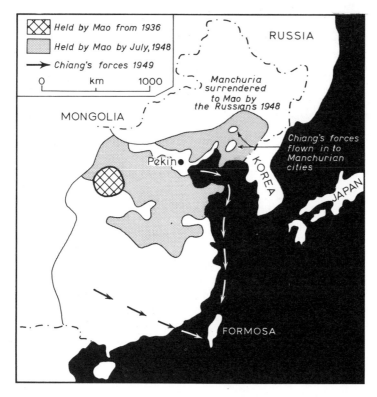

*The Chinese civil war,*
*1948–9*

Mao's troops enter Nanking, a great Chinese city, in 1949

The US fell for the story that the Chinese communists were agrarian reformers who wanted to give the peasants a fair deal, and not serious communists at all; thus the US worked for months to persuade Chiang to arrange a coalition government with Mao. The US were well aware of Chiang's failings and urged him to put them right; meanwhile they gave him military support, but not enough to win a war against the communists. In the end they left him to his fate. As for the Russians, Stalin at this time had small trust in Mao's organisation. The Russians handed control in Manchuria to the communists where possible, and gave them some captured Japanese arms; but Mao got no solid support from Stalin, who pressed him to reach an agreement with Chiang.

There was little chance of such an agreement. The communists kept cutting the communications between KMT-held cities. The KMT kept re-equipping their armies with American aid. Chiang would not allow the Americans to interfere with his conquest of Manchuria from the communists; nor would he consider allowing enough communists in the Chinese government to make any serious difference to the KMT's authority. He was confident that he could survive the inflation which seemed to be ruining the KMT-held areas of China, and that he could crush the communists by force. Full-scale civil war began.

Inside three years, Chiang lost the war. He lost the cities of Manchuria and the north; and he lost whatever was left of his people's loyalty. Chiang committed his best troops to these cities, knowing that if he lost them the communists would have a base which he could not hope to conquer; but the troops fought poorly and soon surrendered. By the end of 1948 the cities were in communist hands, along with masses of American weapons. Chiang could not now win; it was a question of how fast he would lose.

In the KMT area, affairs grew steadily worse. American food sent to feed the starving was auctioned by profiteers. Prices soared. The currency was worthless paper. The government made laws fixing wages and prices. They were ignored. Chiang's secret police murdered and tortured his opponents.

It was different in the communist areas. At the end of the war an American friend found Mao in his cave in Yenan (his first base area) wearing an old brown tunic. The KMT took Yenan in a big offensive and for two months Mao shared a cave with vats of stinking pickles. His closest colleague, Chou En-Lai, had holes in the soles of his shoes. But the future of China was in the hands of these shabby men, not of Chiang's bankers. As they saw victory approach they pushed on with their revolutionary policies: peasants' committees were told to share out the land of landlords and temples; peasants' debts were cancelled; peasant courts were to sentence to death their most hated enemies. In fact, the poorer peasants now took the law into their own hands and there were indiscriminate murders.

Early in 1949, after a token resistance, Peking was surrendered to the communists. They were now far from being mere bandits or guerrillas. Well equipped with

Chu Teh, Communist
Commander-in-Chief, and
Mao Tse-Tung
in 1948, close to victory in
the civil war

captured Japanese and American arms, they could take on
the KMT in major battles; but there were few left on the
KMT side with zeal to fight. The KMT, if they surrendered,
could still have survived as a legal party with a share in the
government; but their leaders preferred to fight on; utterly
defeated on the mainland of China, they fled to Formosa
(see pp. 179–180).

On October 1st 1949, Mao became Chairman of the new
People's Republic of China. This was more than a crimson
dawn, it was a new, red sun in the eastern sky.

# Chapter 11
# The New Giants

## 1 Russia and America

In Chapter 6 we saw how Stalin's dictatorship drove his country on to an industrial and military strength which was just enough to hold and turn back, at a terrible cost, the brutal onslaught of Hitler's armies. To make this strength, the revolutionary ideals of 1917 had given way to government by terror and secret police. The dream of replacing warring countries with one united world society had been completely forgotten. The Russian people fought for Russia, and they called their war the Great Patriotic War.

As the triumphant Red Army marched into the ruins of Berlin, what was the condition of Russia? To the Russian people, Stalin was the hero of the hour. Dictator or not, his great drive to prepare backward Russia for war had saved the nation. Few doubted that he had been the architect of the Soviet triumph.

Yet in the hour of rejoicing and the pride of victory, there was a terrible cost to count. The dead and wounded probably amounted to more than 10 million. In the battle areas, nearly 2,000 towns and 70,000 villages had been reduced to rubble. 25 million people were trying to stay alive without a roof left to sleep under. Their jobs had gone too, often enough: 31,000 factories and 200,000 farms were destroyed. Over half of all Russia's horses and cattle were dead. Whatever hopes the Russian people might have had for easier times were bound to be disappointed. The defeat of Hitler did not mean the end of Russia's long time of trial.

Full recovery took about ten years, and two methods were used. One, as we shall see later (see pp. 172–173), was to treat the areas of Europe conquered by the Red Army as an empire. The other was yet another 5-year plan, the fourth (see pp. 95–96). Once again all of Russia's efforts were carefully planned by the government so that industrial and military strength came before everything. Big housing programmes were carried through, but otherwise human comforts had to take second place to steel, fuel, transport, arms. The drive to catch up with the Industrial Revolution had been cruelly interrupted, but not halted. Once again, everyone was expected to make sacrifices. Propaganda and force still combined to make the hard worker the only hero, and the only writers and artists who were allowed were those who praised the hard worker.

So the hard, dull, often cruel dictatorship continued. It was very successful, and if the Russians were disappointed that victory brought no relaxation, nevertheless they probably accepted what had to be done.

By the end of 1947, the heavy industries were nearly back to where they were before the invasion. In 1948, pre-war production figures were beaten. In 1949 the first Russian atomic bomb was tested, long before anyone out-side Russia had thought it possible. By 1950, it was clear that the USSR was second only to the US as a world power. Thanks to the planning and sacrifice of these post-war years, the Russians would be in a position within a few more years to equal the Americans in space exploration and rocketry.

The only failure was in food production. Russian farm-ing, under-manned and under-tooled, still taking second place to industry, continued to be the thorn in the Com-munist Party's flesh. By ill-luck, on top of the war destruc-tion, the worst drought since 1890 hit Russia in 1946, and only desperate and brilliant work by the government kept the cities fed. The farmers were still unwilling to accept communism, with its central planning and collective farms (see pp. 99–101). In spite of all the government's efforts, non-co-operation and even black-market profiteering continued widespread on the land. Meanwhile, the plan demanded that every detail of Russian life was controlled from Moscow offices by Stalin and the Party. Nothing should happen that did not contribute to national recovery. In the long run, the method was successful; but of course, it often led to muddle, mistakes and delays. In farming, it was a very bad policy indeed. Moscow is not the place to decide the date of gathering the harvest in the distant Ukraine or Siberia, as you can see by measuring some of the distances on a map.

The continuation of the dictatorship meant the continuation of the apparatus of terror which Stalin had built in the 1930's (see p. 103). All contact with the rest of the world was cut off. Secret police and Party agents watched over every aspect of life. No career could go far without membership of the Party, No one in the Party could hope to avoid death or the Siberian labour camps unless he shaped his thoughts to unhesitating obedience to Stalin. The worship heaped on him by the Party and the newspapers lifted him to godlike heights.

> Today and forever, Oh, Stalin, be praised
> For the light that the plants and the fields do emit!
> Thou art the heart of the people, the truth and the
> faith!
> We give Thee our thanks for the sun Thou hast lit!

So ran a poem of the 1940's, called 'To the Great Stalin from the Ukrainian People'.

New books always praised him, old ones were reprinted with admiring passages added; he was credited with expert knowledge of everything from science to sewage-works; statues of him sprang up everywhere; a string of towns, mountains, rivers and streets were named after him.

We cannot be sure, but it is likely that after a while some Russians began to get tired of this sort of thing; many more must have been losing patience with everlasting shortages that the drive for heavy industry created. We do know that strikes and riots broke out in the labour camps in 1950 and 1951. A sure sign that there was trouble came in 1953, when it seemed certain that Stalin was about to launch another round of liquidations such as had made his dictatorship safe in the 1930's.

As usual, the first arrests were made on unbelievable charges. Fifteen doctors were accused of being part of a plot to poison leading government and army figures! There were sinister hints that both Americans and Jewish organisations were in the plot. Waves of further arrests followed, and it seemed only a matter of time before the old pattern repeated itself, and the heads of those in high power close to Stalin began to roll.

Before the blows fell, the cloud of fear gathering over Russia suddenly lifted. On March 5th 1953, Stalin died.

America's position after the war was quite different from that of the Soviet Union. There had been no fighting on

Stalin monument – this one was erected in Prague, Czechoslovakia

American soil, nothing of the war's destruction. As she converted her huge industries to war production, her strength actually increased. Unemployment disappeared as 12 million men were taken into the forces and the factories got to work meeting the demand for war materials. The Great Depression became a memory as the government's orders flowed in.

Roosevelt, the poor man's hero, managed to do what no President had done before by winning the Presidency for the fourth time running in 1944. But he only won by 25 million votes to 22 million, a sure sign that the worst of the poverty was over.

Harry Truman, who succeeded him in 1945, was a man little known to the public. Many people feared that he was not the stuff that successful Presidents are made of, but they were wrong. When elections came round again in 1948, he won again for the Democratic Party. It was he who steered his country through the last months of the war, and his Presidency saw the development in Europe of a great contest for supremacy between the USA and the USSR, and the waging of a new war in Asia by American forces under the flag of the United Nations. The post-war history of the United States is closely tied up with the 'cold war' and the Korean War.

## 2   The cold war in Europe

When the fighting in Europe came to an end in 1945, the Russian armies were in occupation of Latvia, Lithuania, Estonia, Bulgaria, Romania, Hungary, Poland, Czecho-slovakia, and parts of Finland, Germany and Austria. In Yugoslavia and Albania communist governments had taken over as the Germans withdrew.

The three Baltic states, Latvia, Lithuania and Estonia, were made part of Russia. They had been part of the pre-1917 Russian Empire, lost in 1918 (see p. 30), recovered in 1940 and made member republics of the Soviet Union. Recaptured again, they returned to this status. Neighbouring Finland had been fighting her own war against the same fate since 1940; hence she had become an ally of Germany. Now she was able to settle for survival and the loss of territory.

Bulgaria, Romania and Hungary had been active in the Axis cause; Poland and Czechoslovakia had been among Hitler's victims. All five shared the same fate, inclusion in what amounted to a new Russian Empire.

In Poland, the presence of the Red Army, which naturally insisted on freedom to stay on Polish soil so that it could maintain communications with occupied Germany, guaranteed what the Russians wanted, a friendly government. National leaders who had spent the war in London rather than Moscow were now squeezed out of a government of Stalin's puppets (see pp. 153–154). A carbon copy of Stalin's Russia was created, complete with secret police terrorism and a Polish Stalin, President Bierut. In occupied Hungary, Romania and Bulgaria, the same events took place by 1948. Czechoslovakia, a Nazi victim, enjoyed the evacuation of the Red Army and proper elections, in which the Communist Party got nearly half the votes cast. At the 1948 elections, the powerful Czech Communists were able to prevent opponents standing for election against them, and so seized power by revolution. They then delivered the country over to Stalinism.

Not only did these satellite nations, as they came to be called, become imitations of Russia, with forced industrialis- ation, collective farms, low wages, and the enslavement of art and literature to Marxism; their wealth was used ruthlessly by their desperately impoverished conquerors. Polish coal went to Russia at one-tenth the price offered for it by Denmark. Hungary and Romania lost half the profits of their most valuable industries under a scheme by which the Russians 'shared' the effort with them by 'providing' plant already in existence but taken from German hands at the time of the liberation.

This advance of Russian power in eastern Europe caused great alarm in the USA. The high communist vote in Czechoslovakia gave rise to the fear that more European nations might choose to join the new Russian empire. The old danger of 1917 and 1940 threatened again, the danger of a hostile power in command of the whole of the Old World.

In Great Britain, where communism had never been strong, the elections of 1945 had produced a landslide win for the Labour Party. In the same year in France, the Communist Party won more seats in Parliament than any other single party; the Italian Communist Party had an enormous membership. In Greece there was civil war (see p. 154), and only the intervention of British troops was holding off communist victory. When the British govern- ment told the US in February 1947 that it could no longer afford to fight this battle, the Americans were forced to decide what they were going to do about it

President Truman made his decision by announcing what was to become known as the Truman Doctrine. The USA, he said, would 'support free peoples who are resisting attempted subjugation by armed minorities or outside pressure'. He meant by this that the USA would make its strength available anywhere to fight communism, whether it came from Moscow and Stalin or, like the Greek case,

The new Russian Empire in
Eastern Europe after the
Second World War

Map legend:

1945 frontiers — · —

"Iron Curtain" 1948 ———

Divided cities ◆

Countries becoming
Communist 1945-48

0 km 200

from independent communist revolutionaries working within their own country. In fact, American policy made the mistake of not seeing that the two things were different. As far as Truman was concerned, all communism was Russian, and America in 1947 declared war on communism.

The first weapon in this new war was American wealth. Communism thrived in Europe where it gave hope to the poor. Prosperity would discourage it. At the same time, if western Europe could be restored to economic health, her factories and trade re-started, then the US too would benefit, for she was a trading nation which could profit from a rich market.

So the Marshall Plan was born in June 1947. It was a scheme to cure the sick economies of war-shattered western Europe with a blood-transfusion of American dollars. The European Recovery Programme, as it was called, was spread over the years 1947 to 1951. Sixteen European nations between them received aid from the US to the value of $12,500 million in these years.

There was a condition. The European countries had to take steps to make their economies work together rather than in competition with each other. The American planners knew what advantages had come from being the United States, and were hoping to see one day something like a United States of Europe developing along the same lines.

The Russians were invited to the first discussions of the Marshall Plan; but they would have nothing to do with it. The Truman Doctrine had been taken very badly by them, and they were now very suspicious. What would it mean to be helped by a colossally rich enemy? Would co-operation by European countries mean that western Europe would continue to be industrial and eastern Europe continue to be agricultural? Such a plan was of no interest to Stalin, whose life had been devoted to industrial development.

The Russian suspicion seemed to be justified the following year, when the Americans responded to this coldness by making it clear that their aid would not be made available to countries which elected communist governments. To a lender it might seem common-sense to refuse to lend to someone you fear is an enemy; to a borrower this might appear to be interference with free elections. By 1948 it was clear that the wartime alliance was over, replaced by a simmering hatred so close to war that it became known as the cold war.

The tension was at its worst in the places where the two armies stood face to face, occupied Germany and Austria and their capital cities. At the Potsdam Conference (see p. 154), rough plans had been drawn up for the future of the defeated German nation, but as the suspicions grew, the agreements were forgotten. In Churchill's words, an 'iron curtain' divided Europe where the armies met in their zones of occupation.

The western Allies were haunted by the memory of their

own part in bringing Hitler to power after the First World War by ruining Germany, and this time they wanted to restore Germany to self-respect, purified of Nazis and able to pay its way. Russia's only memories were the sort that demanded revenge, and her need was desperate. She took out of Germany and Austria everything of value that she could lay her hands on. The case of Austria was particularly annoying to the westerners, who regarded that country as an innocent victim of the Nazis. In this atmosphere, every attempt to decide the future of the two countries ended in more wrangles.

In June 1948, the situation worsened. The Americans were determined to bring their part of Germany at least into the Marshall Aid scheme, and they began to restore German self-government in the western occupation zones. Then they put a new coinage into circulation.

In a country where soap and cigarettes were more reliable currency than the old coins and notes, this had to be done before there was any chance of returning to normal life. But the Russians did not intend to let the western zones take such an important step without their agreement, and therefore decided to keep the new currency out of their zone. They sealed the frontiers. The break was complete.

But 145 kilometres inside the Russian zone lay the city of Berlin, and that too was divided into zones of occupation. The new coins were issued in Berlin's western zones. This was a direct challenge to the Russians, and they took a grave view of it. By acting without them, the westerners, they said, had broken the agreement to rule Berlin together. Therefore they no longer had any right to be there, deep in the Soviet zone. War seemed very close.

The Russians were very careful. They immediately closed the roads and railways into Berlin, but 'for repairs'; if the westerners could not feed their troops and the two million people of their zones in Berlin, they would have to withdraw from the city. The air routes could not be closed 'for repairs'; that would need an unmistakable act of war, and the Russians did not go so far. The westerners seized on this, and in a brilliant feat of organisation kept Berlin supplied by airlift until May 1949, when the land routes were reopened. At the height of the airlift, planes landed in Berlin every two minutes, day and night, for weeks without interruption.

As the winter of 1948–9 saw the cold war come so near to breaking out into the Third World War, the United States became even more committed to establishing itself in Europe. Marshall Aid might be the beginning of the process of recovery in western Europe, but it was no answer to what were feared to be vast armies lurking on the Russian side of the iron curtain. The armies were not all that vast, and Russia was too busy recovering from the last fight to want another one, but Stalin's secrecy added to America's fear, and the USA was encouraged by the governments of western Europe, who were afraid of facing the Red Army without American support.

So a bond was sealed in April 1949, in Washington; a 20-year treaty between the USA, Belgium, Canada, Denmark, France, Great Britain, Holland, Iceland, Italy, Luxembourg, Norway and Portugal. By this North Atlantic Treaty, these nations undertook to treat an attack on any one of them by a foreign power as an attack on all of them. As the foreign power everybody had in mind was the USSR, and as the USA was the only member capable of fighting the USSR, the treaty was an announcement that the US would undertake the defence of Europe if the Soviet Union should attack it.

To make this possible, the treaty created an Organisation, NATO, which welded the armed forces of the European members and the American forces in Europe into a single whole under American supreme command. It was the most complicated military alliance the world had ever seen, and the first time in United States history that an alliance had been made in peace time.

In due course Greece and Turkey joined the alliance. It deadlocked the situation in Europe, for at the same time America pressed ahead with its plans for an independent, self-governing West Germany, the German Federal Republic, which was eventually to be brought into the scheme of things in western Europe. The Soviet Union answered by founding the German Democratic Republic in the eastern zone. There were now two Germanies, and the line which divided them divided the two worlds of the new giants. The problem of access to West Berlin was never properly settled.

However, at the end of 1949, the victory of Mao Tse-Tung in China (see p. 167), together with the stalemate in Europe, caused the centre of attention to move to Asia. Only after the death of Stalin brought new ideas into Russian policies, and the NATO powers went so far as to propose recreating the German army, did the division of Europe come near to causing war again (see p. 188).

One other cause of the cold war must be mentioned. The atomic bomb, the horrible weapon which had been used against Japan in 1945, greatly affected the events of these post-war years. The only defence against it seemed to be the threat of retaliating in kind, and by 1949 the Russians had equipped themselves with the weapon. Three years later Britain did the same, and the destructive power of the bombs was steadily increased. If another war should start, it looked likely that these bombs would be used. The fear they created deepened the suspicion and distrust between the nations.

And finally, there was one other important result of the cold war. The United Nations could not become, after all, a league of big powers keeping the little ones in order (see p. 155). Instead the meetings of the Security Council became a cold war battlefield, and the veto was in constant use, especially by the USSR, which had to struggle against the pro-American bias of the UN. Bitter quarrels and very little action make up most of the story in these years. For example, the United States offered to hand over all nuclear weapons to the UN. The Russians refused this, on the reasonable ground that the UN was American-dominated, and proposed instead that the weapons should simply be destroyed and abolished. This in turn was unacceptable to a nation which had chosen to rely on the power of nuclear weapons to balance what it believed to be enormous Soviet 'conventional' forces.

The UN, however, marked up some useful achievements. Although the Security Council failed to set up an international peacekeeping force, UN officers did play a vital role in the Middle East and the Congo (see pp. 159, 262, and 254). Most important, the great powers used the meetings of the UN to air their quarrels, and so seemed to be appealing to the opinion of the little nations. This tended to increase the sense of self-importance and confidence among the lesser members, and paved the way for exciting moves by them in the 1950's.

It was in the United Nations, when it was compared with the old League of Nations, that the chief lesson of the post-war years could be learned. For in the days of the League, the USA had not been present, and the Soviet Union had played only a minor role. Now these two nations dominated everything; the once mighty Europeans took second place in the world.


## 3   Asia, the USA, and the Korean War

In December 1949, the remnants of the Chinese Nationalist army were swept from the mainland to take refuge on the island of Formosa (see p. 167). As the cold war reached its most dangerous months, the world's most populous nation joined the communist camp.

The American people needed time to accept what had happened. The Truman Doctrine had taught them to regard any new communist government as yet another of Stalin's puppets (which was a long way from the truth in China). American support in propaganda and guns had for years gone to Chiang Kai-Shek, so the new Chinese government was not at all disposed to be friendly. To most Americans, Mao's victory appeared to be a defeat for America.

Some wiser heads, high in the American government, were aware how rotten Chiang's rule had become, and started work on the idea that the USA ought to make friends with the new China, and so split the communist countries. But it takes time to prepare the American people for the news that their country is changing sides; time to persuade government colleagues that it is necessary to change sides; even more time to win the trust of a suspicious ex-enemy.

There was not enough time. Only six months after Mao's communists took over China, all plans were thrown into confusion by the sudden explosion of war in Korea.

In the Second World War, the US had borne the brunt of the battle for the Pacific. When the war was won, they assumed, in the person of General MacArthur, complete control over Japan and her Pacific Islands. The Pacific was to be America's ocean; never again did she want to fight her way across it.

Korea had been ruled by the Japanese since 1910, and it too was occupied by the victors of the war, though as Japan's victim it was promised early independence. Russian troops advancing through Manchuria had taken the Japanese surrender in the northern half of Korea, and

American troops in the southern half. The 38th parallel, or line of latitude, marked the dividing line.

As they had done in Europe, both sides set up governments to their own liking inside their zones of occupation, and could by no means agree on reuniting the country. As the cold war developed, border incidents grew in number on the 38th parallel, not between Russian and American soldiers, who had left, but between the home forces of the two Koreas.

Both sides, of course, blamed the other whenever there was trouble, and complaints were brought to the United Nations. UN observers were sent to the parallel to try to keep the peace.

On June 25th 1950, these observers reported a full-scale invasion of South Korea by the North Korean army. Was this move made under Stalin's orders, a Russian thrust in the cold war? We do not know enough to be certain. In any case, it was a breach of the peace, and the business of the UN Security Council, which that very day asked North Korea to withdraw its soldiers. Two days later it was clear that North Korea's armies were overrunning the South.

President Truman was now faced with yet another threat of communist expansion, and again his view was that it was part of a Moscow plan. He made a swift decision. He would fight. He ordered the US Air Force and the US Navy to go to the help of the South Koreans, and sent the US Seventh Fleet to guard Formosa and Chiang Kai-Shek from the Chinese. That decision, of course, put paid to any plans for befriending the new government of China.

On June 30th, with the North Koreans still advancing, the Americans realised that an army would have to be landed to save the South. They chose to persuade the UN to declare war against the aggressors, and then landed their armies in the name of the United Nations. Many of America's friends sent soldiers, but the UN forces were overwhelmingly American, and American generals were in command.

By fighting under the UN flag rather than their own, the United States gained a great propaganda advantage. Why did the Russians not use their veto in the Security Council to prevent this? From January to August of 1950, the Russian seat on the Security Council was empty. The delegate of the USSR had walked out in protest when the

American-dominated Council had failed to dismiss Chiang Kai-Shek's representative in favour of a man from the new People's Republic of China government. (This change also needed time. There would have been enough Security Council members in favour to see it through by the end of 1950 if it had not been for the Korean war.)

Realising that if the Russians had used their veto, the UN would not have been able to act at all in Korea, the Americans rushed through a change in the UN rules while they had the chance. This 'Uniting for Peace' resolution ordered that if peace was endangered and the Security Council failed to do anything about it, then the General Assembly, where the small nations had control and there was no veto, could take the matter over.

In 1950, when the majority of nations in the General Assembly were allies of the USA, this looked like a rule which would be very useful to her. But when, after a few more years had passed, and many new African and Asian nations joined the Assembly with their own ideas, it began

*The Korean War*

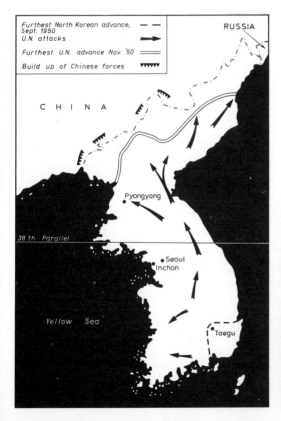

Furthest North Korean advance, Sept. 1950 — —
U.N. attacks ➤
Furthest U.N. advance Nov. '50 ═══
Build up of Chinese forces ▼▼▼▼

RUSSIA

C H I N A

Pyongyang

38 th Parallel

Seoul
Inchon

Yellow Sea

Taegu

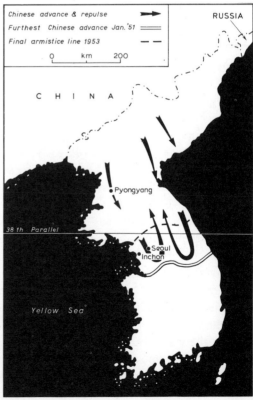

Chinese advance & repulse ➤
Furthest Chinese advance Jan. '51 ═══
Final armistice line 1953 — —

0    km    200

RUSSIA

C H I N A

Pyongyang

38 th Parallel

Seoul
Inchon

Yellow Sea

to look as if the Uniting for Peace resolution might have dented the original idea of the UN; the idea of big powers on the Security Council keeping the small powers in order.

Meanwhile, what was happening in the war? It took the American army some time to get matters under control, but by the end of September the North Koreans had been pressed back to the 38th parallel. The question was, what next? The Americans were commanded by the hero of the war against the Japanese, General Douglas MacArthur. He wanted to go on and conquer all Korea, to reunite the country by force. The American government agreed with him, and persuaded the UN to accept the idea, although the war had been started by the North Koreans trying to do exactly the same thing from their side!

The armies swept forward; by mid-October they were approaching the Yalu River, the Chinese frontier, and the end of their task. Suddenly they were confronted by a new enemy, halted, and forced back. The Chinese felt threatened by the American advance to their frontier, and the Chinese Red Army had been sent to the rescue of North Korea. The Americans suffered a series of crushing defeats. By the time they recovered from the Chinese onslaught at the end of 1950, the front line was back around the 38th parallel, and negotiations had begun.

The negotiations were to continue for two years while fighting went on. The fault lay with both sides. The Chinese believed that they were in the best position, and were not anxious to stop fighting without being given wide gains. The Americans, not used to failing to win complete victories, also found it hard to give much away, particularly as they knew that if it came to it, they could destroy China with atomic weapons. But if they did, would Russia launch an atomic attack on the US?

Most of the American people, and General MacArthur, were for crushing China, and if need be Russia. Truman and his government, with backing from their allies abroad, were much more cautious. The opposition party, the Republicans, did not miss this chance of gaining popularity with the American people, and attacked Truman for trying to limit the war to Korea.

MacArthur opposed Truman so violently and publicly that it looked as if he might actually attack China himself, in defiance of his own government. In April 1951, Truman

North Korea, 1950
Refugees crawl across a shattered bridge in Pyongyang hoping to escape the Chinese army sweeping south

sacked him. When the General returned home to America, he was given a hero's welcome by the people. It looked as if his rash readiness for world war might make him the next President of the United States.

In the event, the Republican Party did win the Presidency in the 1952 election, in the person of another popular soldier, but one with a cooler head; Dwight Eisenhower. He did, however, put John Foster Dulles in charge of foreign policy, a man who believed in taking a very tough attitude to the communist powers.

A cease-fire on the 38th parallel was at last agreed in July 1953, but the two Koreas remained divided, as they had been before. The war had taken between three and four million lives; the country had been bombed and burnt from end to end.

In the US, first the strain of the cold war, then the losses of the Korean war, turned the people bitterly anti-communist. They voted for the more conservative Republican Party. They admired a tough and dangerous soldier who came near to starting a world war in defiance of the President. And they allowed a wave of hysterical persecution against anyone who was known to believe in progressive ideas, even when it took a huge stretch of the imagination to call those ideas communist.

Naturally there were communists in the US. Many Americans had joined the Party during the depression and had long since forgotten it. Some had not forgotten, and the discovery of one or two spies led to a panic, with the American public ready to believe anything that villainous men and perjured witnesses told them. Senator Joseph McCarthy rode a four-year whirlwind of fame which started with his claim that there were eighty-one communist agents in the State Department (the American Foreign Office). He went on to terrorise and ruin a stream of inoffensive teachers, artists, writers, army officers and civil servants by means of false evidence and slanders, before the Senate found the courage to call his bluff. At the last, before sanity returned, he was hinting that the President himself might not be entirely loyal to America!

So by 1952, just before Stalin's death, the USA was bitterly opposed to communism and the sworn enemy of communist countries, including China. More prepared for war than peace, she was ready to make allies of her old enemies Japan and Germany in order to stop any further growth of communism. Lesser nations had little choice but to choose sides, shelter beneath the wings of the two hostile forces, and hope for the best. Both sides of the divided world were equally convinced that they would win in the end, and were not very interested in finding a peaceful way out of their quarrel.

# Chapter 12
# Western Europe and the
# USA since 1953

### 1   Unity in western Europe

Before 1914, the peoples of western Europe had ruled the world. This was no longer true after 1945. To the east and west two new powers eclipsed the European nations, and if they should fight, as appeared likely, Europe would be merely their battleground. For 400 years the nations of Europe had led the world in technology and warfare. Now their day seemed to be ending. In Africa and Asia their empires were challenged by ever more successful nationalist movements. The cost and the destruction of the Second World War had left them exhausted, disorganised, and desperately short of houses and food.

One thing stood out clearly. European nation had fought European nation almost continuously during their greatest centuries. They had helped to bring on their present unhappy position with two wars in the twentieth century which looked to outsiders like European civil wars.

So the question was asked; what if the leaders and peoples of Europe recognised at last that in a changing world their similarities and their common interests were greater than their differences? European civilisation was still intact, the farms and industries would recover. Why not a United States of Europe to stand equal to the United States of America and the Union of Soviet Socialist Republics? A United States of Europe would be able to feed itself, and if its industries were pooled instead of competing with each other, they would be as big and as efficient as any in the world. They would not then have to rely on captive colonies for guaranteed sales. By this means, Europe could both accept the disappearance of the empires, and continue to play an important part in the world. Even better, it would end the long history of Europe's wars.

Dreams and visions are easily put together. History,

politics, the decisions of proud and complicated nations, are difficult, confused and slow.

The first step was a small one. In 1949, Britain, France, Belgium, the Netherlands, Luxembourg, Denmark, Norway, Sweden, Eire, Italy, Greece, Turkey and Iceland joined the Council of Europe. So many joined so quickly because there was little risk involved. The Council was no more than a discussion group on matters of common interest. It had no power, it could give no orders. It was a disappointment to those keen on a European union. It achieved less than the Organisation for European Economic Co-operation (OEEC), the committee which handled the Marshall Aid money (see p. 175).

Here, in fact, was a strong hint. If the nations were suspicious of giving up their independence and wary of new ideas, it was always possible to interest them in a practical paying proposition, as OEEC showed. The hint was taken by the Foreign Minister of France, Robert Schuman, a believer in the idea of a united Europe.

In May 1950 he announced that the entire steel and coal industries of France and West Germany were to be merged and managed by a committee drawn from both countries. The new state of West Germany had only been created the year before (see p. 177), and many Frenchmen were displeased at the reappearance of this old enemy who had attacked France so often. Schuman's plan would make it almost impossible for France and Germany to fight each other again, and so was welcomed. But the most dramatic part of the announcement was an invitation to other European countries to join the scheme, which was a clear step away from national independence towards a future United States of Europe. Anyone who accepted the invitation had to mean business. Italy and the three Benelux countries (Belgium, the Netherlands and Luxembourg) came forward to join France and West Germany in the European Coal and Steel Community (ECSC). These countries came to be known as 'the Six'. Great Britain did not join. Harold Macmillan, who was to become Prime Minister six years later, summed up the British attitude; 'Our people will not hand over to any supra-national authority the right to close down our pits or our steelworks.'

During the next six years, ECSC proved itself a success. The single management of the whole region's coal and steel made for efficiency and increased production, which pleased owners and governments; prices were kept steady and free from shady fixing; and the Trade Unions were well satisfied with the benefits that the fair-minded management, the High Authority, passed on to the workers.

Meanwhile, as if to prove Schuman's wisdom, other attempts at European unity outside the world of economics were failing. The US wanted West Germany to raise an army for NATO's first line of defence. Once again, many Frenchmen objected. Here was another chance for unity. Would it satisfy French fears of a rearmed Germany if the Six pooled their armed forces into one single defence force? The debate on this plan lasted four years, but it was too much to ask. The French rejected the scheme in the end. In 1955 West Germany became an armed member of NATO, on condition that she would not manufacture heavy warships, submarines, rockets, or any sort of atomic weapons. To help put French minds at rest, the British and Germans promised that there would always be British troops kept in Germany.

The coal and steel merger was a success, the army merger was a failure. The lesson was clear. The way forward was Schuman's way. In 1956 the Six agreed to a new treaty, and created the European Economic Community (EEC), usually called the Common Market. The entire economies of the Six were to be pooled by 1970. Competition, rivalry, customs barriers and duties would all disappear. Wages, prices, social security payments and benefits, these would become the same in all six countries. People would be able to move about, live, and find work, without restriction. A single transport system would ignore the old frontiers.

Included in the arrangements was a European Parliament. This was quietly done, and it had very little power. Those who persuaded their countries into the Common Market had it in mind that one day this Parliament might govern Europe as Congress governs the USA, but they knew not to hope for too much at once. Perhaps the time would come when the economies were merged so completely that it would become pointless for the members to have their own separate police forces, armies, or even governments. Then the European Parliament would be ready and waiting.

Great Britain, divided from the Six by the Channel, remained aloof. Her hopes were pinned to the plan of turning the old British Empire into a world-wide association

General de Gaulle
On the right, at the liberation of Paris, 1944; on the left, recalled to power, 1958

of co-operating free nations, the Commonwealth.

The Common Market, like ECSC, was a great success in its first years. But some tough questions lay in wait for it, and the man to ask them was the man who had saved the pride and independence of France in 1940 (see p. 139), who had ruled liberated France from 1944 to 1946, who had then resigned rather than cut down spending on the army, who now returned in May 1958 to govern France at a desperate moment – General Charles de Gaulle.

Among the European nations, France's combination of wealth, tradition and culture was only rivalled by Great Britain. But the last hours of Europe's greatness had been proud, brave and victorious ones for the British. To the people and soldiers of France the war had brought defeat and shame. After the war, her politicians and their forty parties were so divided and fickle that twenty-six different governments held office between 1944 and 1958. The length of their Prime Ministers' periods in power varied between sixteen months and three days. Meanwhile the army was taking another beating, this time at the hands of guerrillas in Indo-China (see pp. 222–224). When it failed again in Algeria (see p. 254), it turned in a rage on its own politicians, and threatened to invade Paris and seize power. Only one man still had their respect, the sixty-seven year old General who had refused to surrender in 1940. In desperation the politicians asked him to take over. A clever politician himself, he managed to hold the army in check while he did the opposite of what they had wanted and gave Algeria its independence, so freeing France from the wasteful struggle to hold its empire.

The secret of de Gaulle's success, as in 1940, was his unshakeable belief in the greatness of France. He had saved France, now he governed her according to his beliefs; the result was a challenge to the leadership of the United States and some quite new ideas on the subject of European unity.

Until the return of de Gaulle, the aims of the Common Market had been clear, and they had fitted very well with United States plans. First, the rest of western Europe should be encouraged to join. Second, control should pass to international committees which would stand above the interests of individual nations. Third, the new Europe would help world trade by allowing the rest of the world to sell goods in Europe with as few restrictions as possible. The last aim was especially important to the rich United States which depended on selling her products abroad to keep her people in work, and helped the poor countries who needed to sell wherever they could to earn enough to buy the basic equipment of industrialisation. In short, the Common Market aimed not only at enriching the Six, but also at developing trading habits which would bind the whole of the non-communist world together under US leadership.

De Gaulle had different ideas. Among the Six, France was dominant. The Benelux countries were small. Italy was still half an under-developed, backward nation, West Germany was after all only part of the old Germany, and even though it was staging a tremendous industrial recovery, it was feeling all the caution and uncertainty of a country which owed its existence to the convenience of its recent conquerors. In an all-inclusive Europe, France would not be so powerful. Her leadership would be challenged by Britain, and the bigger the Market, the smaller France's influence. As it was, France could use the collective strength of the Six to speak to the world with the voice of a great power.

Things came to a head in 1961. Great Britain, followed by Denmark, Ireland, and Norway, and urged on by the US, at last applied for membership of the Common Market. Austria, Sweden, Switzerland, and Turkey also asked to be associated with it. Britain, with her trading partners of the Commonwealth to look after, was the test case. In spite of enormous difficulties, it seemed by the end of 1962 that the way for her entry was clear. The General had been hoping that the negotiations would fail. Now he had to show his hand. He coldly and bluntly exercised his right of veto on new members.

This statement of policy stopped for a while all progress towards a United States of Europe while a struggle started within the Six about the direction they should take. (At least Britain was now on the side of the European idea, for the Prime Minister in 1961 was the Conservative Harold Macmillan, who had rejected ECSC in 1950; and in 1967 another early opponent of British entry, the Labour Prime Minister Harold Wilson, made Britain's second application to join.)

De Gaulle, in accordance with his view of things, also obstructed attempts to develop an international European government with authority over the nation-states. France was to lead, not surrender its independence. And he also campaigned against the pro-American policy of free and open trade with the rest of the world. A great power should look after its own interests, not those of its rivals.

For this was the heart of de Gaulle's policy. A French-led Common Market was not to be part of America's anti-communist alliance, but a third power, equal to the two giants of the post-war world, and belonging to neither of them.

The other five countries of EEC did not care for de Gaulle's ideas. The West Germans, closest to the Red Army, with the very existence of their country open to question, were inclined to cling to a close alliance with America. The others had seen the Common Market as the way forward to a better world through international co-operation rather than rivalry, and resented the General's high-handed dismissal of their hopes and plans.

The resulting deadlock slowed down progress towards the target of complete economic unity by 1970, and at times the actual break-up of the Common Market seemed possible. The battle was reopened in 1967 by Great Britain's second application, but it met a similar fate.

## 2 The French challenge to American leadership

From the late 1940's to the late 1950's, the world had been dominated by the cold war between the USA and the USSR; most other countries had accepted the leadership of one or the other, and the problem of world peace had seemed to be the problem of making these two call off their feud.

Now the situation was changing. Russia's grip on her empire in eastern Europe was slackening (see pp. 210–215). China was reasserting her power, and communist China was not necessarily to be a friend of communist Russia (see pp. 218–221). In western Europe, France under de Gaulle challenged the leadership of the USA.

The last argument for so many countries which had accepted the leadership of one or other of the giants had been that as the sole owners of nuclear weapons, they could offer protection from nuclear attack. True, Great Britain also had nuclear weapons, but the scientific and military team-work between Britain and the USA was so close (General de Gaulle lumped them together as 'the Anglo-Saxons'), that the British weapons could not really be used independently of American wishes.

In 1962 the French successfully tested their own nuclear bomb in the Sahara, and work on a French rocket force was started. This was a serious problem for the American military planners, who wanted to stop what they called 'proliferation', the spread of nuclear weapons to more countries than already owned them. For one thing, the more countries which owned their own atomic and hydrogen bombs, the greater the chance of an accidental atomic war spreading to take in the whole world. The Americans did not want too many fingers on the trigger.

Even more important to American plans, if the French were determined to be able to look after themselves, the whole American idea of NATO, which was that the forces of the US and western Europe should be completely tied to each other, was in danger of collapsing.

De Gaulle had indeed pursued his aims very cleverly. The United States had no intention of giving up her position in Europe. Her trading interests forced her to keep up all the influence she could on the Common Market. Her ability to fight the Soviet Union, if need be, depended on NATO bases stretching from Turkey to Norway. The Americans believed that this ability to fight had kept the Russians from attacking in Europe, and had therefore stopped the cold war from turning into a shooting war. So the US must stay in Europe and in NATO. But could she, after all the one on whom all the others, including France, would rely if there should be a war, keep control of her European allies? The French could now offer nuclear protection to Germany if Germany should choose to quarrel with the US; in Washington Germany had to be listened to, not dictated to. The General's politics gave France the power to irritate the US far beyond what her economic and military power alone would allow.

But de Gaulle did not stop at loosening America's control in western Europe. He extended his efforts to present France as a third power in the world by reaching out to find friends from the other side. In 1964 he officially recognised the Communist government of China, and exchanged ambassadors with it, something which the US government still refused to do. In 1964 he signed trade agreements with Russia, including purchases of Russian oil, in order, he said, to reduce France's dependence on 'Anglo-Saxon' oil. He did this without consulting his Common Market partners, to their fury. In 1966 he signed more agreements with Russia on science and technology, including arrangements for co-operation in space exploration. Similar agreements were reached with Bulgaria, Czechoslovakia, Hungary and Romania.

He took every chance he could of showing that he was not subject to US policy decisions. In 1963, France would not join the test-ban treaty (see p. 207). In 1966, when America was desperately seeking support for her bitter fight in Vietnam (see p. 226), he roundly condemned the destruction that was being dealt out to Vietnam and advised America to leave, as France had left Algeria.

In 1966 came the greatest blow of all. France was leaving NATO. She wanted to stay an ally of the United States; but the days of the cold war were gone, and things had changed. Now France feared that with her forces mixed with America's, with NATO bases all over France, she could no longer face the risk of being dragged into some war of the US which did not concern her, simply because she was a member of NATO. By 1967, French forces were withdrawn from the organisation, and NATO's bases, equipment and installations had been expelled from France.

'France's determination,' said de Gaulle, 'to be responsible for her own destiny . . . is incompatible with a defence organisation in which she holds a subordinate position.'

## 3   The United States after the Korean War

For the US, the activities of France were irritating, but no more than that. There were problems far more serious on hand for the richest country in the world.

The cold war was not just a struggle between two powerful nations. It was a struggle between two ways of life. Russia was showing the world how fast a communist dictatorship could make a poor, backward country into a strong, powerful one, but the system could not offer very much private freedom or the protection of fair and objective law courts. The nation and its interests had to be put before the interests of any one person.

The US had a natural advantage in her enormous wealth, and could show that her people enjoyed the highest living standards in the world. She also claimed that as a democratic nation she could offer her citizens equality, justice, and freedom. But when they looked closely at these claims, many Americans realised that beneath the appearance of democracy there were many ugly flaws.

The first problem is the size of the country. It is huge. Texas alone is bigger than most European countries. The State of California is nearly 5,000 kilometres from the State of Maine. Parts of Florida are tropical swamp, and parts of Alaska lie inside the Arctic Circle.

How can one body of elected men govern and make fair laws for such vast and different territories? The fact is that politically the USA is a very divided country. The central government in Washington shares its power with the separate governments in each of the States. Americans rightly fear dictatorship from Washington, so far away from most of them.

So it turns out that each of the fifty States of America is very different from the rest in its laws, and looks to the Congress and President in Washington not so much for government as for financial help. Each State government decides who should have the vote, what will be taught in school, what unemployment benefits there will be, and so on. In the Congress, the elected representatives of the States compete with each other in the interests of their home State as often as they work together for the good of the United States as a whole, even when they are members of the same political party. Above all, they see it as their job to stop the President interfering in the affairs of their home State.

In one way, of course, this is very democratic indeed. But it also means that when a State like Nevada decides to get rich by encouraging gambling and easy divorce, or like Alabama is determined to keep Negroes from voting or going to school, it is very hard to do anything about it even if the rest of the nation and its President disapproves. It took a long time for the authorities to put down a notorious gangster like Al Capone (see pp. 106–107), because, as everyone knew, he had captured nearly the whole of the police force and law courts of his State by terror and bribery. It was only when he was discovered to have committed a crime against the Washington government by evading income tax that he could be put in prison.

There is also a great historical difficulty for America, dating from her earliest days. The poor of Europe flooded across the Atlantic and out into the great open frontier territories of the west looking for a chance to get rich in the land of opportunity. In America, getting rich by your own efforts became, and remains, the most admired achievement. In most other countries it is agreed that money-making should be kept under some control, so that the poor and the unsuccessful get a fair share. This idea has been resisted in the US. In the tradition of the old pioneers, a man should look after himself, without laws, pensions or health services to look after him.

For the same reason, there are no strong Labour or Communist Parties in the US. When the poor and oppressed of Europe were banding together in such parties, the poor of America had the alternative of bettering themselves by heading west to the frontier.

This was all very well when there was a frontier. But the system and the tradition lasted into the twentieth century, and America was very slow to admit that in the land of plenty and democracy there were many groups of poor people left a long way behind, a standing disgrace which the critical world was not slow to notice and compare with the situation in the socialist countries.

The worst example was the Negroes, descendants of the slaves freed in the Civil War of 1861–5. In that war, the central government had imposed its will on the slave-owning States of the south, and forced them to abolish slavery. But since then those States had managed to pass laws which kept the Negroes out of the schools and the polling booths; and the anger of the defeated slave-owners had survived in the south and elsewhere as a blind hatred of Negro Americans. The result was that by 1958, when the Negroes made up a tenth of the total population, they earned on average only a little more than half what the average white American was making. Even though one-third of the Negroes were by this time living in the northern States, the ignorance and poverty forced on them meant that they lived in crime-infested slums. Thus they were trapped in a vicious circle; the overcrowded slum schools robbed them of a fair chance in American society in the north as well as the south.

The Negroes were the largest and most noticeable of the maltreated groups, especially to a world everywhere plagued by problems of race and racial discrimination. There were plenty of others.

Five million people over the age of sixty-five, naturally subject to loneliness and ill-health, earned less than half the money officially estimated as necessary for a decent life.

Another two million Americans, the travelling field workers who gather the harvests of America's fertile fields, were calculated to be working for an average income equal to £300 a year.

Small pockets of decaying industry and agriculture contained many people living very near to permanent starvation.

In the 1950's a critical world and a few consciences at home woke the great democracy up to the realisation that in the richest country in the world, one-fifth of the people

Little Rock, Arkansas, 1957
Troops used by the State
Government to keep Negro
children out of the Central
High School. Later they
went in, protected by
soldiers sent by President
Eisenhower

lived in bitter, unnoticed poverty.

These wrongs appalled many Americans, and even many who were unsympathetic could see that the situation was the worst sort of advertisement for the American way of life. Something had to be done, in spite of the jealousy of the States and the tradition of self-reliance, and only government action and government aid could meet the problem.

The Negroes, however, were numerous and vocal enough to start taking action for themselves. City riots by frustrated Negroes dated back to 1919; in the 1950's and 1960's they grew fiercer and more frequent. Peaceful demonstrations took place in which Negroes and white sympathisers entered forbidden hotels and restaurants to protest against the colour bar. In the northern towns, where the Negroes were growing in numbers and were not prevented from voting, it became clear to the politicians that they would need to pay attention to Negro demands if they wanted Negro votes.

A crisis came in 1957 at Little Rock, in the State of Arkansas. The Federal Government in Washington ordered an end of the practice of sending Negro children to separate schools where the standards were lower than the white schools. The Governor of Arkansas used angry mobs and State troops and police to stop Negro children entering the white school at Little Rock. President Eisenhower answered by using his soldiers to take control of Little Rock for many weeks, while brave Negro children went into the school protected by bayonets.

It was an important victory for the Negroes in their fight for equality, because they had forced the central government to come out clearly on their side against the States. But it was only the first big victory on a long, hard road which they would have to follow before they could win complete equality everywhere.

The drama at Little Rock made a great stir in the United States, and may even have helped the election of John F. Kennedy to the Presidency in 1960. A rich man himself, his policy was to use government funds against the American tradition, to help the poor and oppressed. Many of the measures he prepared were carried through by his successor, President Johnson, after Kennedy was assassinated in 1963. They included aid to distressed and forgotten areas, laws to guarantee the Negro the right to vote whatever State he lived in, higher minimum wages for poorly paid jobs, and medical assistance from public money for the aged.

These were all measures which were startlingly advanced in America, but still far behind what had become normal practice in Europe. Johnson was keen to extend the work. He said his aim was to build the 'Great Society'. But progress was halted because he was faced with a choice. The wealth of even the USA is not endless, and there was another war being fought against communism in Asia. Increasingly Johnson devoted his attention and his funds to winning the war in Vietnam (see pp. 224–227) and the 'Great Society' was forgotten. Disappointment, disillusion with Johnson, and horror at the seemingly endless destruction in Vietnam encouraged the discontented to show their feelings, sometimes with violence. The Negroes' frustrations exploded. In 1967 rioting, shooting and burning broke out on a frightening scale in several cities with concentrations of deprived Negroes, and massive forces of police and soldiers were used against the rioters.

## 4 The United States and the world

President Eisenhower was elected in 1952 on a wave of resentment caused by America's failure to win an easy and complete victory in the Korean War (see p. 184). From 1952 to 1960, he and his Secretary of State, John Foster Dulles, followed a policy of great danger and little profit.

They tended to base their plans for defence against the Soviet Union on what Dulles called 'massive retaliation', the threat of all-out nuclear war as the answer to a Russian attack. Considering that Russia was capable of giving as good as she got in nuclear war by this time, the policy did not really make much sense, and created a situation in which every little incident on the communists' frontiers might turn into a nuclear war.

Dulles also had ambitions which went beyond defence. A religious man with a deep personal hatred of communism, he always hoped that he could lead the US to liberate eastern Europe from the USSR. This was at the time when the eastern European countries were freeing themselves from Russian control, (see pp. 210–215) so giving Dulles some grounds for his plans; and although they never came to anything, it was certainly the USA which was causing most of the trouble between the two great powers in the 1950's.

Matters were made more confused by the President, who was a real believer in peace. He hoped to end the danger of war by coming to top-level settlements directly with the Russian leader Khrushchev at what were called 'summit' meetings.

These took place at Geneva in 1955 and at Paris in 1960. After raising the world's fears by brandishing their terrifying nuclear weapons, the leaders now raised false hopes by meeting in a blaze of publicity which was used more for propaganda than for real settlement of their differences. The first meeting was friendly enough, but achieved nothing. The second was a disaster, broken up in a fury by the Russians after they had shot down and shown the world an American U.2 spy aircraft, one of a fleet which had been flying over Russian territory and photographing it for years.

When Kennedy became President in 1961, he brought ideas just as tough, but more realistic. He accepted the existence and the power of the Soviet Union. He was ready to try to reach a proper understanding with the Russian leaders, based on both sides recognising that neither would allow itself to be weakened. He convinced his nation that peace would not come through dramatic summit meetings, but slowly through many small, careful agreements on all the small quarrels that arose. Nor, if fighting came, would there be victories and annihilation of the enemy; the purpose would be to make the enemy agree to your demands not to destroy him.

In this spirit he met the greatest test and triumph of his short career as President; the Cuba Crisis of October 1962. Revolutionary Cuba, less than 100 miles from the coast of the USA, had been forced by the American attitude to turn to the Soviet Union for help and protection (see p. 244). Kennedy wanted to make it clear that Cuba was out of bounds to Russia, without provoking a war. His first attempt was a great failure. He helped a group of exiled Cubans to invade their homeland, so that they could overthrow the revolutionary government. The invaders were defeated and his scheme exposed.

But in the autumn of 1962, American spy planes discovered that Russian missile bases were being built on the island. This was something he had to try to stop, and he threw down a challenge to the Russians. He ordered the US Navy to stop and inspect all ships going to Cuba, and to turn back those with missile equipment.

For a week the world held its breath, waiting for news of shooting between Russian and American ships which would spark off a world war, while the leaders of the two nations argued it out in the UN and by letter and telegram. The Russian ships in the Atlantic bound for Cuba first stopped, then submitted to inspection from the air. Finally the Russian government gave way altogether and agreed to remove the missiles in return for a promise that America would leave Cuba alone in the future.

Honour was satisfied, and Kennedy had shown that he meant business without actually threatening to use nuclear weapons; though things might have gone much worse if he had guessed wrong about how determined the Russians would be to keep their missiles in Cuba.

The President, however, had guessed right, and shown that tough, controlled action, accompanied by a willingness to strike agreements suitable between two equally

Cuba, 1962
A US spy plane's picture of a Russian missile site under construction. Above – Kennedy speaking on television announces the blockade of Cuba

MISSILE ERECTOR · CABLE · MISSILE SHELTER TENT · TRACKED PRIME MOVERS · OXIDIZER TANK TRAILERS · FUEL TANK TRAILERS

strong countries, could replace the bluff and bluster of atomic power and grand summit meetings of previous years. From the Cuba crisis onward, Russia and America dealt with each other with more calm, greater respect, and better understanding of each other's point of view. Both knew each other's strength, both feared a catastrophic world war, and both were having trouble at home and with their allies. It seemed as if they were coming to see that they had more to gain from accepting each other's existence than from hopes of world domination.

Not that this meant the end of the danger of war. The pattern of a world divided into a Russian and an American block was changing; with different patterns there were different dangers. As we shall see in Chapter 14, an apparently unimportant little commitment against communism in Vietnam, undertaken at the time of the Korean war, slowly turned into a hideous glue-pot for the United States, even more destructive, costly and dangerous than Korea.

# Chapter 13
# The USSR and the Communist World since 1953

## 1 The USSR after Stalin

As soon as Stalin died, there was a new gaiety in the public appearances of the remaining top government officers. They had been as frightened by Stalin as everybody else, and wanted no more dictatorship of that sort. They announced that from now on they would rule collectively.

The most important of them were watching each other very carefully. They were Lavrenti Beria, head of the secret police, Marshal Bulganin, head of the army, Nikita Khrushchev, a brilliant organizer only recently given high office in Moscow, Georgy Malenkov, for some time Stalin's right-hand man, and the icy Minister of Foreign Affairs, Molotov, who had been near the centre of Soviet government since the Revolution.

Khrushchev, Beria, Malenkov and Bulganin pay their respects to the dead Stalin

All these men were ambitious, but most of all they wanted to stop any one of their number rising to Stalin's position of power; this seems to explain the mysterious trial and execution of Beria in December 1953, for he was the likeliest among them to re-establish a tyranny.

The victims of the dictator's final purge (see p. 170) who were still alive were released. Their arrests, the new government said, had been illegal; from now on the rights of the people were going to be respected. This amounted to a public announcement of the end of government by terror.

Malenkov, the new Prime Minister (called in the USSR Chairman of the Council of Ministers), relaxed slightly the unrelenting drive for heavy industry and improved the supply of food and consumer goods into the shops. Slowly, discussion and the airing of ideas began to return to Russia – not, of course, freedom to oppose the government or the Communist Party, but a great improvement on the days when the only opinion heard on anything was that reflecting the official view.

The change was dramatically confirmed at a private meeting of Communist Party members from all over Russia and the rest of the world, the famous Twentieth Congress, in 1956. Khrushchev dared to tell the Russian people, through the ears of the Party, the truth about the tyrant they had been trained to worship. The shame of the Stalin years was fully exposed. A dazed Russia heard the new leaders denounce the long, miserable tale of lies, terror and tyranny.

At the same meeting, and in the same mood, important changes were announced. The muddle, corruption and red tape of the civil service which had tried to run all Russia from offices in Moscow was admitted. From now on, there would be more local government. There was to be no more ridiculous worship of government leaders. The activity of the secret police was to be reduced. Proper courts of justice and fair trials were promised. Workers were to be free to change their jobs when they wished. Wages were increased and working hours cut.

Many of these relaxations, presented as a righting of wrongs done by Stalin, were only possible because of his work. For the price of his brutal reign, the USSR had first won survival in the war against Hitler, and then, by 1956, recovery from the frightful devastation inflicted by that war (see p. 168). Now that Russia had a fully-equipped modern army, nuclear warheads and rockets, and a great fleet, it was safe for his successors to decry his methods. Now that the basic necessities of life were organised it was possible to make more luxury goods and cut the working week.

Great as the changes were, there was no question about the continuing firm rule of the Communist Party in Russia. Nor was there any sign that the people wanted anything else. All that was happening was that things were becoming more human and reasonable.

The difference between Stalin's Russia and the new mood is shown by the rise and fall of Nikita Khrushchev between 1955 and 1964.

After 1953, the government was carried on by two powerful committees: the Presidium of the Supreme Soviet, the top committee of the elected government, and the Presidium of the Central Committee of the Communist Party, the top Party committee. All the top men were on both these committees, and instead of meekly obeying a dictator's orders, they now argued about policies, voted on them, and accepted majority decisions. At this high level, if nowhere else in Russia, proceedings had become democratic.

Malenkov's new economic policy even caused a bitter debate for and against between the two leading newspapers, *Pravda* the Party's newspaper, and *Izvestia*, put out as the official government paper.

This difference between two organizations which under Stalin had been one and the same gives us a clue to understanding how Khrushchev managed to emerge as sole leader in 1957.

Malenkov was a sophisticated man from a well-to-do family, very different from the traditional figure of the self-educated revolutionary worker that the Communist Party was supposed to bring to power. He did not choose his friends from among such men, but from the new middle-class of Soviet Russia, the wealthy experts who managed industry and technology for high salaries and steered clear of dangerous meddling in Party politics. From such men Malenkov got his ideas and his preference for consumer goods and home comforts over the former grim devotion to Soviet might.

The Party he ignored. Stalin's waves of terror had left it staffed with time-serving hypocrites who survived because of their talents as yes-men. This apparently useless organisation was handed into the care of Khrushchev, Stalin's successor as First Secretary of the Party, as his share of the collective leadership.

Khrushchev, the son of a miner, the ex-factory worker who was twenty-three before he could read, was an organising genius. He worked night and day, using all his experience and knowledge of the country to restock the Party with young enthusiasts, until after only a few months it was once again the best, most powerful, organisation in the USSR.

So the row between *Pravda* and *Izvestia* was really the first sign of a battle between Malenkov and Khrushchev. In 1955, Khrushchev's Party voted Malenkov out of the Prime Minister's chair, and Marshal Bulganin into it. Krushchev's attack on Stalin at the Twentieth Congress the next year was part of this struggle for power, for it contained strong hints to Khrushchev's Party followers that Malenkov and Molotov, as well as the dead Beria, were partners in Stalin's crimes.

The final round came in 1957, at a meeting of the Party Presidium, where Khrushchev's opponents managed to out-vote him, and it seemed that they would have him sacked from his job as Party Secretary. Swiftly, he took an action more democratic than could have been possible in the old days – he called a meeting of the larger Central Committee of the Party, the body which elected the Presidium in the first place.

The Central Committee voted to keep him in power, and sacked Malenkov and Molotov, who were accused of being 'anti-party'. The following year, Prime Minister Bulganin lost his job on the same charge. Naturally, it was Khrushchev who succeeded him, so becoming, like Stalin before him, master of both the Party and the State.

Even so, the defeated men went, not to their graves, but to minor posts far from Moscow. Terrorism had not returned.

For the six years in which he enjoyed this power, Nikita Khrushchev became the centre of world attention. A warm, exciting and witty personality with a violent temper, he was always in the headlines.

His greatest impact was on Russia's relationships with other countries. As a communist leader, he could not give up the idea that one day the whole world would become communist; but ever since 1917 this had been taken to mean that communism would advance by violence, either through revolution or war. This was one of the causes of non-communist governments assuming that Russia would always be their enemy, and therefore at least one of the causes of the cold war.

In the age of the atomic bomb, it made less and less sense; the danger was that war and violence would lead to the end of civilisation of any sort.

Khrushchev recognised this, and took advantage of the new mood in Russia to relax this attitude too. He introduced the idea that there might be many different roads to socialism, including peaceful change through elections. He was abandoning the idea that there had to be more wars. Russia would settle for a peaceful competition to see which side could offer the better example, confident that eventually the world would choose communism.

This new policy, called the policy of peaceful co-existence, was Khrushchev's contribution to ending the worst of the cold war. Of course, he remained careful to preserve his country's full strength and readiness in case war should come, and it was not until the USA had a President equally ready to accept that Russia could not be destroyed that real progress resulted (see pp. 199–201).

Unlike Stalin, Khrushchev was an eager traveller. In 1959 he visited China and the USA, where he spoke to the United Nations. In 1960 he was in Afghanistan, Burma, France, India and Indonesia. All over the world he struck trade and aid bargains which opened up Russia to the world and made her more a living part of it than before. In the same spirit there were many small relaxations. For instance, radio jamming, the blocking of broadcasts to Russia from other countries, almost disappeared.

Those countries which had made nuclear weapons were constantly exploding test bombs as experiments, until radio-activity from them was so poisoning the world's air that sanity demanded that testing, at least above the ground, should be stopped. As always, no one wanted to give anyone else an advantage by being the first to stop. Then Russia declared the end of her testing in 1958, and the

Khrushchev on tour in France in 1960, with a gift of corn. Behind him is his interpreter.

USA followed; but in 1961, first Russia, then the USA, started again, perhaps hoping to produce a weapon so powerful that no one could equal it. When it became clear that this could not happen, that there were no advantages to be gained, in 1963 the leading nuclear nations and many others signed an agreement to stop testing bombs above ground. Unfortunately, the Test-Ban Treaty, as it was called, although it showed that the two giants were becoming content to live and let live, did not end the testing and improvement of bombs, for neither France nor China would take part in it. They, too, were determined not to be stopped from catching up with the United States, the Soviet Union and Britain.

One cold war trouble-spot seemed impossible to remove; there still remained, in the middle of Communist East Germany, left over from the failure to settle the future of Germany in 1945, the western outpost of West Berlin (see p. 176). West Berlin was a centre for NATO propaganda and spying, and provided an open escape route from East Germany to West Germany. Apart from the annoyance to the leader of East Germany's Communist Party, Walter Ulbricht, because half his capital city was owned by a foreign country (i.e. West Germany), East Germany was being ruined by the steady flow of workers going west through Berlin in search of better conditions. This was the reason for the overnight appearance of the Berlin Wall in August 1961, a barrier which stopped the leaking away of labour by sealing West Berlin off from East Germany.

Khrushchev's policy of peaceful competition with America meant that a sort of publicity campaign was needed, and Russia was brilliantly successful in demonstrating her might in the most eye-catching way possible, space exploration. During the Khrushchev years, Russia went ahead of America in the space race. The first artificial satellite went up in 1957, and the first astronaut to go into orbit was Yuri Gagarin, in 1961.

Inside Russia, Khrushchev continued the improvements which had followed the death of Stalin. Even after the disgrace of Malenkov, the promoter of consumer goods, the stocks in the shops went on improving. Gradually Stalin's victims, condemned as traitors, were restored to their true place in the history books. In 1961, the criticism of Stalin, which had been supposed to be a secret within the Party in 1956, was officially made public, and his body was removed from its shrine beside Lenin. The town of Stalingrad, the site of the great victory, returned to its name of Volgograd. There were even hints that before long communism would be so firmly established that dictatorship of the Party (see pp. 20 and 42) might be ended. Writers, artists, scientists and economists dared, very carefully and slowly, to offer more new ideas, criticisms, their own opinions. Still nothing anti-communist was allowed, of course, but such things made a future return to Stalinist dictatorship very much harder.

The final proof of this came when Khrushchev himself was pushed into retirement by his colleagues at the top of

Berlin, 1961
The wall which divides the city has already become a 'sight' for tourists on the Western side

the Party tree. The full story is not known, but it seems that the Prime Minister's partners saw his popularity, his growing habit of taking action without first consulting them, and his reliance on relatives in the government, as the first steps in a return to one-man rule. He had had his failures, too, in Cuba (see p. 200), and in China (see p. 220). Above all, he had set out personally to cure Russia's great, everlasting headache, agriculture (see pp. 99–101 and 169). In spite of new plans, massive grants of money, and reorganisation, he, in turn, failed to prevent failures and shortages. The USSR still had to buy wheat from Canada and Australia.

Whatever the cause, the change was peaceable. Khrushchev was on holiday on the Black Sea in October 1964 when both the Presidiums met on consecutive days and voted him out of his posts because of 'ill-health and advancing years' and replaced him with Alexei Kosygin as Prime Minister and Leonid Brezhnev as Party Secretary; once again, the two jobs were separated.

## 2   The Communist world

In the early days of communism, even for a while after the Russian Revolution, part of the plan for a better world had been the early disappearance of the different nations – all the world would be one. Stalin had returned to patriotism and nationalism, ending that dream with the cry of 'Socialism in one country'.

On the other hand, since the occupation of the Red Army and the setting up of the puppet governments in Eastern Europe (see p. 172), it was also true that any communist of Poland, Czechoslovakia, Hungary, Romania or Bulgaria who thought that his country could be both communist and independent of the USSR was either dead, jailed, or silent. The Red Army and the secret police had seen to that. Yugoslavia, which had carried through its own revolution without Soviet help or Red Army occupation, had alone kept its independence and followed its own road. In the others, power lay with Russian advisers, Stalinist stooges, and the ever-present threat of the Red Army.

Eastern Europe was restless under foreign rule. Before Stalin's death, the factory workers of Czechoslovakia, mostly communists, had struck and rioted against Russian-imposed rationing, low wages and long hours. The puppet Communist Party of East Germany could not control similar riots in 1953, and Red Army tanks had to come to its rescue.

Clearly the Russians were unpopular. Each of the little Stalins was in a shaky position after the death of his master, and they were further endangered by the attitude of the new Russian leaders. Two events triggered off a new round of revolts.

In 1955, Khrushchev visited independent Yugoslavia, which until then the Russians had treated as an outcast.

Stones against Russian tanks
This scene is from East
Germany in 1953

While he was there, he respected Marshal Tito, the Yugoslav leader, as an equal.

Then came the Twentieth Congress and the attack on Stalin. The response in Poland was immediate. On June 28th 1956, in Poznan, workers rioted against food shortages and low wages. Their complaints, the Polish Communist leaders knew, were justified, the result of chaos on the farms caused by collectivisation, and the unfair prices paid by Russians for Polish produce. They sent for the long-disgraced Communist leader Wladyslaw Gomulka.

Long ago he had spoken out in favour of Polish independence from Stalin, and he was lucky to be still alive. While the threat of revolution mounted in the streets of the capital and the industrial cities, he was put at the head of the government, and the Russian advisers were dismissed.

Khrushchev flew into Warsaw, and the Red Army started to close in on the capital; but Gomulka managed to convince Khrushchev that his new programme of Polish independence, increased freedom and better conditions for the workers and farmers, and an end of the persecution of the Roman Catholic Church, was not the end of co-operation with Russia, but the only hope of keeping the Polish Communist Party in power.

The people of Poland were willing to accept half-independence, to stay communist and an ally of Russia, provided they were governed from Warsaw in the interests of Poland instead of from Moscow in the interests of Russia. The events which soon followed in Hungary showed their wisdom.

Here there was the same excitement among the people, led by the factory workers, students, and writers, and the same worried debates among the Communist Party leaders. When they got the news of the Polish success, the Budapest crowds seized control of the city and forced their leaders to go much further, demanding nothing less than neutrality in the cold war and military help from NATO powers to guarantee it! This was more than Khrushchev could stand; Hungary might be lost to communism altogether, especially as the old democratic parties were to be revived and brought into the government. This time he ordered the Red Army into action. A brief, brutal sortie into Budapest in October 1956 crushed the city and the revolutionaries, and restored a Moscow-directed government.

The difference between events in Poland and Hungary showed what Stalin's death and the changes in Russia meant for the Russian empire in eastern Europe. As soon as Stalin was rejected and the independence of Yugoslavia admitted, Moscow had to come to terms with the peoples ready to rebel against shortages and the leaders within the national Communist Parties in whose hearts patriotism was stronger than their loyalty to Marx or Russia.

This much was possible, for, thanks to Stalin, the USSR could at last manage without bleeding her conquests; from about 1955 she was in a position to reverse the process by giving them aid, such as the Marshall Plan had given western Europe.

What was not possible was military desertion. The Eastern European Mutual Assistance Treaty, known more easily as the Warsaw Pact, had been created in May 1955 as the Russian answer to NATO. None of its members could be allowed to think of a non-communist government, or of weakening the defences by turning neutral.

Nevertheless, the changes inside Russia had started some thinking in eastern Europe. Those countries where the Red Army was close at hand had to be careful to avoid the fate of Hungary, but Albania, which like Yugoslavia had turned communist without Russian help, and was a long way from possible invasion, was the next to act.

Long before communism came to Europe, Albania's problem had been to save herself from being taken over by her neighbour Yugoslavia, a poor country, but a great power compared with tiny, backward Albania. The Albanian Communist leader Enver Hoxha had therefore been a nationalist from the beginning, but had chosen friendship with Russia as soon as his enemy Marshal Tito quarrelled with Stalin. Now the new Russian leaders were ready to befriend the Yugoslavs again; so Hoxha became the determined enemy of the USSR and Khrushchev's new approach to world affairs. He could not have done it, of course, if he had not been able to replace Russia with a new friend, China, another country which was rapidly falling out with the USSR (see next section).

Next to make trouble was Romania, this time about plans for COMECON, an east European equivalent of the west's Common Market. Each member was to undertake to specialise in certain types of industry, in the interests of efficiency. That meant that they would have to rely on trading with each other to get goods in which they were not themselves specialising, and so would never be completely independent of their neighbours.

Just as France under de Gaulle objected to this process, so did backward agricultural Romania; she had her own plans for becoming fully industrialised and self-reliant.

The Romanian fight against being made dependent on COMECON started in 1958, although no one outside knew about it until 1963, when she was threatened with being thrown out of the organization altogether. Her answer to that was to strike a bargain with Yugoslavia, (not a COMECON member, of course), to build together Europe's biggest hydro-electric power station. This defiance was followed by a threat to join Albania in supporting China in the great battle by now raging for leadership of world communism, and that was enough. As in the Common Market after de Gaulle had made his views known, progress on COMECON slowed down badly.

In 1964, the Czechoslovak Party announced that it had been mistaken over the last fifteen years in slavishly following the lead of the USSR, and that from now on it would adopt many of the less rigidly controlled planning methods used in Yugoslavia.

Just as the relaxing of the cold war had meant that in the west some nations had challenged American leadership, and tended to go their own way, so nationalism reappeared among those nations which had become known as mere satellites of Soviet Russia. But just as de Gaulle had no serious intention of changing sides in the struggle between two different types of society, neither was there any question of communism itself being abandoned in the east.

## 3  China

In the same years that Russia's hold on eastern Europe was weakening, the independence movements there were given a helping hand by an even more important quarrel between Russia and China. From the moment that China became communist in 1949, the rest of the world jumped to the conclusion that Peking would also be Moscow's obedient servant. A few years had to pass before China's new government was able to show that there had never been the least chance of such a thing.

Victory in the last civil war (see p. 167) was only the beginning for the Chinese communists. The whole country was left in chaos. Mao Tse-Tung and his army were immediately concerned to secure themselves in power and popularity by giving China peace, order and honest government for the first time in forty years.

For twenty of those years, Mao had fought a guerrilla war. He had won because everywhere he fought he had offered the suffering peasants a completely new deal. Now his land reforms were put into practice over the whole nation, not in the rush and panic of war, but with the careful organisation of a permanent government. This was the real revolution which stood Chinese society on its head. The hated landlords were put on trial in every village, humiliated, and often killed. Always they were deprived of their land, and it was shared out among the peasant families. Everyone now paid rent – a fair rent, and they paid it to the government. No one could own more land

215

than he could work himself with his family.

Thus, by bringing justice to the villages, the loyalty of the majority of China's millions, the poor peasants, was won. To these ignorant, illiterate, superstitious masses the Communist Party of China brought leadership, education, consultation, encouragement, and self-respect. Well over half the Party's 17,000,000 members in 1960 were born peasants.

The government organisation was the same as in other communist countries. Complete control remained in the hands of the Party, and the Party was controlled by its leaders. There was all the usual police persecution of known enemies of communism. But since the rule of Chiang Kai-Shek had driven most of China's scholars and honest civil servants into Mao's camp, no large scale terror was necessary.

The new rulers wanted more for their country than peace and a fair deal for farmers. They wanted, of course, the Industrial Revolution and all its benefits. China must be a great modern, industrial power; her people must enjoy the benefits of modern, technological civilisation. And they aimed to do it even faster than Russia had done, with what help they could get, but mostly by their own efforts.

The first need was wealth, the money to build mines, factories, dams. There was vast wealth under the ground in oil, coal, and other minerals, but the only wealth actually ready to hand was the produce of the farms; and the peasant farmer was hopelessly out of date. A Chinese hectare commonly yielded half or even a quarter of the wheat an American or European hectare would give. Before anything else in China could be modernised, the farmers would have to be able to feed a factory population and provide profits for the nation to invest. That meant large-scale farming; and that meant collectivisation.

So the peasants found themselves being encouraged to pool their time, tools, and newly-won land with their neighbours, to make bigger, more efficient units. By 1957, the collectives were established; the average farm was made up of two hundred or so families and their land.

If the peasants were worried that they might be losing the land so long coveted and so recently won, if they feared to become no more than labourers on state farms, worse was to come. The results of the collectivisation were encouraging, the country's need for higher food production desperate. In 1958 the government went a step further. The collectives were pooled again into 25,000 vast communes of 20,000 people working the land for weekly wages like a mobile army, with central stores, shops, nurseries, schools and dining-halls.

This was going too far, too fast. The peasants did not like the divorce from their beloved land. To make matters worse, China was smitten from 1959 to 1961 with a series of floods, droughts, typhoons and locust plagues. News from inside China began to dry up; there were signs of trouble in the villages. Then came the official announcements of a slackening of the drive in agriculture and a return to fifty-family collectives in 1962. The communes were kept only in name. Just as the jealous peasant had slowed Russia's progress, he was dictating the pace in China as well.

Slowed down as the tremendous ambitions of Mao might be, it was still the fact that China was being pulled up by its boot-straps. By 1956 her seventy thousand factories and two million shops were nationalised and under government control. Making do with endless supplies of human labour in place of expensive equipment, the nation set out in pursuit of industrialisation. Cement, coal, steel, machine tools, lorries, locomotives; the production figures went up. Roads and railways lengthened, great dams appeared to control the floodwaters of the Yellow River, 'China's Sorrow', and set them driving dynamos.

The communist method was again proving itself the best for modernising a poor, backward country. But it is important to realise the size of China's problem. With 20 million new mouths to feed every year, and the food supply still threatened by natural disasters, she was a long way from the security and power of the leading nations in the 1960's.

The achievement of the communist government of China since 1949 may well be the most important event in the history of the twentieth century. For five hundred million wretched peasants, famine, war, banditry, disease, ignorance, superstition and slavery, were ended or brought under control at astonishing speed. No limits could be placed on the future possibilities for the Chinese people.

But this was still a nation where the average income was £50 a year, and ploughs were drawn by women for lack of horses, let alone tractors.

Why, then, did the Chinese leaders choose to devote their hard-pressed resources to developing and testing first an atom bomb in 1964, and then a hydrogen bomb in 1967?

The whole story of China's troubles since 1911 had been at bottom a nationalist story, a struggle to save China from foreign control, to make China an equal of the great powers (see Chapter 5). If the peasants backed the communists when they smashed the landlords, the educated Chinese turned to them when they showed themselves the most successful and dedicated fighters of the foreigners who spurned, robbed, and invaded China. Mao, his men, and their masses of supporters, had communism in their heads and patriotism in their hearts. With the help of communist planning, methods, and party control, China would be restored to what she ought to be, to what the Chinese had always believed she was, the most powerful, civilised land in the world, an example to the rest.

Even communist Russia was never really thought of as a

Beating the drum of industrialisation. Chinese factory workers celebrate their achievements safe friend. Before 1917, Russians had been among the first to take advantage of China's weakness (see p. 190). Even after 1917, Stalin's advice had been as much a hindrance to Mao as a help (see p. 85). He had never really thought much of Mao's chances, and even after 1945 had given preference to Chiang's Nationalists. The men who took China in 1949 carried no Russian guns; their weapons they had captured for themselves from the Japanese and the Kuomintang.

Anyway, Mao was not a proper communist. (He claimed to be the *only* proper communist.) Instead of building a revolution on factory workers (there weren't enough of them in China), he built it on peasants, until then looked on as the enemies of communism and revolution.

The difference is much more important than it might at first seem. To other Asian countries without industries, dragged down by huge, poverty-stricken masses of hungry peasants, Chinese communism and Chinese leadership offered something much more realistic and attractive than good wishes and financial help from Russia. From the moment Mao started to rule in China, Peking became a rival to Moscow as leader of the poor against the rich, of poor countries against rich countries.

When, around 1960, the rivalry developed into an open, fierce quarrel between them, it became more important still.

Things came to a head over Khrushchev's policies in Russia, (see p. 206), which were meant to set a pattern for communist opinion everywhere, but to the Chinese were not only unacceptable, but even dangerous. Khrushchev, benefiting from nearly 40 years of Russian hardship, cheerfully relaxed the dictatorship and the austerity. Mao, less than ten years into a much bigger problem than Russia had ever faced, could not listen, or let his people listen.

Khrushchev was ready to co-exist with America, to call off the world struggle rather than risk nuclear war. When he said communism could spread peacefully, he meant that he might stop financing and encouraging violent revolution in Asia and Africa.

To the Chinese, this was treachery. Russia's struggles were over, Russia was rich and strong – so Russia was ready to be friends with China's arch-foe, the USA, the supporter of Chiang Kai-Shek, the enemy of the Korean

War. For the benefit of the two great powers, the cause of the poor of Africa and Asia would be forgotten.

China denounced the Russian leader bitterly and insultingly, and began to go her own way. Russian money stopped going to China. Thousands of Russian technicians were withdrawn, with harmful effects on the drive for industrialisation. Conferences broke up, insults in the papers grew harsher. The Russians insisted on the dangers of nuclear war. The Chinese pointed out that if it came, it would be Chinese communists who would survive in the greatest numbers. Precious funds and brains were diverted to the amazingly swift development of Chinese nuclear weapons and rockets. The Test-Ban Treaty was ignored by China, who saw it only as a plot by the Soviet Union and the United States to keep China weak.

In 1962, the Chinese army launched a short, victorious campaign against the Indian army in the Himalayan mountains. The attack was called off before it had achieved anything of importance, and it is hard to guess its purpose. Probably the intention was simply to remind the poor nations, of whom India was a leading member, that China was the leader of the future. Russia sent India help and support during the fighting. In the same year, during the tense and dangerous Cuba crisis (see p. 200), China offered the USSR only insults and unfriendly criticism.

From 1966 onwards a propaganda campaign was launched, designed to give Mao the same public adoration and worship from the Chinese as Stalin had once demanded from the Russians. China was sealed off from foreign eyes, just as Stalin's Russia had been, and the outside world knew less and less of what was going on.

By 1967, the split was so deep that Russia and China could properly be called enemies, and both were guarding the frontier between them very carefully. The Russian leaders could get on better with American leaders than with Chinese at a time when the Chinese and US armies were in danger of coming to blows again as the war in Vietnam developed (see pp. 224–227).

This great split in the communist camp ended the age of undisputed leadership by the Soviet Union. The chance to choose between Moscow and Peking was a gift to nations looking for a chance to escape Russian influence, as Albania and Romania showed. Outside the area of com-

China, 1967
Party members in a propaganda 'spectacular' in praise
of Mao Tse-Tung

munist rule, in Africa and the Middle East and in South
East Asia, the two competed against each other for influence.

So in the years which followed the death of Stalin, the
aims of communism were questioned, it ceased to be a
united movement, and took on different meanings in
different parts of the world. The danger of war between the
USA and the USSR might be less, but that did not mean that
war itself had become less likely, as China's militant beliefs
showed.

# Chapter 14
# South and South East Asia since 1945

In Chapter 10 we saw how the Japanese capture of the European colonies in South East Asia, followed by the surrender in 1945, had given the nationalists of the region an unexpected chance. Everywhere communist or nationalist groups, sometimes the two together, declared their countries free and independent and set up their own governments.

The victorious Europeans, returning in triumph to disarm the surrendered Japanese, ignored these claims. In some cases they even used the Japanese soldiers to help throw the native interlopers out.

In the war, South East Asia had been one of the lesser battlefields; but now, as peace returned to Europe, the Asians had their own war to fight, on their own soil. At first they did not seem very important, but gradually these wars became the focus of world attention. The Asian guerrillas' successes underlined the weakness of Europe; America, Russia, and the big neighbour, China, became interested in the contests between communists and nationalists which accompanied the fight for independence. Whose side in the world competition would the new nations join?

## 1 Vietnam

In 1944, thirty-two guerrilla soldiers travelled through the mountains from south China into their native Vietnam, occupied now by the Japanese. They were sent by a political party called the Viet Minh, an organisation which united those rebels against the French, communist and nationalist, who had escaped to China. The party was organised by the veteran communist Ho Chi Minh, and the thirty-two men were led by Vo Nguyen Giap, once a nationalist, now a communist.

There were many Vietnamese patriots glad to welcome them. The raiders' numbers grew fast. By 1945, when the Japanese were ordered to lay down their arms, Ho and the Viet Minh were able to take over nearly the whole country before France had mustered an army to reclaim her colony. It was 1946 before the French were able to attack the Viet Minh and drive them back into the northern mountains.

For three years, little happened. The Viet Minh fought occasional skirmishes with French patrols in the mountains, and the French soldiers worried less and less about 'General' Giap. (They could never think of a Vietnamese as a real general, so they always used inverted commas like this.) Nationalists and communists quarrelled and were often busier hunting and murdering each other than fighting the French.

In 1949 the victory of Mao Tse-Tung in China changed the situation completely. The Viet Minh now had a powerful friend at their back behind the mountains, offering money, training, a safe base, and the advice of China's experienced, victorious warriors.

A new phase of the war started. The Viet Minh became fully communist in its aims and adopted Mao's methods. Ignoring the towns, and as far as they could ignoring the French troops (who concluded that they must be cowards), they advanced stealthily through village after village, persuading the poorest peasants to rise against their landlords and seize the land for themselves. Once a village had risen like this, it was committed to the Viet Minh and against the government. The villagers became guerrillas, and before long the young men were joining the regular Viet Minh armies in the jungle.

By the time the French woke up to what was happening, they found themselves left with only the cities, the roads, and about half the countryside. The rest was Viet Minh, hiding armies equipped with French weapons taken in endless little ambushes where the 'cowardly' rebels never fought unless they were certain to win. It was the story of the Chinese civil war all over again.

The French, however, still had nothing but contempt for their invisible enemy, a ferocious guerrilla at night, just another friendly peasant by day. They thought of them as bandits who would be utterly destroyed the minute they attempted a full-scale, pitched battle.

In fact, the Viet Minh had built a superb army in the jungles. The bravest and best of the country had flocked to its ranks as its successes grew, and it was fed by the villages where it had overthrown the tyrannical landlords. This barefoot, bamboo-helmeted army, with its supplies moved by night on huge columns of bicycles pushed by peasant porters, was courageous beyond measure, superbly disciplined and organised, and as ready for a showdown as the over-confident French.

Their moment came in 1954. The French General Navarre committed the best of his army to a great entrenched fortress in the valley of Dien Bien Phu. Giap accepted the challenge, brought his armies together and beseiged the French. After months of desperate fighting, the French surrendered, and the Viet Minh marched ten thousand of them into captivity. No longer did the French scoff at the Viets, or put their general's title in inverted commas. They were beaten and ready to leave.

This was not the end of war in Vietnam. While the French were leaving, it was agreed to divide the country in two, for two years only. The north would be ruled by the Viet Minh, and the south by the Emperor Bao Dai, descendant of the ancient rulers of Vietnam, and until 1954 kept as a puppet of the French. At the end of the two years, the people were to decide the future of Vietnam by a free vote.

What this arrangement amounted to was government of the northern zone by communist patriots, and of the southern zone by anti-communist patriots, for Bao Dai was soon overthrown in favour of a republic under a President, Ngo Dinh Diem. Fearing that the communists would easily win the elections, Diem refused to allow them in the southern zone. The country stayed divided into north and south, and in the south Diem trod the same path as Chiang had followed in China, from nationalism and anti-communism into dictatorship, terrorism, and corruption.

By 1960, Diem was so hated, the likelihood of elections so remote, that the guerrilla war had started all over again. Ex-Viet Minh, and new supporters driven into rebellion by Diem, formed a new party in South Vietnam, the National Liberation Front, to fight the President's tyranny. The President naturally claimed that this new war was a communist invasion from the north, and dubbed the guerrillas

Ho Chi Minh (centre) and General Giap (extreme right) use a model to plan the siege of Dien Bien Phu

'Vietcong' or Vietnamese communists. It was true that they were reinforced and supplied from the north; but this deliberate confusion between the long, long struggle for independence, unity, and honest government in Vietnam, and the much exaggerated threat of advancing world communism made matters worse for Vietnam.

If the story so far had been all there was to tell, this second war would soon have been over, for the tactics which overwhelmed the French would soon have thrown out Diem and his press-ganged army. But Diem had found a powerful friend, an ally even stronger than the French – the United States of America.

The Viet Minh's war against the French reached its climax at the same time as the Korean War (see pp. 180–184). It had seemed a natural thing for the Americans to help the French, who argued that they too were checking the spread of communism. When the French were beaten, the Americans transferred their support to Ngo Dinh Diem, hoping that they were helping to create a democracy, as they had hoped to when they supported Chiang Kai-Shek in China. They came to realise that Diem, like Chiang, was no democrat, and helped to get rid of him in 1963. But they could not find a popular leader to replace him. Believing that their prestige and security were at stake, they tried to bolster up the south Vietnamese governments, sent more and more troops to South Vietnam and began bombing North Vietnam in February 1965. But the National Liberation Front and North Vietnam refused to give up the fight.

*The War in Vietnam – end of the French phase – Left-hand map*

*The War in Vietnam – United States phase, mid-60's – Right-hand map*

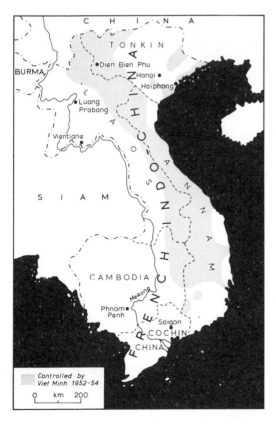

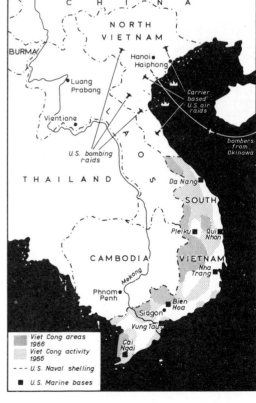

A Vietnamese woman stands with two of her children among the bombed ruins of her house

Like Mao Tse-Tung in his battle with the Japanese, they believed that, in the end, they would overcome the foreign invaders.

## 2   Indonesia

Although the devastation in Vietnam overshadowed other events in the region, the surrounding countries were also finding their way to independence. The peoples of the Dutch East Indies had thrown off European rule and created Indonesia between 1945 and 1949. The French withdrew from Laos and Cambodia after Dien Bien Phu. The USA left the Philippines (see p. 162). The British left Burma at the same time as they left India; Malaya and the great port of Singapore were freed of British control in 1957 and 1963.

All of these newly independent countries faced the same sort of problems. Their leaders were men who had seen the power and wealth of the industrialised nations, and were now determined to modernise their own countries. But the material they had to work with was discouraging. Their people were mostly poor peasants, in villages where new ideas could only be absorbed very slowly. They were short of the money needed to provide education and time for people to study. They were trying to make a twentieth century nation out of farmers, to do in a generation what had taken hundreds of years in Europe. If they succeeded, of course, South East Asia might become more important in the world than Europe.

The South East Asian leaders found, as the Chinese had found before them, that elections, parliaments, oppositions, the apparatus of democracy, often did not mean very much in their situation, where the greatest need was for unity and firm government, even dictatorship. What they needed were new ways of governing, ways of keeping the people's consent and interest at the same time as forcing them through uncomfortable changes.

Indonesia, with perhaps the greatest difficulties, shows the problem very clearly. A hundred million people, half of whom could neither read nor write, lived in 3,000 islands strung out over 5,000 kilometres of ocean. Attempts at governing through a parliament produced eight major political parties, and many more small ones, all competing, none able to govern. Only two groups had power or support all over the huge area – the Army and the Communist Party. All the others were local in their appeal. But these two national groups hated each other, and if one came to power it would probably attack and massacre the other.

So it was that the remarkable nationalist President Sukarno was able to rule from 1950. A brilliant politician, he managed to keep the two from each other's throats and give them both a share in high government jobs; he managed to keep himself safe from both of them by use of another talent – propaganda and mob oratory. He was the idol of the people in his capital city, Djakarta, and woe betide anyone who tried to overthrow him.

Unfortunately, he was so busy staying in power and keeping his balance on this dangerous tight-rope, that he had little time to do much good for the country, and concentrated rather on living a luxurious life himself.

His chief trick was inventing enemies to occupy the nation's mind. He had the Dutch businessmen driven out, and so ruined what industry he had. He had the Chinese shopkeepers attacked, and damaged trade and commerce. He launched an undeclared and meaningless war against Malaya and Singapore, completing the destruction of his country's trade.

It was too bad to last. An inflation like China's after 1945 (see p. 166) broke out, unemployment and famine spread, transport broke down. At last Sukarno fell off the tight-rope in 1965. As his popularity weakened, both the communists and the generals prepared to take over. In October 1965, the communists helped by one or two military units, attempted to take over the capital in the night; they managed to murder six generals, but even so the army recovered. It struck back with a wave of arrests and killings in which anything up to two or three hundred thousand communists and Chinese residents may have died. Then, having destroyed its only rival, it deposed Sukarno and took over the government. But it found the ruin left by Sukarno hard to cure. By 1967 the best it could offer was the execution, by firing-squads, of businessmen who were overcharging.

As in Vietnam, the outcome of Indonesia's search for a future was a matter of great concern to the great powers, as it was all over South East Asia. The choice between democracies and dictators, between planning and free business competition, made allies and enemies among the great nations who were quarrelling about such matters among themselves. Particularly, there was friction between the obvious appeal of Chinese communism, the highly successful answer to the Asian problem, and the enmity of the United States towards any spread of Chinese influence. As if its own problems were not enough, South East Asia was a battlefield for old powers with their old worries. The war in Vietnam might well turn out to be the first of many of its kind.


## 3   India

Britian's Indian empire ended in 1947. Two new states emerged; India, which included all the states with majorities of Hindu people, and Pakistan, made up of the chief Moslem areas except for Kashmir, where most of the people were Moslems but the ruling prince wished his state to join

India. The new Indian government made this an excuse for forcing Kashmir to submit to Indian rule. Who should decide, the prince or the people? The problem poisoned relations between India and Pakistan.

Gandhi had lost his life through trying to heal the hatred between Moslems and Hindus. He left a carefully-chosen political heir – Jawaharlal Nehru, the president of the Congress Party which had led India's independence movement. Nehru was independent India's first Prime Minister and for the next fifteen years he carried the burden of responsibility for the government of the world's most numerous democracy.

Nehru was born a high-caste Hindu. He had been to school and university in England. His work for the Congress Party had cost him nine years of his life spent in British prisons. Loving Gandhi like a father, he was, after Gandhi, the most popular leader of Congress. Lacking Gandhi's intimate contact with the villages where 80 per cent of his people lived, Nehru was deeply interested in world affairs and ambitious to be a world statesman. This distracted him from carrying out his other ambition – the social revolution which he promised to the people of India.

The social revolution which Nehru proclaimed was to make India a socialist country where the people would be well fed, free and equal before the law. The blight of chronic starvation and the crippling restrictions of the caste system and Hindu laws on the inferiority of women: these replaced the British imperialists as the enemies facing the Congress Party. To face these enemies Congress would need a really strong central government which could organise peaceful but revolutionary change for the whole vast country. To create such a government Nehru took the lead in working out a new Constitution for India.

According to the new constitution all Indian adults would have a vote in elections for a parliament for the whole country, and to this parliament a strong central government would be responsible. The hundreds of states were regrouped into workable units, each with its own parliament and governor. All the princes were retired on pensions. Caste restrictions were banned.

As soon as possible Nehru held India's first general election (1951–2). 173 million people were entitled to vote. It was quite a task to organise an election on this scale but the elections were fair and peaceful. Nehru campaigned energetically on a programme of religious freedom, an end to the caste system, education for all and the development of India's economy on socialist lines. Congress won control of the central parliament.

Five years later there was another jumbo-sized election, but the results showed that many Indians were disappointed with Nehru's achievements. It was true, Congress again won control of the Indian Parliament, but 12 million votes went to the communists. Such a large communist vote was a slap in the face for Nehru and the Congress Party. People were voting communist because they expected the communists to really do something about India's social problems. Nehru's promises had not all been kept. His achievements in the previous ten years fell far short of the social revolution he had proclaimed.

Indeed Nehru's career after 1947 was a mixture of success and failure. He succeeded, unquestionably, in launching the Indian Republic as a parliamentary democracy allowing freedom of opposition. He succeeded in securing religious freedom for people of all faiths whilst in Pakistan and China, Islam and Communism were becoming state religions. As for the Hindu caste system and untouchability, caste Hindus and untouchables actually sat next to each other in the primary schools. Women were given equal status with men in new laws in which Nehru took a keen interest, and his own daughter was to be Prime Minister two years after his death, which occurred in 1964. So much for the bright side. Now let us look at the dark side, the failures which account for India's growing lack of confidence in Congress and its leader.

The Congress Party had faded from a popular independence movement into a clumsy combination of sometimes shady and often reactionary interest groups. Congress supporters had all agreed about getting rid of the British, but when it came to running India themselves, they were revealed as divided by class, caste, language and religion. Compared to Mao's communists Congress was like an old blunderbuss compared to the latest machine gun.

On behalf of Congress Nehru promised socialism. But landlords and businessmen were too powerful inside the party for socialism to make much progress. Somehow the most profitable sections of industry were left in private ownership; somehow the landlords dodged all the laws for land distribution. The old ruling groups clung to power and used it to give themselves more privileges. The high castes seemed to win most of the local elections. Congress ministers preached socialism but travelled in Mercedes cars or private railway coaches. Even Nehru moved from his small private house into the huge palace of the old British Commanders-in-Chief. So much for socialism.

In one way India's new rulers were worse than the old. The British had been strict in obeying rules and laws; their officials rarely took bribes. Under Congress rule the spread of bribery became a national scandal. Nehru's finance minister had to resign after a million pounds of government money went astray. While big businessmen bribed government officials, humble peasants bribed the village police. An observer discovered that 'when the villagers take their melons to Lucknow in carts, they usually go at night, and often they fail to have lights on their carts. This is against the traffic rules, but the police let them pass – after taking a few melons from each cart'.

The saddest failure was over the most basic problem of all – the food supply. While people were starving they could take no interest in politics or religion. The man who could feed them would be their deliverer. So Gandhi had taught; would the Congress government be the deliverer? Could it make India grow enough food to give all its people an adequate diet and save millions from a living death? Congress launched three 5-year plans with the chief aim of making India self-supporting in food production. The plans achieved a great deal: dams for irrigation, the improvement of seed and cattle breeds, credit to pay the peasants' debts and marketing boards to get them better prices. Yet all the improvements could not keep pace with the soaring population figures which left the planners with 30 million more mouths to feed than they had reckoned. Famine still haunted the villages where tens of millions were living on a starvation diet. In 1960–1 the average food intake per person in India was about 500 grammes a day. This is about half of what people were eating in the richer countries such as Britain. With twice as many people as Russia, crowded into a seventh of the space, India still could not feed herself. Indian farming remained technically backward and the Hindu prejudice forbade two techniques which would have helped the food supply: the slaughter of surplus cattle, to save food for human beings, and birth control, to limit the size of families and check the growth of the population. The village masses were still sunk in their ancient ways of thought. Twenty years after independence, only a quarter of them could read and write. Whatever Nehru's laws might say, they still accepted their wretched life as fated from birth according to the caste system. The first step to saving them was to make them realise that things could be better. This first step seemed to be the hardest one to take.

In spite of these problems at home, the Indian leaders thought that their country had a part to play in world affairs as a great Asian state. In 1946, before India became independent, Mr Nehru said that 'in the sphere of foreign affairs India will follow an independent policy, keeping away from the power politics of groups aligned one against another'. In other words, India did not want anything to do with the cold war between the two giants, America and Russia. This policy became known as neutralism and was taken up, not only by India, but by many other countries which became independent after World War II, such as Sukarno's Indonesia, Nasser's Egypt and Nkrumah's Ghana. In 1955, the African and Asian countries organised a big conference at Bandung in Indonesia, and most of the governments represented there came out in favour of neutralism.

To America and her allies, however, it often looked as if the neutrals were not really neutral at all, but pro-communist. How else, it was argued, could you explain such things as, for example, Nehru's bitter attack upon the Anglo-French invasion of Egypt in 1956 (see p. 262) and his failure to condemn the Russians for their brutal suppression of the Hungarian revolution (see p. 212) which took place at the same time? In fact, there was a very simple explanation. Most of the neutralist countries had had very little experience of the Russians and the Chinese, but they had been ruled by one or other of the European colonial powers. Indeed, many of their fellow-Africans and Asians were still ruled by them. They were still suspicious of the European powers (and their American ally) and they were more interested in freeing the remaining colonies from European control than in fighting communism. Russia and China supported the end of colonial rule too – if only to embarrass their opponents in the cold war – and this made them natural allies of the neutralists.

As far as India was concerned, however, the picture began to change in 1958–9 when serious quarrels began with China over the frontier between the two countries. The Indians stood by the border which had been worked out by the British when they had ruled India, but the Chinese claimed that this included areas which had been seized from China when she was too weak and defenceless to resist. (Until 1951, for example, the Chinese government had had hardly any control over Tibet, even though it was supposed to be a province of China.) Matters were made worse in 1959, when there was a revolt in Tibet against Chinese communist rule, for the Chinese suspected that the Indians had had something to do with it. Attempts to settle the quarrel failed and, in October 1962, heavy fighting broke out between the two countries in the wild and mountainous border area (see p. 220). The Indian forces were badly beaten and the Chinese took over much of the territory that they had earlier claimed. Britain and America offered military aid to India, which was accepted, although the fact that the Soviet Union sent help as well enabled Nehru to claim that he was still a neutral in the cold war.

But, as we have seen, by 1962 the cold war was very different from what it had been in the beginning. The communist powers were no longer united (see Chapter 13), and Russia's conduct showed that she was more interested in bolstering up India to prevent China from becoming too powerful in Asia than in helping a fellow-communist country. Russia's attitude was even more obvious in 1965, when fighting once more broke out between India and Pakistan over the disputed province of Kashmir. When it looked as if the Chinese might try to profit from India's difficulties by taking over more Indian territory, Russia quickly stepped in to try to stop the fighting. Early in 1966, Russia arranged a meeting between the Indian and Pakistan leaders at Tashkent in the Soviet Union and an agreement was reached between the two sides which, while it did not settle the dispute over Kashmir, took the heat out of the situation.

When K. M. Panikkar, the first Indian ambassador to

Indian civilians, fleeing from the advance of Chinese troops, board a boat to cross the Brahmaputra

China, arrived there in 1948, he reported to his government that 'it was understood that China as the recognised great power in the east . . . expected India to know her place'. That was in the days before the communists took over power in China, but their attitude has been the same. On one subject at any rate – the belief that China should be the dominant power in Asia – there was to be no disagreement between Chiang Kai-Shek and Mao Tse-Tung.

# Chapter 15
# Latin America since 1945

In Chapter 4 the story of the Mexican revolution was used to lead us into the history of Latin America before 1945. Now, the revolutions in Bolivia and Cuba will be described as they are a key to the understanding of Latin American developments since 1945.

## 1 Bolivia

From the West Indies and Mexico the Spanish conquerors of the sixteenth century spread down the west coast of South America. There they found the fabulously wealthy Inca empire, and high in the Andes a mountain full of silver. The lure of precious metal brought Spanish settlers to the Andean land now known as Bolivia (after Bolivar the Liberator). When the silver ran out, they found tin, and forced the Indians to mine it. Over the centuries the poor farming land of Bolivia's high plateau, jungles and savannahs passed into the grasp of the Spaniards and *mestizos* (see p. 69). The Indians, still a majority of the people, toiled for starvation wages in the mines, or on the estates stolen from their ancestors. They seemed not to want anything better. Factory-made goods did not attract them: all they bought were sewing machines (which helped them to do without factory-made clothes) and chamber pots. So they did not try to save, or earn more. Any savings they had were wasted in regular drinking orgies. The country's richest farming lands concentrated on growing cocaine – the Indians chewed the leaves, to dull the pain of their miserable lives.

Yet Bolivia is the only Andean country to have had a really dynamic revolution. The Bolivians have faced up to the problems of all Andean countries: dependence on one raw material export (tin), Army control of politics, foreign control of mines and Indians barred from political life.

How did revolution come? The ruling Creoles and

*Bolivia: site of an Andean revolution*

mestizos weakened their position by fighting a disastrous war against Paraguay in the 1930's. The Indians, forced to fight in a cause they did not support, kept their guns when the war was over. The mine workers knew about explosives. They found a grim leader, Juan Lechin, communist and soccer star.

The miners did not start the revolution. The fuse was lit by some Spanish-speaking intellectuals who launched a new political party, the MNR (National Revolutionary Movement), pledged to nationalise the chief tin mines and give the land to the Indians. Although the Indians were disqualified from voting because they were illiterate the MNR won the 1951 elections, but it did not have a majority of the votes. This gave the army an excuse for taking over. But next year Lechin's miners fought the army, and beat them. The MNR took over the government. They cut the army's numbers severely, and nationalised the big mines. They gave the *haciendas* to the peasants. Indians got the vote, and equality before the law. Foreigners were encouraged to prospect for more raw materials, to reduce Bolivia's dependence on tin.

Mexico's revolution dragged on for forty years. Bolivia's revolutionaries were in a hurry: perhaps they were too impatient, as they soon hit trouble. The value of tin in world markets fell, whilst the tin miners claimed higher wages and shorter hours – now the mines were theirs, why shouldn't their life be easier? There was only a slow rise in food output and the country's transport was so bad that foreign food was still cheaper than Bolivian food. The government spent more than it could afford; money lost its value (see p. 113); workers demanded still higher wages. At one time the President went on hunger strike to persuade the miners to cut a wage claim.

The MNR found an unexpected fairy godmother – the US. American aid saved them, and for years paid one-third of Bolivia's budget spending. The US were not always enemies of Latin American revolution, especially when the losers were mostly local mine owners, as in Bolivia, rather than US business companies, as in Guatemala or Cuba.

US dollars and technical experts could not make every dream come true for Bolivia. The ills of centuries could not be cured in a year or two. Furious at the slowness of progress, Bolivians staged mass demonstrations in 1959 against the Americans, accusing them of propping up feeble governments. As a result US aid was cut but not altogether ended.

An Air Force general replaced the MNR President in 1964. Communist guerrillas started a jungle war against him. The MNR's appeal for Indian support and the Indians' return, after 400 years, to the foreground of their country's political life: these events pushed Bolivia into a new but troubled phase.


## 2 Cuba

Travellers say that only two names are recognised everywhere in Latin America – the Virgin Mary and Fidel Castro. Castro was the leader of the Cuban Revolution of 1959, which made a completely new departure by looking for help outside America altogether, to communist Russia and China. Cuba was the jewel of Spain's old Caribbean empire. Its rich soil, worked by *mestizos,* descendants of negro slaves and poor Spanish settlers, grew lush tropical crops, especially sugar, making fortunes for the Creole plantation

owners. No wonder it took longer here than elsewhere to
get rid of Spanish rule – and Cuba's powerful northern
neighbour, the United States, lent the Cubans a hand in
1898.

The long fight against Spain left two problems for Cuba –
the Army and the US. The army was like a jack-in-the-box
– no one could put the lid on it. The US citizens bought up
the Spaniards' sugar plantations and turned many poor
Cubans off their land; the peasants were worse off than
ever. The US took an extra interest in Cuba since they
bought almost all the sugar crop, and also Cuba was handy
to America's coast and on the sea route to Panama. The
Platt Amendment (see p. 77) allowed the US to interfere
in Cuba whenever they thought it necessary. Would Cuba
lose its independence and be swallowed up by its northern
neighbour?

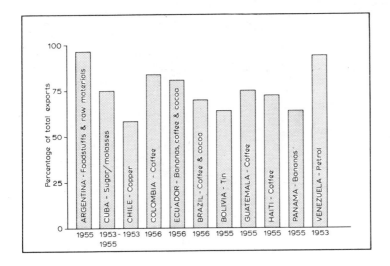

Havana's airport is named after Jose Marti, apostle of Cuban independence, killed in the war against Spain. Marti wrote: 'The country which buys lays down the law: the country which sells has to obey ... A nation which wants to die sells to a single country: a nation which wants to live sells to more than one.' Until 1959 Cuba seemed to want to die. The sugar companies, often US-owned, always depending on sales to the US, owned up to three-fourths of the arable land; 70 per cent of agricultural workers earned rock-bottom wages on the sugar plantations. Rising population drove thousands of landless, workless, families to squatters' shanties on other people's land, or along roadsides. The peasants lived in filthy huts with palm-tree bark walls; less than half of them had toilets of any kind. They could not afford to eat meat, fish, eggs, or milk, and the children's pot bellies showed they suffered from intestinal parasites as well as poor diet. People said, 'Only the cattle are vaccinated.'

In 1952 Cuba had one of its many revolutions. Colonel Batista, who had started as an army sergeant and for twenty years had been either President or the power behind the President, seized power for himself. He ruled Cuba as a tyrant, though he was careful to be popular with the right people – the trade unions controlling the workers in Havana, the plantation owners, the Americans. The US-owned Cuban Telephone Co. loved him so much, they gave him a solid gold telephone. As for the miserable country-dwellers, he expected no trouble from them.

The promise of a better life for them was laid up in Cuba's Mexican-inspired constitution of 1940. This – which had never been put into operation – called for minimum wages, guaranteed employment, social security, an eight hour day, one month's paid holiday a year for all workers, and the break-up of the plantations. In its name, a gang of young revolutionaries attacked a Cuban army base in 1953, hoping to spark off a mass uprising against Batista. They were arrested, many tortured and killed, some tried and gaoled. Their leader, the lawyer Fidel Castro, called at his trial for a share-out of land to the peasants and the nationalisation of the American-owned electricity and telephone companies. He was imprisoned, but three years later Batista set him free in an amnesty. (Batista was bad enough, but no Hitler.) Castro left for Mexico, to train for rebellion. In 1956 he and a handful of companions set up a base for guerrilla war in the mountains of the Sierra Maestra. Castro now called for an end to interference from the US and the Cuban army in Cuban politics, elections within a year, land distribution, and a fast industrial build-up.

Batista claimed that Castro's rebels were unimportant bandits. He even said Castro was dead – until Castro gave an interview in the mountains to the *New York Times* correspondent. Later Castro's men hit the world headlines by kidnapping Juan Fangio, the racing driver, in Havana itself. The rebellion snowballed. Batista was fast losing control. On the first day of 1959 he fled from Cuba, and the bandits became the government.

Castro's success is explained in a do-it-yourself guide to guerrilla warfare written by his best general, Che Guevara, for the use of other Latin American revolutionaries. Ordinary people could overcome an army equipped with aircraft and tanks, he wrote, if they set up strong bases, in the countryside, not the cities. The first base was set up by the original group of rebels. This tiny army had two tasks: setting the example of taking up arms against Batista – and showing what the rebels meant to do once they had won. Rebel soldiers ambushed the army, dynamited roads and railways, but they also shared out the land to the peasants in their base area, and launched campaigns for health and education. They were, says Guevara, 'breaking the moulds' of the old way of life.

Thus inside the base area the rebels were sure of their

popularity. Outside it, they started by asking the people not to betray them to the government; gradually they trusted them with messages, supplies, and guiding; finally they called on them to join in mass action against the government. Guevara was deliberately importing the revolutionary methods of Mao Tse-Tung from China to Latin America.

Batista's US-armed troops struck at the base areas, but the guerrillas avoided pitched battle until the very last stage. Batista's aircraft were powerless against enemies who moved only at night, and his tanks, useless in the wild mountains, were easy victims of traps. Using hit-and-run tactics, attacking chiefly at night, then melting away, the rebels gradually wore down the army, strengthening themselves by the capture of guns and ammunition. Batista could not get to grips with his enemy. Province after province fell from his grasp. His troops drifted away to join the rebels. Soon Castro could come down from the mountains, take the field with full-scale armies, and call on the townspeople to rise against the tyrant.

Castro did not mean to be just another army dictator. His army was already starting the promised revolution. Trials and mass executions in public of leading Batista supporters showed he was in earnest. The executions were condemned abroad, but were mostly forced on him by the Cuban public. In one town riots and a general strike broke out because two 'Batistianos' got prison instead of death sentences.

*Cuba and its neighbours*

Castro demobilised Batista's army. The revolutionary army manned his National Institute of Agrarian Reform, which was to supervise the land share-out and organise farming co-operatives, spreading modern techniques, building modern housing and schools, lending money to the peasants, and promoting the cultivation of crops other than sugar so that Cuba could feed itself and have something else to export.

The main impact of Cuba's revolution was in the countryside, but the cities felt it too. Castro cut all rents by half, forced speculators to sell land for building, turned the luxury hotels over to the use of Cubans instead of tourists, and stopped the national lottery. Batista's friends had made fortunes out of the gambling habit. The lottery's funds were to be used for house building, and now it sold savings certificates instead of lucky numbers.

Castro's revolution soon ran into trouble. When the landlords and speculators saw their fortunes shrink they attacked Castro as a communist. Thousands emigrated to the nearby United States and plotted rebellion against Castro – he was still too popular for peaceful opposition to have much chance. More serious was the attitude of the United States government itself. At this time the United States government was concerned about the spread of communism (see p. 199). Communism in Latin America, on the US doorstep, was especially unwelcome. In 1954 the US was faced with a possible communist government in Guatemala, where the left-wing President Arbenz confiscated the US-owned United Fruit Company's estates and looked for communist support. The US got rid of him by stage-managing a right-wing rebellion. A dictator could expect US support, so long as he kept order and protected US investments. It was just after the Guatemala affair that seven Latin American dictators signed Mr Dulles' OAS resolution (see p. 77) affirming their faith in representative democracy!

The United States encouraged this humbug while listening readily to the dictators' arguments that any men who wished to keep their country's wealth at home, and use it for the mass of the people, were communists. Latin Americans saw how badly their countries needed to build their own industries – how unlikely private enterprise was to do this wisely – how their governments could not afford

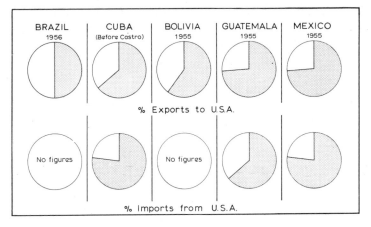

BRAZIL
1956

CUBA
(Before Castro)

BOLIVIA
1955

GUATEMALA
1955

MEXICO
1955

% Exports to U.S.A.

No figures

No figures

% Imports from U.S.A.

*The United States' economic grip on Latin America*
In 1953 three-fifths of the foreign money invested in Latin America was from the us, and the chart shows how the us dominated foreign trade in five Latin American countries

to do it unless there was a better return for their exports. If us firms owned the estates and the transport, if the us, buying most of the products, refused to arrange higher prices, how were new industries to be built? It seemed as if the us was aiming to keep Latin American economies backward.

United States reactions to the Cuban revolution fitted this pattern. Until Batista's control was on the edge of collapse he was able to buy arms from the us. Afterwards his friends were asked to give evidence before the us Senate and allowed to use us territory as a base for plots and air-raids against Castro's government. Castro stiffened taxes on foreign landowners and started to confiscate the plantations. The us owners complained to their government, which began to suggest that Castro and his men were like Cuban melons – green (liberal) outside, red (communist) underneath. Castro and Eisenhower failed to agree on compensation for the landlords, and when Castro proceeded to take over the telephone and electric companies the us ambassador was called home. Rich Cubans, feeling the pinch of land reform, joined vigorously in accusing Castro of communism, and in Florida exiles still plotted violence.

In 1960 the frost in Cuban–us relations sharpened. Air-raids by Cubans from Florida enraged Castro. His speeches attacking the us government for allowing the raids prompted Eisenhower to play one of his strongest cards – to cut the amount of sugar the us would buy from Cuba that year. This threat to bankrupt Cuba was daringly countered – Castro sold the sugar to the ussr instead. Now who was going to lay down the law?

Castro feared the same fate as Guatemala's President Arbenz, and in fact the US now began secret, active help to the Florida exiles. But Castro would not back down. When the American and British-owned oil refineries in Cuba refused to handle the Soviet oil he was buying, he confiscated them.

That autumn was election time in the US. Nixon and Kennedy, the presidential candidates, competed as to who was tougher against Cuba's communists. To help the Republican campaign and to hurt Castro, the US government banned all exports to Cuba. Castro was coming to depend on Russian trade to replace the US. He countered the export ban by nationalising all US-owned businesses in Cuba.

The Democrat Kennedy won the election, and accelerated planning for a counter revolutionary invasion of Cuba – although the US as a member of the OAS was pledged not to interfere for any reason with any American government. The invading force landed at the Bay of Pigs in April 1961, (see p. 200), expecting ample help from the Cuban people – but Castro had no difficulty in rounding up the invaders. He seemed as popular as ever with Cuban workers and peasants.

How true were US charges against Castro? His rebellion had begun without communist support. Cuba's official communist bosses got on quite well with Batista. Later they came to Castro's side, and Castro's own brother, and Guevara, were both convinced communists. Communist influence in the Castro government increased in time, and in 1959 one of Castro's most trusted governors resigned in protest against this and was gaoled for twenty years.

Yet Castro may not have wanted to tie Cuba to Russia's tail. US policy gave him no choice. As he came to depend more on trade with the communist world his government moved nearer to the communist style. Anti-Castro newspapers closed. The government controlled all broadcasting; the universities ran compulsory courses on Marxism. The promised general election never came off. Housewives who banged pots in the street to complain about food shortages were answered by a parade of soldiers and tanks.

Russia was supplying Castro with guns, bombers, and, in 1962, with missile bases which could be used to attack the US. Bases on Cuba showed vividly that the cold war had come to Latin America. Kennedy blockaded Cuba and told the Russians to take their missiles out: he got overwhelming support from the OAS. For hours world war threatened, but Khrushchev withdrew the missiles – without consulting Castro.

This affair dented Castro's prestige in Latin America. Cuba seemed to have become a Russian puppet – no better off than when it was a US puppet. And US fears that Castro's example would inspire more anti-US revolutions in Latin America were not yet borne out. On the other hand Castro successfully defied the US by creating America's first communist-ruled state.

Kennedy tried to learn from his dealings with Cuba. He saw that the Latin American countries were demanding industrial development and land reform, to give the masses dignity, health and education. If they could not get United States help in this, they might look elsewhere. Kennedy supported and expanded a new scheme which Eisenhower's administration had worked out to help Latin America. He gave the scheme a headline-catching name, the Alliance for Progress. To join the alliance and qualify for US aid a country must produce a national plan showing what it proposed to do to give its people homes, work, land, health and schools. The US was clearly in favour of reform unless they thought it was communist reform! Kennedy's successor, President Johnson, sent troops to the Dominican Republic to stop a suspected communist take-over. In the very same year, 1965, Johnson supported the right-wing Marshal Castelo Branco when he made himself dictator of Brazil. Branco had thrown out a left-wing President on the ground that he was going communist. To many Latin Americans these moves looked much the same as the 'big stick' policy of fifty years before (see p. 77).

# Chapter 16
# Africa and the
# Middle East since 1945

## 1  The end of European control

In most African colonial territories after 1945, political
parties emerged to work for the downfall of European rule.
The Portuguese, Belgians, and Spanish banned all African
political activity in their territories, while in South Africa
the Europeans committed themselves to white overlordship
over the African majority. The British and French authorities could not behave like this. After all, they were supposed
to have been fighting Hitler to stop him from building an
empire of unwilling subject nations; and they had promised
as members of the UN to treat their colonies as a trust held
for the good of the Africans. The British planned to hand
over authority in their colonies to the Africans – but the
British would judge when the Africans were ready for this.
The French aimed to turn their African subjects into French
citizens. As they grew more civilised they would qualify as
French citizens, and would be represented in the French
parliament just like any French town or department. The
stage seemed to be set for a peaceful transfer of power. This
was not to be.

In North Africa a million French settlers would fight
rather than lose control of Algeria's fertile land to 7 million
Africans. In Egypt the British felt unable to trust the
Egyptians with controlling or owning the Suez Canal. In
Kenya the Africans were desperately short of farming
land (see p. 58) and would not wait for the British, whom
they suspected of working hand in glove with the wealthy
settlers. In the Congo and Rhodesia mineral wealth had
attracted strong European interests with wires to pull
in European capitals. In West Africa British and French
governors feared bloody clashes between rival tribes and
religions if the white men hurried their exit. So freedom
would not be given as a present.

West Africa had the most promising prospect for African
nationalism in 1945. There were few settlers, so the land

*Independent Africa*
Countries which appear in
*white* are dealt with in detail

Map labels:

Conquered by
Israel 1967

ALGERIA

EGYPT

GHANA

ABYSSINIA

KENYA

CONGO

Occupied by
South Africa

SOUTH
AFRICA

— · — Frontiers of independent
states

Areas still ruled by
European countries (1967)

0        km        2000

was still owned by the Africans, who had profited from the
wartime boom – with government help they had sold the
goods themselves, through marketing boards (see p. 114)
instead of through European traders who agreed amongst
themselves to offer low prices. Not much burdened with
colour-conscious settlers, and wealthy by African standards these lands led tropical Africa in securing the 'political
kingdom' for Africans.

First was the Gold Coast. In 1946, it was given, by the
new British Labour government, a constitution providing
for an elected Legislative Council with an African majority.
After this big step towards an African government, things
did not move fast enough for the people. They found that
they still had to pay through the nose for foreign goods
from foreign traders: the promised development of their
own country dawdled. Kwame Nkrumah (see p. 157),
educated in American and English universities, and a

close friend of the French African leaders, followed the tactics of other twentieth century revolutionaries by organising a political party, based on the masses, to demand immediate self-government. Boycotts of foreign traders, and street demonstrations, led to riots and shooting, and gaol for Nkrumah; but he was succeeding in forcing the British to hurry up and transfer power to the Africans. He was in gaol again at the time of the Gold Coast's first general election – his party won a resounding victory. The Governor released him from gaol and asked him to take over as leader of Government business. A sudden change! Within a year he was Prime Minister.

This was in 1951, but independence did not come for six years more. Why the delay? The Gold Coast had a problem shared by many other nations struggling out of the chrysalis of European control. It was deeply divided in itself – there was a prosperous coastal area, and the more backward Ashanti lands, far from the sea, where the ancient tribal system was still strong. Should there be one strong central government for the whole country, divided as it was, or a federal system which would still allow the chiefs control of their tribes? Hoping to solve this problem the British delayed granting independence. It was six years before an uneasy compromise was worked out. In 1957 the Gold Coast, now known as Ghana, became the first British colony in Africa to achieve independence.

Unfortunately for Ghana, in his decade of power Nkrumah was led by success into the path of dictatorship. He began in 1959 with the expulsion of foreign journalists whose reports were not to his taste, pressure on judges to return the 'right' verdict on his political enemies, and hounding his chief political opponent out of the country. There followed a steady stream of treason trials, deportations, and imprisonments without trial. The constitution was changed to allow only one candidate in presidential elections. A youth movement was created, the Young Pioneers, whose members were taught to chant, 'Nkrumah is our leader, Nkrumah never dies.'

Nevertheless he was tremendously popular – until Ghana ran into economic trouble brought on by the corruption and inefficiency of his government. In 1966 the cost of living was over half as much again as it had been in 1963. Ghana's foreign debts in 1957 were £20 million, in 1966

£400 million. Theft and mismanagement of public money was becoming notorious. In February 1966, while Nkrumah was away on a visit to Peking, the army seized power and the generals took over. They promised to clean things up and restore civilian government within two years. They accused Nkrumah of having made an illicit fortune of £2 million, and put a £10,000 reward, dead or alive, on his head. They put 53 state business concerns up for sale. There were no takers – Ghana's public enterprises were too rotten from filching and mismanagement to be worth buying.

Ghana had an easy journey to independence, compared with Kenya, where 20,000 European farmers exploited the rich and healthy highlands. Not a handful of deaths as in Ghana, but thousands; not weeks of prison, but years, for Kenya's future President, Jomo Kenyatta (see p. 59). When the Axis surrendered in 1945, Kenyatta returned home, hoping to combine all Kenya's tribes in a movement demanding independence. Neither the settlers, nor the British government, sympathised. The settlers knew that the overcrowded Kikuyu would not leave Kenya's best land in European possession after European political control was gone. Even when the government was sincerely trying to help, the Kikuyu suspected treachery. For instance, the Kikuyu lands, like many native reserves, were being ruined by soil erosion (rain washing away the fertile topsoil) which could be checked by terracing. The government encouraged the Africans to terrace their hillsides but met with no response – the Kikuyu feared that the white men would confiscate this land, once terracing had increased its value.

Some Africans were not prepared to wait, and trust in peaceful methods; they were desperate for more land; others had fought in the war and could not settle to tribal life; others had left the tribes, and drifted into criminal violence in the towns. Such men as these formed a secret organisation, Mau Mau, to drive the Europeans out. Their supporters, mostly from the Kikuyu tribe, took oaths secretly at night, and those who could not take them, or would not pay money to support Kenyatta's independence movement, were sometimes beaten up or murdered.

The government told Kenyatta to condemn Mau Mau; and so he did – in public; but the government suspected him of still secretly organising Mau Mau. By 1952 Mau Mau oaths included a promise to kill white men. Kenyatta and other Kikuyu leaders were arrested, and charged with organising Mau Mau. The prosecution witnesses were not very convincing, and Kenyatta denied any connection with the criminal oath-taking – he argued that Mau Mau was being used as an excuse to strangle his movement, which had been only demanding 'the rights of the African people as human beings'. The court sentenced him to seven years hard labour.

This did not improve the situation. Mau Mau oaths and brutalities gew more loathsome and widespread. The whole Kikuyu people seemed infected. There were cases of settlers hideously murdered by long-trusted Kikuyu servants. The settlers rushed to the gun shops, the British moved troops to Kenya. Mau Mau killed 32 settlers, 63 soldiers, and nearly 2,000 of the Africans who would not join them. British forces killed many thousands of Mau Mau supporters and suspects. Cruelty bred cruelty. Mau Mau murders were answered with the machine-gunning of suspects, and at Hola Camp British guards beat some prisoners to death. Like the French torturers in Algeria (see p. 254) and the South African police at Sharpeville (see p. 259) they were discrediting their claim to be more civilised than the Africans.

Mau Mau was crushed in the end. The government at last began to bring Africans into positions of authority. But two big obstacles to the growth of a free, united Kenya remained. First the British would not allow any African organisation with branches outside more than one small area. This rule was made, Africans believed, on purpose to prevent the Africans from uniting against the settlers. The result was that each town or tribe had a separate political party. The Kikuyu remained loyal to Kenyatta – still a prisoner, for the second obstacle was the British refusal to free the only man who could command support throughout Kenya.

After years of delay, Kenyatta was released, and Kenya did achieve independence in 1964, but British policy had created a deep conflict between Kenyatta's followers and the rest. It was expressed in a quarrel over how strong Kenya's central government should be. Should it have real authority, or should most of the power, over only eight million people, be divided among seven regions, each with a separate parliament? Kenyatta wanted a strong central government and as soon as the British left he chiselled away the powers of the regional authorities. In 1963 Kenyatta's party won a general election and the ex-convict became his country's first President. Like his old friend Nkrumah, he soon banned all political parties except his own; in Kenya the other parties were quite willing to come under the President's umbrella, as they thought he did not mean to show favouritism to his own people, the Kikuyu.

The British in Ghana and Kenya made mistakes – but at least they had been preparing for years to hand over authority to the Africans, and had arranged that this happened gradually. The Belgians neglected this, and inflicted four years of civil war on the Belgian Congo as a result.

After 1945 the sale of copper boomed, but it was chiefly the Belgians who profited. Half the children in the capital were undernourished – so said a United Nations survey in 1956 – and meanwhile the British and French colonies were advancing towards self-government. In 1958 General de Gaulle returned to power in France (see p. 189). He offered the French colonies a choice: association on equal terms with France in a French Community, or complete independence. By 1960 all the colonies had chosen independence. The Belgians could not insulate the Congo from its neighbours. They set up elected local councils. Out of these emerged two political parties calling for independence. One, favouring a strong central government, was inspired by a young clerk named Patrice Lumumba. The other wanted a federal system, which would leave the provinces, such as Katanga, running their own affairs. Lumumba won recognition by other African independence movements as his nation's leader when he attended the African People's Congress at Accra, Ghana's capital.

The Belgians had no intention of using armed force to keep political control of the Congo. In 1960 they decided to hold elections for an independent government. They expected to remain in control of their investments, mines and factories. After all, the new government would have to depend on Belgian officials and experts, and in Katanga the Belgian-owned Union Minière, the company which owned the copper mines, was bound to pull the strings. So the

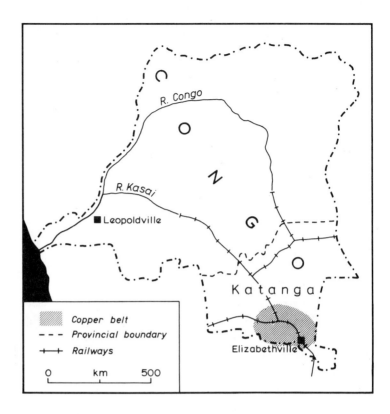

Belgians packed their bags and left — so suddenly that magistrates left half-way through a case! The elections gave no clear majority. Lumumba's party alone had support throughout the Congo, but he won only about one-fourth of the seats. He managed to form a coalition government.

But the volcano was about to erupt. Congo's army mutinied against its Belgian officers. Europeans were beaten up in the streets. Law and order broke down. The Belgians flew in troops to protect Belgian citizens. In Katanga, the provincial government, led by Moise Tshombe, and backed by some local tribes and the Union Minière, declared itself independent. This meant that the central government would be ruined — it depended entirely on Katanga's copper exports for revenue. Tribal wars broke out, as people fell back on the old tribal loyalties they had been forgetting. The Katanga government hired European soldiers to protect it. The army seized power in the capital, Leopoldville (now Kinshasa) and arrested Lumumba. Later he was murdered in Katanga. Clearly, outside help was needed if the new state was ever to make a fair start.

253

The United Nations sent expert help of all kinds and called for the withdrawal from the Congo of all foreign troops, including the mercenaries. If the mercenaries left, Katanga's independence would collapse. They stayed. The UN sent an international force to Katanga and fighting developed between them and the mercenaries. Trying to arrange a cease-fire, the UN Secretary-General, Dag Hammarskjold, was killed in an air crash. The British and French governments attacked the UN for using force, but the United States was backing the UN – the US feared that if the UN did not see to the establishment of a strong central government in the Congo, Russia might take a hand. Early in 1963, after heavy fighting, the Katanga government broke up and the Union Minière agreed to pay taxes to the capital. Katanga would not after all form a separate state from the rest of the Congo – or at least, not yet.

Belgium had kept the Congo as a colony, run by outsiders, who combined profit-seeking with care for the people's welfare. French colonial policy was different, in giving the colonies the chance to develop as overseas provinces of France. Nationalist movements in the colonies turned down this chance. They demanded, and got, independence. Only in North Africa, where European settlement was heavy (see p. 59) did the French resist this demand by force.

When news of the German surrender of 1945 reached Algeria there were nationalist demonstrations. The police fired on one of these, and riots spread throughout the country. One hundred Europeans were killed. The settlers and the army joined forces to restore order, with terrible brutality. Estimates of the Algerians killed range from 1,500 to 45,000.

For years afterwards the Algerians tried to reach agreement with the French on their country's future. By 1954 some were tired of waiting. They formed the FLN (Front de Libération Nationale) and launched a rebellion. At first this had the support of only a few extremists, but the harsh attitude of the French soon changed this. Their army treated the rebels as agents of international communism, and their paratroop commander allowed his men to use torture. The FLN reckoned that more than a million Algerians were killed in the eight years of fighting. Many died in French concentration camps, many under torture.

The FLN treated the French, and any Algerians who got in their way, with equal savagery.

The French used half a million troops but could win no final victory. East and West of Algeria were Tunisia and Morocco which had recently achieved independence from France – further off was independent Egypt. All three helped the rebels and treated the FLN as Algeria's true government. The war dragged on. The settlers and the army blamed the French governments for weakness and defeatism – it was Algerian settlers who started in 1958 the movement which overthrew the French government and brought General de Gaulle back to power as President (see p. 189).

The settlers expected the wartime champion of Free France to fight the war more vigorously. Instead, he offered the Algerians self-determination. The settlers revolted again – this time to overthrow de Gaulle. But in mainland France, de Gaulle won majority opinion for his policy, and the generals found that against de Gaulle their own men would not support them. Soon de Gaulle and the FLN leaders were hammering out the details of self-determination, while the despairing settlers and some army leaders set up a secret terrorist organisation to carry on their fight to the bitter end, against the Army and Algerians.

The war ended in 1962, leaving Algeria with a ruined countryside, and an eighth of its people dead. The war's agony spilled over in quarrels amongst the FLN leaders, and civil war threatened, until mass demonstrations and strike threats brought the rivals to their senses. Thousands of European settlers returned to France and Algerian labourers took over their estates. The new government went on to confiscate all settlers' land, as well as some belonging to rich Algerians. The confiscated land was to be handed to self-governing communities of the workers on each estate.

## 2 The Union of South Africa

In the twenty years after the Second World War, the rule of the one-fifth of South Africans who are white over the four-fifths who are black or brown or of mixed descent, was not seriously shaken. Here was Africa's largest white minority, digging in. From 1948 the official policy of the government was 'apartheid', the Afrikaans word for separation. These laws show something of what apartheid meant to the Africans.

   (i) According to the Pass Laws, every African must carry at all times a reference book containing an identity card. Fingerprints are taken when the books are issued.

  (ii) No African may visit a town for more than three days without a permit.

 (iii) Jobs are classified according to colour. Desirable jobs are reserved for whites. African trade unions are separate from European. Africans must not strike. (Penalty three years in prison, £500 fine.)

 (iv) Different racial groups must live in different areas. (This meant turning thousands of families out of their homes.)

  (v) Only whites are represented in Parliament. The only vote Africans have is for the parliaments of the tribal reserves (renamed Bantustans) where the chiefs, chosen by the government, and government officials have the whip hand.

 (vi) Mixed marriages and all sexual relations between the races are illegal.

(vii) All public places – cinemas, theatres, hotels, restaurants, sports-grounds, buses and trains, are either banned to non-Europeans or have separate facilities for them.

(viii) Education for non-Europeans is controlled by a white minister. (Dr Verwoerd, chosen Prime Minister in 1958, said this was to make sure that Africans learned not to seek equality with Europeans but to serve their own people.)

 (ix) The government has the right to ban all racially-mixed meetings, even in a church.

How did apartheid come to be government policy? During the Second World War, and until 1948, the United Party was in power. Its leader was Jan Smuts (see p. 56) who granted that the whites must stay on top in South Africa but believed that it was wrong to deny citizens' rights to all the Africans – after all, he said, they were carrying South Africa on their backs. Most English-speaking whites supported Smuts' party, whilst its rival the National Party was aiming at solid Afrikaner support.

Gold miners, some of the manpower behind the wealth of Southern Africa

Since Afrikaners outnumbered English-speakers, this would give the Nationalists control of the country. Apartheid, the Nationalists reckoned, would win this solid Afrikaner support.

The Nationalists leaders believe, like the Nazis, in racial purity. (During the war they were openly pro-Nazi. A South African court declared that Verwoerd's newspaper was a tool of the Nazis, and future Prime Minister Voerster, who was imprisoned as a Nazi sympathiser, declared: 'We stand for Christian Nationalism, which is an ally of National Socialism.') They saw that the development of city life was mixing the races, as Africans left the countryside – where they lived either in tribes or as wretchedly paid labourers on Afrikaners' farms – to seek city work. This mixture, they argued, was a threat to white purity – the only way out was for the white minority to stay in power, and remove every trace of non-European political rights. The Negroes must live quite separately – except for working for white bosses in farms, mines and factories.

This programme won the election of 1948 for the National Party, and they set about putting it into action. The first target was non-white representation in parliament. In 1948, the Indians and Africans had a few white representatives, and the Coloureds actually voted in the same way as whites. After a six-year tussle with the law courts and the South African senate the Nationalists abolished these white representatives and crossed off all the coloured voters.

Then they tried to reorganise the African population according to the old, dying tribal system. Africans could not own land in South Africa, except in the tribal reserves – about 10 per cent of the area, already overcrowded, and with soil so poor through erosion that the people could not grow enough food for themselves. The Nationalists planned to build these reserves up into Bantustans which could govern themselves (under strong white supervision) and act as homelands for the Africans.

There was a complication. The whites could not survive without plenty of badly-paid African workers. (In 1957, African families in Johannesburg earned an average of £18 a month.) These African workers would have to live in the white men's cities – unless all the factories and mines could be moved to the edge of the Bantustans, and the white housewives all gave up their African servants. In fact, in 1951, more than half the supposed natives of the largest Bantustan lived outside its area.

The apartheid laws were naturally hated by the Africans. In the 1950's they trusted in the law-abiding resistance led by the African National Congress. In 1952, led by Chief Luthuli, the Congress launched a passive resistance campaign (see p. 65) – Luthuli urged his people to accept prison rather than the tyranny of the Pass Laws. Refusing to obey a government order to resign from his chieftaincy or from the Congress, Luthuli said he wished to join his people 'in the spirit that revolts openly and boldly against injustice and expresses itself in a determined and non-violent manner.' The government sacked him and put an end to the campaign with a law punishing all non-violent law breaking with whippings and up to three years' imprisonment.

In 1959 the tightening of the Pass Laws and enforcement

of race-separation in living areas prompted a new campaign. The Africans demonstrated in mass against the Pass Laws. In 1960 the police fired on one such peaceful demonstration, at Sharpeville. The news of the eighty-three innocent lives lost at Sharpeville and elsewhere provoked a wave of strikes. The government declared a state of emergency, and arrested thousands of suspects. Some were kept for months without trial. Chief Luthuli publicly burned his pass; under arrest, he was beaten up by a policeman. The Africans' organisations were banned. African opposition went underground. The leaders began to advocate violent methods. In 1961, Chief Luthuli won the Nobel Peace Prize, but his life's work, for true democracy and a true union of all the communities of the land, seemed to have failed.

Even harsher laws and punishments answered the Africans' secret resistance. When the Africans started a sabotage campaign the law was changed to make sabotage equal to treason (penalty: death) and a law for the 'suppression of communism' allowed the government to ban any organisation furthering the achievement of any of the objects of communism. As communists aimed to get rid of apartheid, this law meant that any group which worked against apartheid could be smeared as pro-communist and banned.

To the north of South Africa lay the British colony of Southern Rhodesia. In 1923 the settlers had turned down a chance to unite with South Africa (see p. 57). At that time they feared the Afrikaners more than the Africans. Since then, although in theory still ruled by London, they had self-government in practice and their own army and airforce.

As the tide of African nationalism swept towards them, the whites of Rhodesia felt more and more inclined to find security and protection by taking South Africa's road of white supremacy and racial dictatorship. What was more, like the South Africans, they were wealthy and numerous enough to do it.

The British government had a real problem. It would have to give independence to Southern Rhodesia along with the rest of its African empire. But should it hand over at once to the Europeans, and so deliver the Africans into bondage, or wait and force the Europeans to allow Africans to take the country over before independence?

The white Rhodesians decided not to wait. In 1965 they declared themselves independent, and waited to see what the British government would do. Caught napping, the best the British could offer to bring the Rhodesians to order was United Nations sanctions (see pp. 35 and 128). These caused some discomfort to the Rhodesians, but South African help was quickly forthcoming and the new nation survived long enough to begin the work of modelling itself on its powerful southern neighbour.

## 3  Egypt

Home a mud-brick hut with three rooms shared with the animals; food, black bread and vegetables; children with flies crawling round their infected eyes; the whole family chronically ill, infected by the filthy Nile water. A farm too small to feed the family, most days spent using a wooden plough or 'shadoof' on someone else's land – this was life for seven out of ten of Egypt's people, for most of its 6,000 year history. One of these poor country-dwellers of the Nile valley – known as *fellahin* – was the grand-father of Gamal Nasser, in 1942 a promising captain in the Egyptian army, fighting at El Alamein (see p. 146).

Young Nasser had grown up in an Egypt still dominated by the British. Egyptian nationalists of the middle-class Wafd Party secured a treaty with Britain in 1936 (see p. 61) which gave Egypt independence (and Nasser his chance to train as an officer – the British wanted promising young men of all classes in their new ally's army). But Britain kept a garrison in Egypt, to protect the Suez Canal. Would a Nazi victory help the Egyptians to get rid of the British altogether? As Rommel advanced on Cairo the British suspected Egypt's king, Farouk, of planning to form a pro-German government. British tanks surrounding his palace showed him this would be unwise. To men like Nasser, Farouk's obedience to the British proved how far their country was from true independence.

After the war, Nasser organised a secret association of army officers pledged to reform the Egyptian government and throw out the king, whose luxurious life was an inter-national joke. In every respect, Egypt's situation cried out for revolution. The rising population worsened the condi-tions of the *fellahin*, whilst the great landlords grew yet richer. The Wafd, after winning so-called independence for Egypt, had become the tool of a few wealthy landlords and businessmen. The British still garrisoned the Suez Canal. More than 60 per cent of Egyptian business was foreign owned.

The Wafd government, which dared not tackle Egypt's other problems, yielded to popular hatred of the British by launching a terrorist campaign in the Canal Zone. In 1952, a British attack on an Egyptian police H.Q. led to riots which burned down much of central Cairo – the Muslim Brotherhood, an association of fanatical Muslim terrorists who wanted power for themselves, was at work. Farouk could find no one who would govern for him – but he was on the trail of Nasser's revolutionary organisation: Nasser put his plans into action. The capital fell to him like a ripe apple. Only two soldiers were killed. Farouk abdicated, and with 204 pieces of luggage left for Europe to spend the fortune he had salted away in Switzerland.

Nasser's men now dealt with their rivals, the communists and the Muslim Brotherhood. Nasser was a socialist, but he regarded communists as unpatriotic puppets of Moscow. After a riot in one of the chief cotton mills, he hanged two of the leaders, to discourage left-wing violence, and soon Egypt's leading communists were behind bars. An attempt to assassinate him gave Nasser a neat excuse to round up the Muslim Brotherhood's leaders. Six were hanged. The officers' revolutionary council banned all the political parties, and announced that they would stay in control for three years before holding any elections.

Nasser's first moves to help the *fellahin* only scratched the surface of the problem. He cut drastically the rents they had to pay, and shared out amongst them about 10 per cent of the fertile land – this came from the largest estates, which Nasser confiscated from the landlords, who had mostly supported the Wafd party. Most *fellahin* got no land, and the new law on rents was hard to enforce. Nasser postponed grasping this thorny issue. Instead, he let himself be tempted by the role of international champion of Arab nationalism. As a champion of the Arabs Nasser found it hard to resist the pressure of Arab opinion driving him towards a full-scale second round in the struggle against Israel (see p. 158). Along the Israeli frontier each side was rivalling the other in night sabotage raids.

Nasser wanted the Arab and African states to stay neutral in the cold war, taking sides with neither Russia nor the United States and its allies. Iraq, on the other hand, had joined Britain, a US ally, and four other Moslem countries in a military alliance, the Baghdad Pact (1955). Egypt now stood out as Iraq's rival for leadership in the Arab world.

Yet Nasser was trying to borrow money from Britain and the US to build the Aswan Dam (which would vastly increase Egypt's farming land, make it possible to control the Nile floods, and provide power for industry). At the same time, to show his independence, he bought weapons from communist Czechoslovakia. Since the American government reckoned that Nasser could not afford to pay the interest on the loans as well as the cost of the Czech arms, the British and Americans cancelled their loans for the dam in 1956. Nasser's answer was to nationalise the Suez Canal Company (owned by British and French shareholders) and tell his people that though the imperialists might choke in their rage Egypt would use the canal's earnings to pay for the dam. The Arab world gloried in this bold defiance.

The British and French now planned to ruin Nasser altogether. The French resented his support for the FLN (see p. 255); the British hoped to recover control of the canal. With Israel they organised a joint attack on Egypt (though the British and French pretended that their expedition was just an 'intervention' to 'separate the combatants'). Once again as in 1948 (see pp. 158–159) the Israelis thrashed the Egyptian army, but the UN, led by the US and USSR, condemned Egypt's three invaders, and the British and French withdrew in disgrace. The Russians agreed to help build the Aswan Dam.

Nasser's Egypt, with its land reform policy and its defiance of the western powers, inspired other Arab and African countries. Nasser hoped to set up a United Arab Republic (UAR). In 1958 he was able to form a union of Syria and Egypt. Meanwhile President Eisenhower had suggested that the collapse of French and British power in the Middle East had left the area dangerously open to the communists. He offered US military aid to countries which felt threatened, and made it clear that he thought Nasser was no better than a communist. In the summer of 1958 the Lebanon was on the edge of civil war between the pro- and anti-

The Glories Of
The July Revolution

٢٠ من مايو ١٩٦٠.
تربية اجتماعية
أ- أمجاد الثورة
ه- لماذا يعتبر يوم ٢. من يوليو عيداً قومياً
٦- ما هو أضخم منشأ... تقوم به الثورة؟
... ناصر قناة السويس؟

President Nasser (pointing) shows Prime Minister Nehru (white hat) around on a tour of Egypt 1960

Nasser forces. When it seemed that the Iraqi army might be sent against Nasser's allies in Syria and the Lebanon, the army rebelled, the king and prime minister were assassinated, and an Iraqi republic proclaimed. Britain and the US rushed troops to prop up their remaining friends – Britain to Jordan, the US to Lebanon.

The Iraqi revolution seemed the high tide of Nasser's success. It looked as if he might preside over a real united republic of all the Arab states. But this was only a dream. Even the union with Syria collapsed within four years. The Syrians felt overshadowed by the Egyptians; Syria's powerful middle class hated Nasser's socialism. When the Syrians backed out, Nasser realised that only union between countries which had similar social systems could hope to last. After the break-up of the UAR the government took over the whole of Egypt's import trade, and the sale of cotton, the chief export; also all banks and insurance companies and hundreds of business firms. Taxes on higher incomes were stiffened, to wipe out extremes of wealth. Egypt embarked on the first of two 5-year plans aiming to double its income by 1970.

At the same time Nasser was trying to find ways of getting ordinary Egyptians to take charge of their own affairs; they were so ignorant and backward, so used to selling their votes and taking orders. Nasser, like Nkrumah and Kenyatta, would only allow one political party, but he tried seriously to involve the masses in its working. Improving the life of the *fellahin* was a formidable task. The government made a start by building hundreds of clinics to treat the *fellahin*'s illnesses, and working to bring clean water to all the villages (though it was hard to persuade villagers not to prefer the infected Nile water). In thirteen years, Egypt's health expenditure multiplied four times.

As for land reform, breaking up the huge estates could not solve the problem – there simply was not enough land to go round. Nasser looked to the Aswan Dam and irrigation schemes to provide more land; and to industrial growth to provide more jobs for the rising population. The most socialist aspect of the land reform was the compulsory co-operative farms set up on confiscated land. To make sure the land was used scientifically, these were government-supervised; each farm had three huge fields, each with a crop rotation of cotton/maize or rice/clover; and each peasant had a share in each field. This rotation, unlike the older methods, rested the soil and caused some spectacular improvement in yields. Alas, the entanglements of foreign affairs again spoiled these efforts.

Egypt remained officially at war with Israel. A large army and airforce helped to keep the *fellahin* poor, but when put to the test of a third round of the battle with the flourishing Jewish state, they proved utterly useless.

After the 1956 fight, only Syria kept up a really determined guerrilla war on Israel's northern frontier, making night raids and shelling farms near the border. Although Israel answered back, the nuisance continued. In 1966 the Israeli army crossed the frontier and flattened a Syrian village. Early in 1967 an Israeli air raid silenced a battery of Syrian guns.

But still the incidents went on. Appeals to the United Nations produced no help; of the two big powers, America was too busy in Vietnam to look after peace in the Middle East, and Russia was not slow to move in – by befriending the Syrians.

So the Israel government made heavy threats of war. The tension built up. On Russian advice, Nasser moved his army up to Israel's southern border to discourage any attack on Syria. Syrian and Egyptian radios blared out counter-threats about destroying Israel, and sneered at Jordan on the eastern frontier for not joining in and completing the circle. Guerrilla activity was stepped up.

In truth, it was madness for Egypt to go to war, and probably Nasser never meant it to happen. He was enjoying a reappearance as the great Arab leader, blustering and gambling his way to undoing the defeat of 1956.

His sneers brought the King of Jordan into line. Under pressure from his people, who were under the radio-spell of the wild anti-Israeli broadcasts, he put the Jordanian army under an Egyptian general and allowed Iraqi troops, also joining the fray, to use his territory.

Having 'saved' Syria and brought Jordan into line, Nasser now ordered out of Egypt the 3,400 soldiers of the United Nations Emergency Force which had been watching the frontier since 1956. Then he closed the Straits of Tiran, the narrow entry to Israel's southern seaport of Eilat.

The Israel government watched all this with intense anxiety; if the Arabs really meant to attack on all fronts, and it looked more and more like it, Israel would be in a poor position. There was Russian friendship for the Arabs. Would the United States protect Israel? The Israelis decided not to risk waiting. They struck first.

The result was one of the most extraordinary military victories of modern times – the 'Six Day War' of June 5th–10th 1967. The Israeli airforce, sweeping in under the Egyptian radar, smashed the Egyptian airforce to pieces on the ground in three hours. That settled the war, because in desert fighting an army unprotected from air attack is doomed. In six days, with hardly any Israeli losses at all, the armies of Egypt, Syria and Jordan were shattered and in flight, their equipment destroyed. Areas of all three countries were occupied, including all of Egypt up to the east bank of the Suez Canal, which, with two armies lining

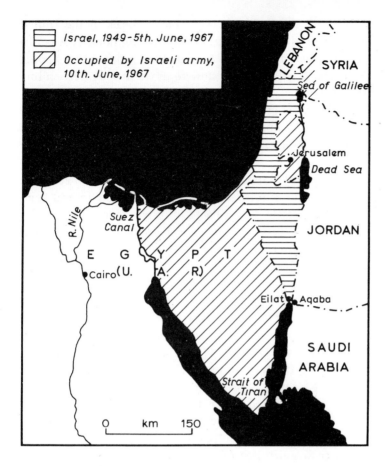

Israel, 1949–5th. June, 1967

Occupied by Israeli army, 10th. June, 1967

LEBANON

SYRIA

Sea of Galilee

Jerusalem

Dead Sea

JORDAN

R. Nile

Suez Canal

E G Y P T
(U. A: R)

Cairo

Eilat  Aqaba

SAUDI ARABIA

Strait of Tiran

0    km    150

its banks, was closed to shipping. Israel gained tremendous confidence and pride from its third great victory over the enemies who had sworn to destroy it from the first.

In Egypt, Nasser managed to stay in power, although he took the blame and offered to resign. In spite of his blunders, the people, far from knowing the whole truth of course, flooded into the streets to demonstrate in favour of him, and he was able to remain.

But what settlement could be made? Russia encouraged the losers by rearming them. The USA, worried at its loss of influence in the Middle East, tended to answer this by giving more support to Israel. The Israelis wanted a peace treaty which would give them guaranteed peace after twenty years of threats and fighting, and they were determined to hold their conquests until they got it. The Arab states, bolstered by Russian support, hung on hopefully and refused to talk about peace until the Israelis cleared out. In the meantime, petty destruction went on along the line where the armies stood face to face while a gallant but helpless set of United Nations observers tried vainly to control it.

# Some Explanations

ABDICATE — Resign from the position of being king, queen or emperor.

AFRIKANER — Person who speaks Afrikaans as his native language. This language developed from Dutch, and is used by people descended from the Dutch settlers in South Africa.

AGGRESSOR; AGGRESSION — Words used in international affairs. A country which attacks another country, and is held responsible for the outbreak of war, is called the aggressor (from a Latin word meaning 'attack') and said to have committed aggression.

AGRARIAN — Concerning the LAWS about agricultural land, that is, land used for food production (crops or livestock).

AMBASSADOR — Person who represents his own country's GOVERNMENT in dealings with another government. He usually lives in the capital city of the foreign country.

ARYAN — The Nazis believed that the Aryans were a superior race originating in India, and that "pure" Germans were Aryans. In fact the word has no such meaning. It means a group of languages. English, Latin and German are all Aryan languages.

ATHEIST — One who does not believe in the existence of a god or gods.

ATOMIC BOMB — Atoms are the smallest units of the elements which make up all the matter of the universe. In this century, scientists learned to split atoms. This splitting releases tremendous energy. Atomic bombs use the energy released by splitting atoms of the element *uranium*.

BOLSHEVIKS — Russian for 'majority men'. In 1903 the Russian SOCIALIST party voted on whether to form a tightly-knit group of revolutionaries (as Lenin wished) or to build up a larger party which could work for a peaceful socialist take-over in Russia. Lenin's views got a majority. His followers then called themselves 'Bolsheviks'.

| | |
|---|---|
| BOURGEOIS | A French word, originally meaning 'town dweller'. Used chiefly by COMMUNISTS to refer to the 'middle CLASS' of business and professional people and their way of life. |
| BOYCOTT | Technique often used in political agitation. It means a ban on all contact with the victim or victims; the boycotters will not speak to them, help them, buy from them, or sell to them. |
| BUDGET | A government's annual forecast of how it proposes to raise and spend money, and to steer the ECONOMY. |
| CABINET; CABINET GOVERNMENT | The group of chief ministers in a GOVERNMENT is often called the 'cabinet'. If a country's CONSTITUTION includes cabinet government, these ministers share responsibility for all major decisions. If a minister disagrees with a Cabinet decision he is still obliged to support it in public, or else resign. |
| CAPITAL; CAPITALIST; CAPITALISM | Money or resources which can be used to create more money and resources is called capital. For example money in a bank can be invested in SHARES which will collect interest. A house can be let to tenants who pay rent. A businessman might divide his capital into *fixed* (buildings and machinery) and *floating* (money and materials). A person who owns capital is called a capitalist. Capitalism is an ECONOMIC system where most of the capital is owned by private individuals. Compare SOCIALISM. |
| CAPITAL GOODS | Equipment, such as railways, steel mills or motor works, which can be used to produce *more* goods. |
| CATHOLIC; ROMAN CATHOLIC | Person who accepts the teaching of the Catholic CHURCH, that Christ chose St Peter as the chief of his apostles, to be the first of a series of men who would represent him on earth. Compare POPE. |
| CHURCH | Organised group of people having the same religious beliefs. Usually reserved for Christian groups. |
| CHURCH OF ENGLAND | In the 16th century King Henry VIII claimed that he, not the Pope, was head of the Christian Church in England. Those who accepted this became the 'Church of England' which had many privileges, some of which still survive. |
| CIVILIAN | Anyone who is not in the armed forces of a country. |

| | |
|---|---|
| CIVIL SERVICE | All the organizations which work for a country's central GOVERNMENT, carrying out its POLICY, whatever political party is in power; not including the armed, or fighting, services. |
| CLASS | Set of people who are basically alike in their ECONOMIC situation e.g. big CAPITALISTS; middle-class people with a little CAPITAL; working-class people with very little or no capital. Class differences are often more or less inherited, and show in different styles of speech, manners, customs and beliefs. |
| COALING STATION | Until after the First World War, coal was the chief fuel of the world's navies and merchant ships. Coaling stations were bases where ships could refuel from coal dumps. |
| COMMISSAR | The BOLSHEVIKS used this word for anyone to whom they gave some special task. For instance it was used instead of the BOURGEOIS word 'minister'. |
| COMMUNIST INTERNATIONAL | Organization of world communist parties accepting Bolshevik leadership, set up in 1919 to promote more communist revolutions. Considered a menace to civilization by the FASCISTS and by many CONSERVATIVES. Disbanded by Stalin in 1943. |
| CONGRESS | (a) any assembly of people who meet to discuss or settle some problem in which they share an interest. (b) the FEDERAL LEGISLATURE of the U.S.A., made up of the SENATE and the House of Representatives. (c) Indian political movement which worked for independence from Britain and after 1947 became the ruling PARTY in India. |
| CONSTITUENT ASSEMBLY | Meeting of representatives of a country, aiming to revise their country's CONSTITUTION, or give it one after a dictatorship or rule by a king. Such assemblies often meet after a REVOLUTION. |
| CONSTITUTION | The set of rules or laws which decide how any association of people is to be run. Any club may have a constitution. Most do, to avoid endless quarrels about how to carry on the club's affairs. In history, the most important constitutions are those of STATES. The Americans drew up a written constitution in 1787, and |

the French after 1789. Since then, many countries have copied their example. Not all constitutions give a reliable picture of how the state is really run. Stalin issued a 'democratic' constitution for the USSR just as he was eliminating all threats to his own dictatorship. Britain has a long series of LAWS and traditions but no single written constitution.

CONSUL

The ancient Roman REPUBLIC elected two consuls each year to command its armies and run its government. Nowadays a consul represents his own country in a foreign country, but is chiefly concerned with looking after businessmen and tourists, not international affairs. Compare AMBASSADOR.

CONSUMER GOODS

·Almost everything you would normally buy in a shop would count as consumer goods. They can be used (consumed) but not to make anything else.

CONVOY

column of vehicles, ships or aircraft, carrying goods or people, and escorted by armed forces.

COOPERATIVES

Shops, farms and other facilities which are owned by their users, who share any profits they make; very important in modern farming as co-operation can provide farmers with facilities (tractors, dairies) which they could not afford as individuals.

CORRUPTION

If there is corruption in a CIVIL SERVICE, army or law court it operates unfairly and inefficiently, because the people in it will accept bribes or presents, or give way to threats.

CREDIT; CREDITOR

From a Latin word meaning 'believe' or 'trust'. A creditor lends money or goods to people whom he trusts to repay him at a later date. In return for this service he will probably charge interest. If people or countries have paid their debts to their creditors reliably, they will have 'good credit', that is, they are likely to find creditors easily. Creditors may be private individuals, businesses or governments.

CZAR, TSAR

Russian for Emperor. Nicholas II, the last Czar, abdicated in 1917.

DELEGATE

Person chosen by a local group (factory, village, union branch etc.) to represent them and put their point of view, not his own, at an assembly.

| | |
|---|---|
| DEMOCRAT | From Greek words meaning 'the people rule'. A person who believes that the GOVERNMENT should be controlled by all the people, not just by a ruling CLASS. |
| DEMOCRATS | One of the two chief political PARTIES in the U.S.A. In this century the Democrats have often been more sympathetic to labour interests and recent immigrants than the REPUBLICANS. |
| DEPARTMENT | In France, a local government area with its own chief town. The central GOVERNMENT appoints a 'Prefect' to take charge of each department. This system dates from the French Revolutionary period. |
| DEPORTATION | Compulsory transfer of a person by a GOVERNMENT from one part of a country to another, or out of the country altogether. Used to control political enemies by the Italian FASCISTS and Russian Communists. |
| DESTROYER | A light, fast warship armed mainly with torpedoes; used as a screen for heavier ships, to hunt submarines and to CONVOY merchantmen in the two world wars. |
| DISARMAMENT | Giving up or cutting down a country's armed forces. Disarmament was forced on Germany after both world wars. |
| DOLE | Popular word for an unpopular system – government payments to the unemployed in Britain between 1918 and 1939. |
| ECONOMICS | From a Greek expression meaning 'household rules'. Everyone who plans his or her earning and spending is using 'economics' in this original sense. Nowadays the word usually means the study of very large scale earning and spending – by whole INDUSTRIES, or CLASSES, or countries; also of how a country's wealth is produced and shared. |
| ECONOMIST | Expert on ECONOMICS. Such people may be expert at running their own home, or household, 'economically', that is, without waste. If they are professional economists, they may advise business firms, or GOVERNMENTS, on how to run *their* ECONOMIES. |

| | |
|---|---|
| ECONOMY | (a) making sure a person, or business, or country, is run without material waste (as in 'economy drive'). <br> (b) the system used in a country for organizing the production and sharing of wealth (as in 'the British economy'). |
| EMBARGO | Ban on exports or imports, enforced by a government. |
| EMPIRE | Sometimes one country conquers its neighbours or areas overseas, and rules them whether they wish for this or not. Sometimes royal marriages may lead to several kingdoms being combined. Either way, the result is an empire, where one GOVERNMENT claims authority over areas which at one time had their own, separate governments. In an empire, there are usually people with different languages and histories from the ruling government. Thus nationalism has been a powerful enemy of empires. |
| EQUALITY | Before the French Revolution, different ranks of people (e.g. peasants, clergy, merchants) had different privileges in French LAW. The French revolutionaries demanded that everyone should be equal in law, or have equality. |
| ESTATE | Not always a housing estate. In the countryside the word refers to the property of a landowner; usually a big house, a park, a farm, and farming land worked by tenants. |
| EXPLOIT; EXPLOITATION | Make a profit out of some natural resource such as a piece of land, a coal deposit, or a supply of human labour. |
| FACTION | A sub-group within a larger group such as a PARTY. Factions may form in loyalty to a leading personality, or to a belief which the members share and wish to promote. |
| FALLOW | Farming land left with no crop for a season. This is a primitive method of resting the soil. |
| FASCIST | The 'fasces' were the rods carried before a magistrate in Ancient Rome as a sign of his authority. In modern Italian 'fascio' means 'group' or 'bunch'. Mussolini's fascist PARTY began as a network of groups which adopted the 'fasces' as their badge. The name 'fascist' was used for his followers and imitators in other countries; that is for violently anti-communist movements aiming to set up a one-party STATE. |

273

| | |
|---|---|
| FEDERAL | Some countries such as Brazil or the U.S.A. are too large and various to be run by one central GOVERNMENT. Others such as Germany have a long tradition of strong local authorities. Countries like this may be divided into STATES which have their own complete government system. The people of all the states choose a FEDERAL government which deals with matters, such as foreign relations, which affect more than one state. Such matters are set out in a CONSTITUTION. |
| FEUDAL | A feudal ECONOMY is based on land-holding. Land is granted by the SOVEREIGN to his lords, who grant it to their followers. At each step, services such as fighting or work in the fields are promised in return for the land. |
| FILIPINO | Native of the Philippine Islands. |
| FOURTEEN POINTS | Basic aims to be embodied in a peace settlement after the First World War, suggested by the U.S. President Wilson in January 1918. On disarmament and colonial problems the Points were much more lenient to Germany than the eventual peace treaty. They did not refer to REPARATIONS at all; but the Allies made it clear before the *armistice* that they would want reparations. |
| FUELLING STATION | Base where ships can take on oil fuel (see COALING STATION). |
| GESTAPO | Shortened from Geheime Staatspolizei (Secret State Police). The Prussian secret police set up by Goering. In 1934, Himmler, perhaps the vilest Nazi 'leader', was put in charge of them. Their actions could not be challenged in German law courts. In 1936 they were extended throughout Germany. Responsible for many atrocities. |
| GOVERNMENT | The people who control a country and claim to run its affairs. The government may have been elected by the ordinary people, in a DEMOCRATIC system, or have got control of the STATE by some other way. |
| GRAFT | Bribery in American POLITICS |
| GUERRILLA | Irregular soldier. Guerrillas wear no uniform and may have no command system. They may fight part-time and at other times do a CIVILIAN job. They often appear when a country is occupied by foreigners, or during a revolutionary war. |

| | |
|---|---|
| HABSBURGS | Ruling family of an EMPIRE based on Austria, Hungary and Bohemia. This empire had a period of glory in the 17th century when it was Europe's barrier against the Turks. After 1815 the rise of nationalism sapped its strength. The last emperor ABDICATED in 1918. |
| HINTERLAND | Area inland from a coastal town (usually a port) which is the ECONOMIC centre of the area. |
| HYDROGEN BOMB | Bomb using the same kind of energy as makes the heat of the sun – that is, the fusing together of hydrogen atoms. Such bombs are of unlimited power. The Americans tested the first large H-bomb in 1954, destroying the Pacific island of Bikini. Compare ATOMIC BOMB. |
| IKON | Russian word for a religious painting, of Christ or a saint. Such paintings are very important in the Greek Orthodox CHURCH to which most Christians in Eastern Europe and Russia belong. |
| INDUSTRY | The organized use of human labour and raw materials to produce goods of any kind. Usually divided into farming and manufacturing. Farming produces basic foodstuffs and some raw materials such as wool; manufacturing produces almost everything we use. In modern times, manufacturing industry has moved from craftsmen's workshops into factories where powered machines are used. |
| INFLATION | Word used by ECONOMISTS to describe the situation when prices rise (or are inflated) so that money of a given face value buys less and less. Drastic inflation may ruin the money system altogether, as in Germany in 1923. |
| INTERNATIONAL | Concerning more than one NATION, or GOVERNMENT. |
| INTERNATIONAL LAW | LAW which concerns the relations between countries, or disputes between the people of more than one country. |
| KAISER | German for Emperor. |
| KULAK | From the Russian word for 'fist' – thus, a 'grasping' person who EXPLOITS others. The BOLSHEVIKS used the word for rich PEASANTS who had enough land to need hired labour as well as their own family. The 'kulaks' were said to be the enemies of the 'muzhiks', the majority of peasants who had no land, or only enough to support one family. |

| | |
|---|---|
| LAW | Rule controlling any activity, from a game to a murder trial. Laws must generally have been accepted by the authority which claims to control the activity, and they mean little unless there is some SANCTION against those who break them. |
| LEFT | In politics, sympathetic towards SOCIALIST or communist ideas. The expression goes back to the time of the French Revolution, when the king's supporters sat to the RIGHT of the president in the National Assembly, while the more extreme revolutionaries who wished to get rid of the king sat to his left. |
| LEGISLATIVE | concerned with making LAWS for a whole country. |
| LEGISLATURE | The organization which has power to make LAWS for a country. In Britain, Parliament is the Legislature; in the U.S.A., Congress. |
| LIBERTY | Freedom; especially from GOVERNMENT interference. |
| LOTTERY | Gambling system in which the customers buy numbered tickets, as in a raffle. Those with lucky numbers win cash prizes. The rest lose their money. Lotteries are used by many GOVERNMENTS for fund-raising. |
| MARNE | River in France, famous as the site of Germany's first major setback in 1914. The French armies, operating from a central position around Paris, struck at the Germans' flank and enforced a fatal change in the German plan of campaign; the Germans withdrew, gave up their attempt at a knock-out blow and had to face a stalemate in France. |
| MEDIAN | The middle of a series. There are an equal number of items above and below the median. |
| MEDIEVAL | (From Latin words meaning 'middle age'). Refers to the period of European history between the fall of the Roman empire in Western Europe (5th century) and the beginning of European expansion overseas (late 15th century). |
| MORALE | State of mind of people in an organization such as a factory or army. If their morale is good, they are confident and energetic but obedient. |

| | |
|---|---|
| NATION | Community of people linked together by shared historical experiences and, usually, the same language. People in a nation generally claim the right to have their own GOVERNMENT. They regard all the other people in the world as foreign. |
| NATIONALISATION; NATIONALISE | Sometimes a GOVERNMENT takes over the ownership and control of an INDUSTRY, either by confiscation (Russia, 1918) or by compulsory purchase (Britain after 1945). The industry is then said to be nationalised. A POLICY of nationalisation is often supported by SOCIALISTS as a check on the power of private CAPITALISTS. Beware of confusing nationalisation with nationalism (see chapter 1). |
| NATIONAL SERVICE | Conscription, or the compulsory training of men, and sometimes women, for armed service. The chief aim of national service is to build up a large trained reserve. |
| NEUTRAL, NEUTRALITY | A neutral country declares that it will not fight in any war unless attacked. Some countries have a long-standing POLICY of neutrality (remaining neutral). |
| NEW WORLD | The Americas. The Spanish and Portuguese explorers of the early modern period used this expression when they realized that Columbus was wrong in identifying America with Asia. |
| NOBILITY | The nobles, or members of the nobility, were those who received favours from kings or emperors. Such favours were usually hereditary (passed on within a family) and indicated by titles like Sir, Prince or Lord. |
| NOMADIC | Wandering without a fixed home, as all the human race was before the invention of farming. Some 'primitive' peoples are still nomadic. So are tramps. |
| NON-AGGRESSION PACT | An agreement not to attack each other, usually made by two countries. Hitler was expert at confusing unfriendly countries by offering them such pacts. |
| NON-LETHAL | Not deadly for human beings. |
| NUCLEUS | (a) The positive electrical charge, and sometimes the neutral particles, at the 'centre' of an atom. Hence nuclear energy, which comes from the breaking up of atomic nuclei. |

| | |
|---|---|
| | (b) The central, organizing 'core' of any structure or organization. |
| OLD WORLD | The Continents of Europe, Asia and Africa; they were at least partly known to Europeans before Columbus' voyages. See NEW WORLD. |
| OPEN FIELDS | Huge unfenced fields, divided into strips which were shared among the farming community, and often redistributed each year or according to the size of families. Open fields were used before private property and modern techniques were introduced. |
| PADDY | Waterlogged field used for rice-growing. Rice paddies are often TERRACED. |
| PARLIAMENT | English word for a LEGISLATIVE assembly. |
| PARTY | In POLITICS, an organization of people who seek GOVERNMENT power so as to carry out some POLICY on which the party members more or less agree. |
| PEASANT | Small scale farmer, working on the land, often not owning the land he works on. Beware spelling confusion with *pheasants*, the birds. |
| PHOENICIANS | A people of the Mediterranean lands in ancient history. They built cities in Palestine and founded Carthage, Rome's rival. They were energetic traders. |
| PLEBISCITE | A vote by all the people of a country, when the GOVERNMENT asks them to show approval or dis-approval of a POLICY, *not* to elect a representative. Often used by dictators to test, or show off, how popular their policies are. |
| PLUTOCRATIC | 'Plutocrat' means a very rich person whose wealth gives him political power. Hitler suggested that plutocratic organizations pushed the Allies into war against the Nazis. |
| POLICY | Plan, or method, or attitude, which anyone supports over a problem in POLITICS. |
| POLITICS | All affairs which affect whole communities and are felt by them not to be just people's private business, but matters for the GOVERNMENT at any level. |

| | |
|---|---|
| POPE | Head of the Roman CATHOLIC Church. Bishop of Rome; believed by Catholics to be St Peter's successor. |
| POWER | A STATE considered as a force in INTERNATIONAL affairs, as in the expression 'Great Power'. Here, military or ECONOMIC greatness is meant. |
| PRESIDENT | Person who 'presides', or is the official head, of any organization, from a football club to a STATE. In REPUBLICS this is the usual title for the Head of State. |
| PRODUCERS' GOODS | Raw materials, tools, transport facilities and other products which can be used to make more goods including CONSUMER GOODS. |
| PROTECTORATE | The situation where a POWER claims to be protecting a smaller, weaker country from interference by other powers. Usually involves interference by the 'protecting' power, but the pretence of independence is sometimes kept up. |
| QUOTA | Share of some product, or of men, that each group such as a factory, or a country, has to pay, or collect, according to the decision of an authority. |
| RADAR | Short for 'radio detection and ranging'. Technique pioneered by Sir Robert Watson Watt of sending out beams of radio waves to locate approaching ships or aircraft. The waves are echoed back by obstacles, enabling distance and direction to be calculated. |
| REFORM | Make some improvement in the running of a country; usually by changing the LAWS. It is often a matter of opinion whether what books call 'reforms' really are, or were, improvements. |
| REPARATIONS | Money to be paid by a culprit who is responsible for damage. The allies who fought Germany in the First World War demanded reparations from Germany and her allies. |
| REPUBLIC | Before the French Revolution, almost all STATES were ruled by kings or emperors. With the spread of the belief that the state stood for the people, royal families were generally discarded and replaced by PRESIDENTS. Countries where the head of state is a president are known as republics. |

| | |
|---|---|
| REPUBLICAN | In American POLITICS, one of the two chief PARTIES. Since the 1850's the Republicans have been the chief rivals of the DEMOCRATS. In this century, American business and farming interests, and people who suspected more recent immigrants, were often Republican supporters. |
| RESERVE | Area kept (reserved) for the coloured people by white settlers. The Red Indians have reserves in North America, and the negroes in South Africa. |
| REVOLUTION | Very drastic change which leaves some area of human life quite different from before. If the revolution changes control of the STATE or ownership of property, there is likely to be violence. |
| RIGHT | In POLITICS right-wing supporters are cautious about making changes, except to stave off LEFT wing revolutions. They respect existing property holders and are unfriendly to SOCIALISM and COMMUNISM. |
| S.A. | Short for Sturm Abteilung (Storm Detachment) – the part-time, brown-shirted private army of the German Nazis. |
| SANCTIONS | Actions taken to discourage or punish LAW breaking: used especially for attempts under the authority of the League of Nations or United Nations to deal with AGGRESSION. |
| SAVANNAH | Open grassland in tropical latitudes. |
| SELF-SUPPORTING | Usually refers to a country; not needing any essential imports; or able to maintain its ECONOMY without help from any other country. |
| SENATE | Any very dignified governing body may use this title, taken from the group of senior politicians of the Roman Republic. It is especially common for the 'upper house' of a LEGISLATURE. For example, in the U.S.A., the Senators represent whole STATES, not smaller con-stituencies, and have privileges and responsibilities which make each individual senator count for more than most representatives in the 'lower' house. |
| SHADOOF | Simple irrigation device, based on a pivoted beam, used in Egypt since prehistoric times. |

| | |
|---|---|
| SHARE | One share is the smallest part of the money CAPITAL of a business company. The shareholder owns a certificate which can be bought or sold, giving him the right to a 'share' in the company's profits. Each certificate was originally sold by the company. |
| SHEIK(H) | Chieftain or king of an Arab people. |
| SOCIALISM; SOCIALIST | Socialists believe that the freedom of an individual to get and use CAPITAL needs to be severely limited for the good of the community he lives in. The STATE, representing the whole community, should own and control at least the chief INDUSTRIES. Socialists also support energetic GOVERNMENT action in such fields as health and education where wealth can easily buy privilege, and poor people lose out. More extreme socialists want cooperation, not competition, to be the basic method of creating wealth. There are many varieties of socialism. Communists claim to be true, scientific socialists. |
| SOVEREIGN; SOVEREIGNTY | A STATE claims sovereignty, or unlimited power, within its borders. The authority which uses this power is the SOVEREIGN. In Britain, the highest authority is PARLIAMENT, which may therefore be called sovereign. Before the French Revolution, kings or emperors claimed sovereign powers in most of Europe. |
| SPECULATOR | Person who risks money in buying and selling STOCKS and SHARES, hoping to profit from their constantly changing price. |
| S.S. | Short for Schutz Staffel (protection squad). This was the black-uniformed organization which gained more power after Hitler disgraced the S.A. in 1934. It acted as Hitler's bodyguard, controlled the concentration camps, and provided field troops in the Second World War. |
| STAPLE | The staple crop or product or export of a country is that on which it chiefly relies. |
| STATE | Usually, the authority which claims to have SOVEREIGNTY over all the land and people in its borders. Note that in a FEDERAL system the States can be overruled by the Federal GOVERNMENT. |
| STOCK | Much like a SHARE, but stocks are sold by 'public' concerns such as town councils. |

| | |
|---|---|
| SYNTHETIC | Artificially made, by applied chemistry, as a substitute for or improvement on a natural raw material such as wool or rubber. |
| TARIFF | Tax or duty on imports. Tariffs may be used by GOVERNMENTS to raise money, or to discourage imports and favour home producers. |
| TERRACING | Method of checking soil erosion (the destruction, by weathering, of fertile topsoil) by building walls along contour lines, with flat fields between. |
| THEORY | Suggested explanation of how or why certain things happen, or will happen. Marx had a theory that CAPITALISM would inevitably be replaced by SOCIALISM. Note that theories may be right or wrong, but what is right in theory cannot be wrong in practice. |
| TREATY | Solemn agreement between two or more STATES. |
| TRIBE | Group of people with the same language, usually related to each other like a chain of inter-marrying families, and often claiming a common ancestor. Some tribes are small, but some are counted in millions and are no different from NATIONS. |
| VICEROY | From words meaning 'in place of the king'. The personal representative of a king or emperor; especially the head of the British GOVERNMENT in India. |
| VIRGIN MARY | In Christian belief, the mother of Jesus Christ. |
| WALL STREET | New York street where trading in STOCKS and SHARES takes place. Hence the name, 'Wall Street Crash', for the sudden collapse in share prices in October 1929. |

# Index

262; union with Syria, 262; 'Six Day War', 265–6

Eisenhower, President Dwight D., 184, 199: and Cuba, 244; and Nasser, 262

El Alamein, Battle of, 146, 260

European Coal and Steel Community (ECSC), 187–8, 191

European Economic Community (EEC) see Common Market

Farouk, King of Egypt, 61, 260: abdication, 261

*Fellahin*, 260–1, 264

Finland, 35–6: war against Russia (1939–40), 138; alliance with Germany, 172

First World War, 21–33: causes, 21–4; Franco-Prussian War and French desire for revenge, 22; German alliance with Austria, 22; rivalry in the Balkans, 22, 24; German imperial and naval ambitions, 22–3
course of war, 24, 26–33: outbreak, 24; stalemate of trench warfare, 24, 26; attacks on Turkish Empire, 26; failure of Dardanelles campaign, 26; struggle for resources, 26; blockade of Germany, 26; submarine warfare, 26, 28, 33; entry of USA, 26–8; Russian Revolution and withdrawal from war, 28–31; German attack (1918) and Allied counter-attacks, 33; defeat of Germany's allies, 33; revolution in Germany and Austria, 33; armistice, 33

Ford, Henry, 49–50

Formosa, 90, 167, 179, 180

France: and American War of Independence, 16; French Revolution, 16, 18, 69; Napoleonic wars, 18–19; Franco-Prussian War, 22; idea of revenge, 22; alliance with Russia, 22; closer friendship with Britain, 23; and outbreak of war (1914), 24; and peace terms, 34; and Russian Civil War, 41; and North Africa, 59–61, 247; Syria and Lebanon, 62; and development of China, 80; army leaves Ruhr, 108
and Stresa conference, 126–7; agreement with Russia, 127, 129; and sanctions against Italy, 128; and German move into Rhineland, 129; popular front government, 130; and non-intervention in Spain, 131; rearmament, 132; and appeasement, 132; and Czechoslovakia, 134; Munich conference, 135, 137; declaration of war, 138; defeat by Germans, 139; Free French government, 139; and United Nations, 155; dependence on USA, 158; withdrawal from Syria and the Lebanon, 158; Communist Party, 173; signs North Atlantic Treaty, 177; and Council of Europe, 187; and ECSC, 187; postwar weakness, 189–90; war against Viet-Minh and withdrawal from Vietnam, 223–6; withdrawal from Laos and Cambodia, 227; independence for former colonies, 252; Algerian independence, 190; challenge to US leadership, 190–4; and the Common Market, 190–1; nuclear weapons, 192; as third power, 193–4; withdrawal from NATO, 193–4; remains outside Test-Ban Treaty, 207; attacks UN use of force in Congo, 254

Franco, General, 131

Gandhi, Mohandas Karamchand, 64–5: in South Africa, 64–5; leads Congress, 65; imprisonment, 65; belief that Britain would lose war, 160; desire to keep India intact, 160; assassination, 162, 230

Germany: Franco-Prussian War, 22; creation of one nation (1871), 19, 21; alliance with Austria, 22; imperial and

India, 160, 162; and Council of Europe, 187; remains outside ECSC, 187; troops kept in Germany, 188; and the Common Market, 188–9, 191; military aid for India, 234; and African colonies, 247–52; attacks UN use of force in Congo, 254; and Rhodesia, 260; and Baghdad Pact, 262; forces sent to Jordan, 263

Greece, 135, 136: Civil War and British intervention, 154, 173; joins NATO, 177; and Council of Europe, 187

Guevara, Che, 241–2, 245

Hammarskjöld, Dag, 254

Hiroshima, dropping of atomic bomb, 150

Hitler, Adolf, 37, 39, 107, 112, 128, 168, 203, 247: attempt to seize power by force, 116; writes *Mein Kampf* in gaol, 116; unsuccessful candidate for Presidency, 117; becomes Chancellor, 117; bans Communist Party, 117; sets up dictatorship, 117; closes trade unions, 118; proclaims himself *Führer*, 118; attack on the Churches, 119; 'Hitler Youth', 121; and Mussolini, 121, 126, 129, 133, 135–6 agreement with Poland, 126, 129; rearmament, 126, 129; four-year plan, 129; and Spanish Civil War, 130–1; occupies Austria and Czechoslovakia, 132–6; Munich conference, 135; turns against Poland, 136–8; and Stalin, 137; Second World War, 138, 140–2, 146; and new European order, 150; commits suicide, 149

Ho Chi Minh, 163, 222, 223

Holland, *see* Netherlands

Hong Kong, 80, 82: in Japanese hands, 144

Hoover, Herbert: organises famine relief in Russia, 43; President of USA, 49; imposes heavy import tariffs, 110; and the slump, 122

Hungary, 210: communists expelled, 37; landowners' dictatorship, 37; part of territory goes to Romania, 38; active in Axis cause, 172; under communist rule, 172; agreements with de Gaulle, 193; revolt crushed by Khrushchev, 212, 233

India, 54, 132, 159–63, 229–35: British East India Company, 12; revolt of 1857, 15; incorporation of Burma, 66; British rule, 62–5; princely states, 62, 63; Hindus and Moslems, 63–5, 160, 230; Congress, 64, 65, 160, 230–2; Moslem League, 64, 160; movements towards self-government, 64; Gandhi's role, 64–5; communal outbreaks, 65; Indian leaders imprisoned, 65; threat from Japan, 145, 149, 159–60 Moslem desire for separate state, 160; British departure, 160, 162, 227, 229; partition, 160; riots and massacres, 162; position of Kashmir, 162, 229–30, 234; Nehru's 'social revolution', 230–1; new Constitution, 230; Congress control of central parliament, 231; caste system ended, 231; spread of bribery, 232; failure of food supply, 231–3; policy of neutralism, 233; frontier quarrels with China, 220; Chinese campaign of 1962, 220, 234; British, US and Russian aid, 220, 234

Indian National Congress ('Congress'), 64, 65, 160, 230–2: Hindu majority, 64; Gandhi's leadership, 65; non-violent disobedience, 65

Indo-China, 66, 140, 142, 163, 190

Indonesia, 13, 163, 227–9, 233: hostility between army and communists, 228; trade destroyed by Sukarno's policy, 229; war against Malaya and Singapore, 229; Sukarno's fall, 229; army takes over government, 229

Iraq, 62, 158: independence, 158; and
Baghdad Pact, 262; revolution, 263
Ireland, 132: Blueshirts, 130; and
Council of Europe, 187; attempt to
join Common Market, 191
Iron Curtain, the, 175
Israel, 266: foundation of state, 159;
victory over Egyptians (1956), 262,
264; Syrian guerrilla war on frontier,
264; and 'Six Days War', 265–6;
support from USA, 266
Italy, 37–8, 59, 121, 190: creation of one
nation, 19; and peace treaties, 34;
Mussolini's network of *fasci*, 46;
violence between fascists and socialists,
46; March on Rome, 46–7; Mussolini
becomes Prime Minister, 47; election
rigging, 47; opposition parties banned,
47; press censorship, 47
and Stresa conference, 126–7; attack
on Abyssinia, 127–9; troops run away
in Spain, 131; Pact of Steel with
Germany, 136, 138; enters war (1940),
139; war with USA, 142; defeats in
North Africa, 146; invasion of Italy,
146; Mussolini's imprisonment and
rescue, 146; end of war, 146–7
Communist Party, 173; signs North
Atlantic Treaty, 177; and Council of
Europe, 187; and ECSC, 187

Japan, 14, 85, 88–93, 222–3: emperor-
worship, 88; admission of foreigners
to Japanese ports, 89–90; copying of
Europe, 90; Chinese turned out of
Formosa and Korea, 90; designs on
Manchuria, 90, 91; Russo-Japanese
War, 66–7, 90; and First World War,
91; and Russian Civil War, 41; permanent seat on League of Nations
Council, 91; naval agreement, 51, 91;
sufferings in Great Slump, 91–2;
penetration of China, 82–4; conquest
of Manchuria and war with China,
86–8, 93, 130, 163–4; civilians lose
control of policy, 93; one-party state,
93
alliance with Axis, 93; Second World
War, 136, 140–2; US anxiety, 141;
Pearl Harbour, 142, 144, 146; threat to
India, 145, 146, 149, 159–60; defeats
by US fleet in Pacific, 146, 149;
campaign in Burma, 149; dropping of
atomic bombs, 150, 178; Japanese
surrender, 150; US control, 179; and
nationalism in South-East Asia, 163
Jews, the, 62: national home in Palestine,
62, 158; Nazi attacks on them, 117–19,
158; Nuremberg Laws, 118; anti-
Jewish laws in Italy, 121; war with
Arabs and British in Palestine, 158;
proclamation of state of Israel, 159
Johnson, President Lyndon B.: and the
'Great Society', 198; sends troops to
Dominican Republic, 246; supports
Branco in Brazil, 246
Jordan, 158, 263: army shattered in 'Six
Day War', 265

Kashmir, 162, 229–30, 234
Katanga: copper belt, 57, 252–4;
independent government, 253–4;
UN intervention, 254
Kaunda, Kenneth, 59
Kellogg Pact, 51
Kennedy, President John F., 198, 246:
policy towards Russia, 199–201, 246;
and Bay of Pigs landing, 245; and Cuba
crisis, 200–1, 246; Alliance for Progress,
246; assassinated, 198
Kenya, 57–9, 247, 250–2: white farmers,
57–9, 250; Asian traders in coastal
towns, 57, 58–9; Mau Mau, 250–1;
British troops in Kenya, 251;
independence, 251
Kenyatta, Jomo, 59, 250–2:

Marx, Karl, and communism, 19–20, 30, 85, 101, 173, 212, 245

Mau Mau, 250–1

Mexico, 28, 70–6, 236

Middle East, the, 61–2, 158–9, 261–7

Molotov, 137, 202: dismissed, 205

Monroe Doctrine, the, 77

Morocco, 61, 146: achieves independence, 255

Moslems, the, 59, 63, 64, 160, 230: fighting with Hindus, 65; creation of Pakistan, 160

Munich conference (1938), 135, 137

Mussolini, Benito, 45–7, 71, 107, 112, 121, 138: left wing journalist, 46; leaves socialists and supports war, 46; attacks peace terms, 45; network of *fasci*, 46; March on Rome, 46–7; Prime Minister, 47; bans opposition parties and starts press censorship, 47; pact with the Pope, 121; and Hitler, 121, 129, 133, 135; anti-Jewish laws, 121; and Spanish Civil War, 130–1; and the Axis, 131–2; and German occupation of Austria, 133; Munich conference, 135; invades Albania, 135; brings Italy into war (1940), 139; and new European order, 150; imprisonment and escape, 146; shot by communists, 147

Nagasaki, dropping of atomic bomb, 150

Nasser, Gamal, 233, 260–6: revolutionary organisation, 260, 261; seizes power, 261; nationalises Suez Canal, 262; land reform policy, 262, 264; and Iraqi Revolution, 263; allows only one political party, 264; Russian support, 265–6; orders UN Emergency Force out of Egypt, 265; and 'Six Day War', 265–6

Nationalism, 15–19: American War of Independence, 16, 18; French Revolution, 16, 18; idea of the nation, 16, 18; national anthems, 17–18

NATO, *see* North Atlantic Treaty

Nazis, the, 39, 102, 107, 111, 116–21: SA, 116–18; rising vote, 116, 117; attacks on Jews, 117–19, 158; all other parties banned, 117; SS, 118, 150, 151; popularity of Nazism, 118; plans for national church, 119; education of young in Nazism, 120–1; in Austria, 126, 133; concentration camps, 150–1; supporters in South Africa, 257

Negroes in USA, 195–8; demonstrations, 197; Little Rock crisis, 197–8; reforms by Kennedy and Johnson, 198

Nehru, Jawaharlal, 230–4: belief that Britain would lose war, 162; desire to keep India intact, 162; proclaims social revolution, 230–1; new Constitution, 230; neutralism, 233

Netherlands, 26, 40: overrun by Germans (1940), 139, 140; signs North Atlantic Treaty, 177; and Council of Europe, 187; and ECSC, 187

Nicholas II, Czar, 29, 41: abdication, 30; shot with his family by Bolsheviks, 42

Nkrumah, Kwame, 59, 157, 233, 248–50, 264: forces British to hasten transfer of power in Gold Coast, 249; his party wins first general election, 249; becomes a dictator, 249; corruption and inefficiency of his government, 249–50; overthrown, 250

North Atlantic Treaty and NATO, 177, 188, 192–4, 212: France's withdrawal from NATO, 193–4

Norway: occupied by Germans (1940), 138; signs North Atlantic Treaty, 177; and Council of Europe, 187; attempt to join Common Market, 191

Organisation for European Economic

occupies Baltic States, 140; and Mao Tse-Tung, 165; continued dictatorship, 168–70, 202–3; apparatus of terror, 170; death, 170, 208; posthumous attacks on him, 203, 205, 208, 211–12; his body removed from its shrine beside Lenin, 208

Stalingrad: battle of, 145–6; reverts to name of Volgograd, 208

Sudan, the, 61

Sudeten Germans, 37, 133–5

Suez Canal and Canal Zone, 13, 54, 61, 158, 247, 260–1: nationalised by Nasser, 262; closed to shipping (1967), 265–6

Sukarno, President, 163, 228–9, 233: destruction of Indonesia's trade, 229; war against Malaya, Singapore, 229; fall, 229

Sun Yat Sen, 87: leader of Kuomintang, 81–2; 'United Front' with Communists, 84

Syria, 62, 158, 263: French withdrawal, 158; union with Egypt, 262, 263; guerrilla war on Israel frontier, 264, 265; army shattered in 'Six Day War', 265

Test-Ban Treaty, 207, 220

Tito, Marshal, 211, 214

Tojo, General, 142

Trotsky, Leon, 30: organises Red Army, 40; in Russian Civil War, 41–2; electrification plan, 95; resigns office of Commissar for War, 102; banished by Stalin from Russia, 95, 102; tries to organise anti-Stalin world communist movement, 103; sentenced to death by Russian court, 103; assassinated in Mexico, 103

Truman, President Harry S., 154, 172: Truman Doctrine, 173–5, 179; and Korean War, 180, 182; dismisses

MacArthur, 182, 184

Tshombe, 253

Tunisia, 61: achieves independence, 255

Turkey, 19, 22, 35, 62, 136: and Egypt, 61; First World War, 26; Arab revolt, 61; defeat (1918), 33; joins NATO, 177; and Council of Europe, 187; and Common Market, 191

United Nations Organisation, 154–6, 178–81, 262, 265, 267: Security Council, 155, 156, 178, 180, 181; and Korea, 182–4; General Assembly, 181; intervention in Congo, 254; sanctions in Rhodesia, 260; Emergency Force ordered out of Egypt by Nasser, 265

USA: War of Independence, 15, 16, 18, 64; Civil War, 19; First World War, 26–8, 33; and German submarine warfare, 26–8; declaration of war (1917), 28; and Russia, 31, 41 Republicans capture Congress, 47; Wilson's breakdown in health, 48; Congress rejects peace treaty, 34, 48; prohibition, 48–50, 106–7, 124; immigration controls, 49; radio and films, 49; mass-production of cars, 49–50; government scandals, 50; Coolidge's administration, 50–1; agreement with chief naval powers, 51, 91; and reparations, 51; and disarmament, 51; and Latin America, 70, 76–8; and China, 80, 84; and Japan, 89, 91 and world crisis, (1929–33): US credit, 106, 108; prosperity in 1928, 107; New York Stock Exchange slump, 108–10; collapse of US credit, 109–10; European debt to USA, 110; Hoover's attempts to deal with slump, 122; unemployment and the squatters' 'bonus army', 122–3; Democrats' electoral victory (1932), 111, 123;